Learning with Generative Artificial Intelligence

This book delves into the core of education's digital transformation, presenting a thorough and empirical examination of generative artificial intelligence (GenAI)'s impact beyond the theoretical and fragmented insights prevalent in current discourse.

Drawing from peer-reviewed and extensive empirical studies, the contributors aim to unveil the multifaceted effects of GenAI (particularly ChatGPT) on learning. They navigate through topics of interaction, assessment, emotion, effect and efficiency, meta-cognition, and ethics, offering a comprehensive exploration of GenAI's educational implications. This book presents a closed loop of learning theory, multimodal data, and learning analytics technology. Furthermore, this book builds and proposes core conceptual models for future learning and identifies potential research directions.

This book will serve as a foundational reference for educators seeking innovative learning and teaching methods and for researchers and technologists who seek to push the boundaries of educational technology and related areas.

Yizhou Fan is an Assistant Professor at the Graduate School of Education, Peking University and an Adjunct Research Fellow at the Centre for Learning Analytics, Monash University. He identifies himself as a learning analyst employing computational techniques to enhance the understanding of self-regulated learning and to develop next-generation learning environments for envisioning future education. In 2023, he received the Emerging Scholars Award and Early Career Research Grant from SoLAR (The Society for Learning Analytics Research). His recent research focuses on human-AI collaboration and the scaffolding of hybrid intelligence.

Learning with Generative Artificial Intelligence

What Empirical Studies Tell Us

Edited By
Yizhou Fan

Routledge
Taylor & Francis Group
LONDON AND NEW YORK

This book is published with financial support from the Society for Learning Analytics Research (Early Career Research Grant 2023), the National Natural Science Foundation of China (No. 62407001) and the National Social Science Fund of China (No. VGA230012)

First published 2025
by Routledge
4 Park Square, Milton Park, Abingdon, Oxon OX14 4RN

and by Routledge
605 Third Avenue, New York, NY 10158

Routledge is an imprint of the Taylor & Francis Group, an informa business

British Library Cataloguing in Publication Data
A catalogue record for this book is available from the British Library

ISBN: 9781041052807 (hbk)
ISBN: 9781041052814 (pbk)
ISBN: 9781003632146 (ebk)

DOI: 10.4324/ 9781003632146

Typeset in LMRoman
by codeMantra

Contents

List of Figures

List of Tables

Preface

The rise of generative artificial intelligence (GenAI) in education is nothing short of revolutionary. It's a game changer that's reshaping how we learn, teach, and engage with knowledge. As educators, researchers, and policymakers explore the potential of this technology, one big question emerges: How can we make GenAI a force for good in education? This book, *Learning with Generative Artificial Intelligence: What Empirical Studies Tell Us*, offers an evidence-based, practical guide to answer that question with a focus on learning.

The inspiration for this book stems from the urgent need for empirical evidence in the rapidly evolving landscape of AI-assisted learning. While theoretical discussions on AI's potential abound, the gap between conceptual possibilities and actual educational outcomes persists. Recognising this disconnect, I embarked on a journey to bridge theory and practice through methodologically rigorous research. This book is the result of extensive collaboration with young and talented scholars and students engaged in the forefront of educational transformation.

This book was born out of a simple yet pressing need: to provide clear, research-backed insights into how AI tools like ChatGPT are affecting learning. While plenty of people talk about AI's potential, fewer focus on what's actually happening in a learning context. Rather than speculate, I aimed to ground this book in evidence. This book's structure is designed to guide readers on a journey from past to future, from concept to empirical studies. It starts with a look at the history of AI in education, from early tutoring systems to today's large language models like ChatGPT, and introduces the research design for this whole book. Then, through rigorous studies and close analysis, we've uncovered how GenAI influences students' behaviour, emotion and motivation, learning outcomes, metacognition and self-regulation, assessment engagement, and perceived values from Chapters 3–8. Each chapter includes an overview of key concepts, insights from the latest research, real-world case studies, and practical advice for the future. Empirical research is woven into every chapter, giving readers a rich mix of data, analysis, and big-picture takeaways. By the end, this book discussed the future vision and key topics of learning with GenAI. Readers will have a clear understanding of where we've been, where we are, and where we're headed in the age of GenAI. I hope these insights will provide educators and decision-makers with the possibilities and evidence they need to make informed choices about using AI in education. By sharing concrete evidence and innovative ideas, I hope to spark conversations that lead to more thoughtful and human-centred uses of GenAI in education.

Every idea in this book is grounded in research. We used a mix of experiments, case studies, and data analysis to get a complete picture of GenAI's impact on learning. By comparing human-led and AI-led learning, we've uncovered unique insights into how students learn differently with AI support. These insights and topics are related to human-AI co-evolution, synergy regulation, generative assessment, metacognitive laziness, and value tension, while this book highlights future research directions such as conversation-based pedagogical agents and new assessment frameworks. The goal is to give readers an evidence-based look and vision at how GenAI is changing education.

This book is for anyone curious about the role of AI in education. Educators will find practical ideas for using GenAI in their classrooms. Researchers will discover new avenues for enquiry and reflection. Policymakers will gain insight into how to shape policy and practice around AI in schools. Technologists will see how their tools are being used and how they could be designed on the ground.

This book would not have been possible without the support and encouragement of many people. I am deeply grateful to my advisors, Prof. Qiong Wang and Prof. Dragan Gasevic, for their valuable guidance and support in my academic journey. I would also like to thank my collaborators, colleagues, students, and research assistants, who played a crucial role in shaping the studies and writing in this book. Special thanks go to Peng Zhang from Peking University for her conscientious assistance in the planning, writing, and editing of this book. I am also grateful to the students, educators, and experts who shared their insights and experiences with me. Their contributions made this book richer and more meaningful.

As we step further into an era defined by digital intelligence, the role of AI in education will only grow in importance. This book is a call to action for educators, researchers, and technologists to think deeply about how AI can support human learning. By weaving evidence with experience, I hope this book inspires new ideas, in-depth discussions, and creative solutions for the future of education. Together, we have the chance to shape a world where technology and humanity thrive side by side.

Dr. Yizhou Fan
December 14, 2024

Contributors

Xinyu Li
Graduate school of Education
Monash University
Melbourne, Australia

Zijian Li
Department of Educational Technology
Peking University
Beijing, China

Huaiya Liu
Graduate school of Education
Peking University
Beijing, China

Kejie Shen
Graduate school of Education
Peking University
Beijing, China

Yuan Shen
Research Center for Data Hub and Security
Zhejiang lab
Hangzhou, China

Luzhen Tang
Graduate school of Education
Peking University
Beijing, China

Zhanghan Wang
School of Education
Shanghai Jiao Tong University
Shanghai, China

Mengtong Xiang
Graduate school of Education
Peking University
Beijing, China

Zixian Yu
Graduate school of Education
Peking University
Beijing, China

Peng Zhang
Graduate school of Education
Peking University
Beijing, China

Yuyue Zhang
Graduate school of Education
Peking University
Beijing, China

CHAPTER 1

Brief History of AI in Education and Transforming Learning with Generative Artificial Intelligence

Yizhou Fan

EXPLORING THE INTERSECTION of artificial intelligence (AI) and education is crucial for developing innovative technologies that can transform learning. This introductory chapter briefly elaborates on how technological advancements have continually reshaped education and then explores the integration of Artificial Intelligence (AI) into education, highlighting four metaphors for human-AI collaboration: AI as a learning tool (automating tasks), AI as a learning tutor (providing adaptive instruction), AI as a learning agent (engaging dynamically with learners), and AI as a thought partner (augmenting human cognition and creativity). These metaphors represent varying degrees of human agency and AI involvement in the learning process. This chapter acknowledges the intertwined opportunities and challenges of integrating Generative AI (GenAI) in education, likened to a Möbius strip where benefits and concerns coexist. Key challenges include data privacy, ethical considerations, over-reliance on AI, biases in AI-generated content, and

DOI: 10.4324/9781003632146-1

issues of equitable access. To navigate these complexities, it calls for robust empirical research to bridge the gap between GenAI's theoretical potential and practical application, emphasising the need to evaluate its efficacy, ethical deployment, and equitable impact across diverse learning contexts. Finally, this chapter outlines the book's narrative logic, moving from historical context to theoretical frameworks and empirical investigations, culminating in insights that inform future research. Integrating historical evolution, theoretical exploration, and empirical evidence underscores GenAI's multifaceted impact on education and advocates for a thoughtful, human-centred approach to its integration.

1.1 THE HISTORY OF AI IN EDUCATION

1.1.1 The Interwoven Development of Technology and Education

The evolution of education has been closely tied to technological advancements. Innovations continually shape how knowledge is transmitted and acquired. For instance, the invention of the printing press revolutionised access to information, making books more affordable and knowledge more widespread (Eisenstein, 1980). This democratisation of learning materials laid the groundwork for mass education and literacy. The Industrial Revolution further intertwined technology and education. The demands of an industrialised society required a workforce with basic literacy and numeracy skills, prompting governments to establish formal education systems (Horne, 1993). Innovations such as the blackboard and the typewriter became classroom staples, enhancing teaching efficiency and organisation.

The 20th century witnessed rapid technological advancements infiltrating educational settings. Radio and television introduced new mediums for delivering educational content, expanding learning beyond traditional classrooms (Cuban, 1986). Tools such as the overhead projector and photocopier facilitated information dissemination. Computers entered education in the 1960s and 1970s, initially used for administrative purposes but gradually becoming integral to instructional practices (Papert, 1980). Seymour Papert's development of the LOGO programming language exemplified the potential of computers to enhance learning by encouraging problem-solving and logical thinking. This period marked the beginning of educational technology (EdTech) as a field, exploring how digital tools could transform learning processes.

1.1.2 Learning Transformation in the New Century

The dawn of the 21st century brought a seismic shift in education, driven by the proliferation of the internet and digital technologies. Traditional models evolved with the emergence of e-learning platforms, allowing learners to access courses online from anywhere (Allen and Seaman, 2013). Learning Management Systems (LMS) such as Blackboard and Moodle facilitated online course delivery and management. Mobile technology also further transformed learning by making educational content accessible on smartphones and tablets, giving rise to mobile learning or m-learning (Traxler, 2009). Educational apps and games became popular tools for both formal education and self-directed learning, engaging learners through interactive multimedia content.

From 2012, massive open online courses (MOOCs) democratised education by offering courses from prestigious institutions to a global audience for free or at low cost (Pappano, 2012). Platforms such as Coursera, edX, and Udacity enabled millions to participate in higher education courses, challenging traditional notions of accessibility and scalability. Pedagogical approaches also evolved. The flipped classroom model gained traction, where students first explore new content outside class, typically via video lectures, and then use class time for interactive activities that reinforce learning (Bishop and Verleger, 2013). Blended learning, combining face-to-face instruction with online activities, became prevalent to enhance outcomes and engagement (Garrison and Kanuka, 2004).

These transformations emphasised digital literacy and 21st-century skills, preparing students for a technology-driven world (Partnership for 21st Century Skills, 2009). Collaboration, critical thinking, creativity, and communication became focal points in curricula, reflecting modern workforce needs.

1.1.3 When Learning Meets Artificial Intelligence

Artificial intelligence has progressively integrated into education, offering new possibilities for personalised and efficient learning experiences. Early implementations focused on intelligent tutoring systems (ITS), aiming to replicate the adaptive nature of human tutors (Woolf, 2010). ITS utilised algorithms to tailor instruction based on individual performance, providing customised feedback and pacing. Advancements in machine learning and data analytics enhanced AI's capabilities in education. Adaptive learning platforms began analysing vast amounts of data to adjust the content difficulty, learning paths, and assessments in real-time (Johnson, 2016). This personalisation aimed to address diverse learner needs, improving engagement and retention (Kulik and Fletcher, 2016). Natural Language Processing (NLP) also enabled the development of AI-driven chatbots and virtual assistants, providing immediate support to students (Fadhil and Villafiorita, 2017). These technologies and tools facilitated administrative tasks, answered FAQs, and assisted with language learning by engaging in conversations.

The advent of Generative AI (GenAI) marked a significant milestone. Large Language Models (LLMs) such as OpenAI's GPT-3 and GPT-4 demonstrated the ability to generate human-like text, opening new avenues for educational content creation and interaction (Mann et al., 2020). These models could produce explanations, answer questions, and generate personalised study materials, enhancing resource availability. However, integrating AI introduced challenges and ethical considerations. Issues of data privacy, algorithmic bias, and transparency became prominent concerns (Williamson and Eynon, 2020). Reliance on AI raised questions about the role of teachers and the potential for technology to replace human interaction. Ensuring equitable access to AI-driven tools emerged as a critical issue, as disparities in technology availability could exacerbate educational inequalities (Van Dijk, 2020). Policymakers and educators advocated for frameworks to guide ethical AI implementation, emphasising inclusivity and fairness.

In summary, the convergence of learning and AI represents a transformative phase in education's history. AI offers the potential to enhance experiences, personalise education, and prepare students for a future where technology plays an integral role. As we embrace these advancements, addressing accompanying challenges is essential to ensure AI's benefits are realised for all learners.

1.2 FOUR METAPHORS FOR HUMAN-AI COLLABORATION

Understanding AI's role in education can be conceptualised through four metaphors: AI as a learning tool, AI as a learning tutor, AI as a learning agent, and AI as a thought partner. These metaphors reflect varying levels of human agency and AI automation (Cukurova, 2025), providing a framework for how AI can support learning—from automating tasks to facilitating deeper cognitive and metacognitive engagement.

1.2.1 Metaphor One: AI as a Learning Tool

AI as a tool is the most traditional metaphor. It represents AI as an instrument extending human capabilities by externalising specific tasks. AI tools automate repetitive tasks such as grading, administrative duties, or providing writing suggestions, streamlining processes, and boosting productivity (Al Naqbi et al., 2024). For example, educators use OpenAI's ChatGPT to generate lesson plans, suggest teaching activities, and draft emails (van den Berg and du Plessis, 2023). Automated essay grading systems like Intelligent Essay Assessor reduce instructors' grading load by providing quick assessments based on language features (Foltz et al., 2013). While efficient, this approach lacks adaptability and does not engage learners beyond set parameters.

1.2.2 Metaphor Two: AI as a Learning Tutor

The metaphor of AI as a learning tutor represents a more advanced role, where AI adapts to learners' needs and delivers personalised instruction. Building upon Intelligent Tutoring Systems, AI provides feedback, direct instruction, and guidance, improving understanding and mastery. Examples include Carnegie Learning's Cognitive Tutor and Duolingo, which utilise algorithms to deliver personalised experiences, adapting exercises and feedback to individual performance (Alfarra et al., 2024). These systems excel in delivering well-structured tasks but are limited in addressing complex social and emotional aspects that human tutors navigate.

1.2.3 Metaphor Three: AI as a Learning Agent

AI as a learning agent shifts focus to AI being actively engaged in the learning process by understanding intraindividual factors such as prior knowledge, emotions, motivation, and the contextual factors in which the learning takes place (Dumas et al., 2020). AI acts not only to provide responses but also to learn alongside students, forming a dynamic partnership (Seo et al., 2021). Learning outcomes result from these interactions, and AI's role in this context is to support and adapt in real time to optimise both learning and its environment. Multimodal Learning Analytics (MMLA) provides a promising approach to better understand, model, and support learning, and MMLA systems integrate AI to analyse various data points, such as learners' physical, emotional, and cognitive states, in order to assess engagement and dynamically adjust content and support (Dumas et al., 2020; Cukurova, 2025). However, MMLA also presents significant challenges, including methodological, practical, and ethical issues related to privacy, bias, fairness, accountability, and transparency (Cukurova, 2025). Therefore, AI also needs to bridge gaps in real-time understanding, promoting a responsive and personalised experience together with human learners as each other's thought partners.

1.2.4 Metaphor Four: AI as a Thought Partner

The most transformative metaphor is AI as a thought partner. Here, AI serves as an agent that supports and augments human cognitive and metacognitive processes, helping individuals think more deeply and creatively (Markauskaite et al., 2022; Khan and Alamäki, 2023; Khosravi et al., 2023). This involves a tight coupling between AI capabilities and human creativity, where both collaborate to explore problems and generate ideas (Zheng et al., 2017; Rezwana and Maher, 2023).

Large language models such as ChatGPT can serve as brainstorming partners, helping learners explore alternative perspectives and generate diverse solutions. For example, in creative writing, students can use AI to propose plot twists or character developments, expanding thinking beyond conventional boundaries (Happle, 2024). For another example, in the SPL system (a socratic playground), GPT-4 acts as a thought partner in revolutionising dialogue-based Intelligent Tutoring Systems (ITSs) by enabling nuanced, context-aware, and adaptive interactions that foster critical thinking and personalised learning (Zhang et al., 2024a). AI as a thought partner fosters an environment encouraging questioning, reflection, and co-creation of knowledge.

These metaphors offer different lenses to understand AI's interplay in education. Each represents a distinct level of engagement, highlighting the range of possibilities for human-AI collaboration. While AI as a tool or tutor provides foundational support, AI as a learning agent or thought partner promises to redefine experiences by promoting richer interactions and deeper outcomes.

1.3 OPPORTUNITIES AND CHALLENGES AS A MÖBIUS STRIP IN LEARNING WITH GENAI

The integration of GenAI in education presents a complex interplay of opportunities and challenges (Yan et al., 2024; Zhang et al., 2024b), akin to a Möbius strip where positive potentials and inherent concerns are intertwined.

1.3.1 Opportunities in Learning with GenAI

GenAI has emerged as a versatile tool in education, acting both as an assistant for performance optimisation and as a facilitator for cognitive growth. Its role in learning spans four main areas (Yan et al., 2024; Zhang et al., 2024b): performance improvement, cognitive facilitation, high-quality answer provision, and interactive learning.

First, GenAI has demonstrated significant potential in improving learning performance, especially in writing tasks. Studies show that students who frequently used GenAI in their academic writing scored higher, as GenAI supported them by generating task content, which they revised and integrated into their work (Nguyen et al., 2024; Lu et al., 2024; Song and Song, 2023). This approach saved time and enhanced efficiency. Additionally, GenAI acts as a cognitive facilitator by providing insights that go beyond students' current capabilities, aligning with Vygotsky's zone of proximal development theory (Vygotsky and Cole, 1978). For instance, using ChatGPT as a co-mentor, students tackled advanced concepts and developed critical, creative, and reflective thinking skills (Villan and Santos, 2023; Essel et al., 2024).

Second, GenAI's ability to provide high-quality answers across various domains, such as sports management, medical testing, and programming, was also a key area of support, as shown in studies like (Keiper et al., 2023; Maitland et al., 2024; Joshi et al., 2024). It ensured completeness and accuracy, contributing to effective learning experiences. Moreover, GenAI fostered interactive learning through dialogue-based interactions, allowing students to engage with the material more deeply. Studies by Villan and Santos (2023) and Dasari et al. (2024) highlighted that interactive feedback from GenAI led to better comprehension and student engagement.

Third, in teaching support, although less studied, GenAI acted as both as a content generator and as a curriculum designer. It produced textual content, interactive exercises, and multimedia, helping teachers meet diverse learning needs and reduce workload (Phung et al., 2023; Yeh, 2024). Additionally, GenAI's responses have been found to be content-complete and pedagogically aligned, indicating its utility in curriculum development. It provided well-structured content and practical pedagogical suggestions, aiding in designing interactive and student-centered learning experiences (Keiper et al., 2023; Villan and Santos, 2023).

Fourth, GenAI also stands out in enhancing feedback and emerging assessment opportunities. Unlike traditional AI tools, GenAI provides detailed, personalised feedback, fostering creativity and improving writing skills (Putjorn and Putjorn, 2023; Yan, 2023). It offers a more adaptive evaluation approach, focusing on individual abilities and providing nuanced feedback. This represents a significant shift from rigid scoring systems typical of traditional AI (Lu et al., 2024; Mansour et al., 2024). Although GenAI has shown substantial promise in feedback, further research is needed to explore its role in adaptive assessments fully.

1.3.2 Challenges in Learning with GenAI

While the previous section highlighted the opportunities, there are also significant challenges in learning with GenAI such as GenAI imperfections, ethical dilemmas, and competency challenges (Yan et al., 2024; Zhang et al., 2024b).

First, GenAI has significant imperfections that undermine feedback quality. Its limitations include providing incorrect, inconsistent, or irrelevant guidance, primarily due to the statistical models lacking true comprehension of content nuances (OpenAI, 2022; Liu et al., 2023). A major challenge is GenAI's tendency towards hallucinations—misleading or inaccurate outputs arising from training data mismatches and the complexity of language generation (Ji et al., 2023). Such inaccuracies can foster misconceptions and hinder learning efficiency (Maitland et al.,

2024; Essel et al., 2024; Song and Song, 2023). GenAI's feedback often lacks personalisation, providing generalised responses that fail to meet individual student needs, which emphasises tailored guidance for effective learning (Bernabei et al., 2023). In comparison, human experts can offer more targeted, interactive support (Dasari et al., 2024). Furthermore, GenAI's reliance on language patterns rather than logical reasoning results in randomness, leading to inconsistent outputs and making it unreliable for educational use (Wan et al., 2024; Hu et al., 2024; Joshi et al., 2024; Hellas et al., 2023). GenAI also faces limitations in data processing, such as handling length constraints and interpreting graphics, hindering its effectiveness in subjects like Quantum Physics (Alneyadi and Wardat, 2024). Emotional intelligence and creativity are other areas where GenAI falls short, often producing limited or incomplete answers (Keiper et al., 2023; Lu et al., 2024).

Second, ethical concerns also arise with GenAI's use in education, particularly in handling ill-structured tasks. These concerns include academic integrity, over-reliance, equality, and student beneficence (Janse van Rensburg, 2024; Urban et al., 2024). Biases, lack of transparency, and unequal advantages are highlighted in various studies (Pinargote et al., 2024; Maitland et al., 2024; Yan, 2023). Additionally, students fear that excessive dependence on GenAI might hinder their critical thinking and intellectual growth (Dasari et al., 2024; Song and Song, 2023).

Finally, mismatches exist between GenAI-enabled teaching changes and users' competencies, resulting in utilisation gaps, assessment challenges, and skill atrophy. GenAI's assistance, without proper user skills, can lead to superficial engagement with AI-generated content (Nguyen et al., 2024). Skill degradation has also been observed, with students experiencing a decline in creativity when using GenAI extensively (Niloy et al., 2024; Bernabei et al., 2023). These issues underscore the need for cautious integration of GenAI into education to avoid over-reliance, ensure equity, and maintain student skill development.

The opportunities and challenges of GenAI are not isolated, and they coexist in a continuous loop, like a Möbius strip (Starostin and van der Heijden, 2007). Benefits such as personalised learning and creativity are linked to challenges of ethical use, privacy, dependence, and access. Navigating these complexities requires a thoughtful, human-centered approach acknowledging their intertwined nature. By embracing both promises and limitations, stakeholders can harness GenAI's transformative potential while mitigating risks, creating more effective learning environments.

1.4 CALLING FOR EMPIRICAL RESEARCH TO CLOSE THE LOOP

Despite GenAI's promising opportunities, a significant gap exists in empirical research providing a comprehensive understanding of its effects. Integration into learning environments has been guided largely by theoretical discussions and anecdotal evidence (Zhang et al., 2024b). To fully realise GenAI's potential, it's essential to ground efforts in rigorous empirical studies evaluating practical outcomes (Zhang et al., 2024b). Current literature highlights opportunities and challenges, but empirical studies are needed to close the loop between theory and practice. For instance, while AI-driven personalisation promises improved engagement, evidence on long-term impact is limited. More research is needed to evaluate efficacy in diverse contexts and determine effects on different learners.

Research should also explore balancing AI assistance with student autonomy to mitigate over-reliance risks. Addressing ethical challenges like data privacy, bias, and equity requires systematic study to develop frameworks guiding ethical AI deployment, ensuring benefits are shared equitably. A robust empirical foundation is needed to bridge potential and practice, ensuring GenAI contributes meaningfully to education's future. This book was planned and written in the context of calling for empirical research to close the loop.

1.5 THE NARRATIVE LOGIC OF THE BOOK

This book is carefully constructed to offer an in-depth, empirical examination of how generative artificial intelligence (GenAI), particularly ChatGPT, transforms learning. This exploration is guided by a systematic narrative logic that moves from foundational historical contexts to targeted empirical research, ultimately aiming to bridge the gap between theoretical concepts and practical educational applications of GenAI.

This book opens by establishing the historical trajectory of AI in education, setting the stage for understanding the profound shifts brought about by GenAI. Chapter 1 provides a comprehensive background, tracing the evolution of technology and its interwoven relationship with education, highlighting pivotal moments that have defined learning transformations. This historical context and overview of the opportunities and challenges of learning with GenAI as a Möbius Strip is crucial for this book, as it illuminates the progression towards the current era of GenAI-integrated education.

The central research framework is introduced in Chapter 2, where theoretical concepts are linked with empirical data to create a solid foundation for the book's empirical studies. This chapter details the methods and analytical paths employed in the subsequent chapters, providing readers with insight into how various facets of learning—such as behaviour, emotion, metacognition, and ethics—are explored through rigorous experiments and multimodal data collection. This framework not only grounds the empirical investigations in theory but also provides a cohesive structure that connects the entire book.

Chapters 3–6 each delve into a distinct dimension of learning with GenAI, addressing the practical aspects of human-AI interaction. Chapter 3 focuses on learning behaviours and interaction patterns, revealing how learners engage differently with GenAI compared to traditional teacher-student dynamics. Chapter 4 shifts the focus to emotional analysis, examining whether ChatGPT can replicate the empathetic interactions typical of human teachers and how these emotional dynamics influence learners' motivation and engagement. Chapters 5 and 6 take a closer look at cognitive processes, examining how GenAI impacts both learning outcomes and metacognitive abilities. Chapter 5 assesses the effectiveness of GenAI in enhancing student performance and facilitating higher-order thinking skills, while Chapter 6 explores the impact of GenAI on metacognition and self-regulated learning, highlighting both the opportunities for promoting reflection and the risks of fostering "metacognitive laziness."

In Chapter 7, this book addresses the role of GenAI in educational assessment, exploring the dual aspects of automating traditional evaluations and opening up new opportunities for formative and summative assessments. The empirical studies presented in this chapter demonstrate how GenAI tools like ChatGPT can enhance the assessment process, offering real-time feedback and facilitating learners' self-assessment.

The narrative culminates in Chapter 8, which examines the ethical dimensions of GenAI-assisted learning, emphasising the value tensions and ethical considerations that arise when integrating GenAI into educational settings. This chapter discusses how the embedded values within GenAI systems may conflict with those of learners and educators, highlighting the need for value-sensitive AI tools and responsible implementation strategies.

The concluding chapter, Chapter 9, synthesises insights from the empirical studies and introduces emerging concepts that are anticipated to shape the future of learning with GenAI. It outlines potential future research directions, including the development of conversation-based pedagogical agents and the design of new assessment frameworks that align with GenAI's capabilities.

Throughout this book, the narrative is designed to cater to a diverse audience, including educators, researchers, policymakers, and technologists. Each chapter builds upon the previous one, offering a coherent progression that transforms fragmented theoretical discussions into a well-rounded empirical understanding of GenAI's educational implications. This logical progression ensures that readers not only grasp the practical applications of GenAI but also appreciate the theoretical underpinnings and ethical challenges associated with its integration into educational practices.

By weaving together empirical evidence, theoretical exploration, and practical insights, this book aims to illuminate the multifaceted impact of GenAI on learning, inspiring a multidisciplinary approach that is essential for advancing digital education in the 21st century.

Bibliography

Alfarra, A. H., Amhan, L. F., Mosa, M. J., Alajrami, M. A., El Kahlout, F., Abu-Nasser, B. S., and Abu-Naser, S. S. (2024). AI-driven learning: Advances and challenges in intelligent tutoring systems. *International Journal of Academic Applied Research (IJAAR)*, *8*(9):24–29.

Allen, I. E. and Seaman, J. (2013). *Changing Course: Ten Years of Tracking Online Education in the United States*. Sloan Consortium, Newburyport, MA.

Al Naqbi, H., Bahroun, Z., and Ahmed, V. (2024). Enhancing work productivity through generative artificial intelligence: A comprehensive literature review. *Sustainability, 16*(3):1166. http://doi.org/10.3390/su16031166.

Alneyadi, S. and Wardat, Y. (2024). Integrating ChatGPT in grade 12 quantum theory education: An exploratory study at emirate school (UAE). *International Journal of Information and Education Technology, 14*(3):389.

Bernabei, M., Colabianchi, S., Falegnami, A., and Costantino, F. (2023). Students' use of large language models in engineering education: A case study on technology acceptance, perceptions, efficacy, and detection chances. *Computers and Education: Artificial Intelligence, 5*:100172.

Bishop, J. and Verleger, M. A. (2013). The flipped classroom: A survey of the research. In *2013 ASEE Annual Conference & Exposition*, pp. 23–1200, Atlanta, Georgia.

Cuban, L. (1986). *Teachers and Machines: The Classroom Use of Technology Since 1920.* Teachers College Press, New York.

Cukurova, M. (2025). The interplay of learning, analytics and artificial intelligence in education: A vision for hybrid intelligence. *British Journal of Educational Technology.56*: 469–488. https://doi.org/10.1111/bjet.13514.

Dasari, D., Hendriyanto, A., Sahara, S., Suryadi, D., Muhaimin, L. H., Chao, T., and Fitriana, L. (2024). ChatGPT in didactical tetrahedron, does it make an exception? A case study in mathematics teaching and learning. *Frontiers in Education, 8*:1295413.

Dumas, D., McNeish, D., and Greene, J. A. (2020). Dynamic measurement: A theoretical–psychometric paradigm for modern educational psychology. *Educational Psychologist, 55*(2):88–105. https://doi.org/10.1080/00461520.2020.1744150.

Eisenstein, E. L. (1980). *The Printing Press as an Agent of Change*, volume 1. Cambridge University Press, Cambridge, England.

Essel, H. B., Vlachopoulos, D., Essuman, A. B., and Amankwa, J. O. (2024). ChatGPT effects on cognitive skills of undergraduate students: Receiving instant responses from AI-based conversational large language models (LLMS). *Computers and Education: Artificial Intelligence*, *6*:100198.

Fadhil, A. and Villafiorita, A. (2017). An adaptive learning with gamification & conversational UIS: The rise of cibopolibot. In *Adjunct Publication of the 25th Conference on User Modeling, Adaptation and Personalization*, Bratislava, Slovakia, pp. 408–412.

Foltz, P. W., Streeter, L. A., Lochbaum, K. E., and Landauer, T. K. (2013). Implementation and applications of the intelligent essay assessor. In Shermis, M. D. and Burstein, J., editors, *Handbook of Automated Essay Evaluation*, pp. 68–88. Routledge, New York, NY.

Garrison, D. R. and Kanuka, H. (2004). Blended learning: Uncovering its transformative potential in higher education. *The Internet and Higher Education*, *7*(2):95–105. http://doi.org/10.1016/j.iheduc.2004.02.001.

Happle, K. (2024). Cre-ai-tivity: The intersection of human ingenuity and AI collaboration in scriptwriting with ChatGPT 4.0. Utrecht University, Master's thesis.

Hellas, A., Leinonen, J., Sarsa, S., Koutcheme, C., Kujanpää, L., and Sorva, J. (2023). Exploring the responses of large language models to beginner programmers' help requests. In *Proceedings of the 2023 ACM Conference on International Computing Education Research-Volume 1*, pp. 93–105, Turku, Finland.

Horne, J. (1993). Education and state formation: The rise of education systems in England, France and the USA. *Sociology*, *27*(2):318–321.

Hu, Y., Goktas, Y., Yellamati, D. D., and De Tassigny, C. (2024). The use and misuse of pre-trained generative large language models in reliability engineering. In *2024 Annual Reliability and Maintainability Symposium (RAMS)*, pp. 1–7. IEEE, Albuquerque, New Mexico, USA.

Janse van Rensburg, J. (2024). Artificial human thinking: ChatGPT's capacity to be a model for critical thinking when prompted with problem-based writing activities. *Discover Education*, *3*(1):42.

Ji, Z., Lee, N., Frieske, R., Yu, T., Su, D., Xu, Y., Ishii, E., Bang, Y. J., Madotto, A., and Fung, P. (2023). Survey of hallucination in natural language generation. *ACM Computing Surveys*, *55*(12):1–38.

Johnson, L. (2016). NMC horizon report: 2016 higher education edition.

Joshi, I., Budhiraja, R., Dev, H., Kadia, J., Ataullah, M. O., Mitra, S., Akolekar, H. D., and Kumar, D. (2024). ChatGPT in the classroom: An analysis of its strengths and weaknesses for solving undergraduate computer science questions. In *Proceedings of the 55th ACM Technical Symposium on Computer Science Education Volume 1*, pp. 625–631, Portland, Oregon,USA.

Keiper, M. C., Fried, G., Lupinek, J., and Nordstrom, H. (2023). Artificial intelligence in sport management education: Playing the AI game with ChatGPT. *Journal of Hospitality, Leisure, Sport & Tourism Education*, *33*:100456.

Khan, U. A. and Alamäki, A. (2023). Harnessing AI to boost metacognitive learning in education. eSignals PRO.

Khosravi, H., Denny, P., Moore, S., and Stamper, J. (2023). Learnersourcing in the age of AI: Student, educator and machine partnerships for content creation. *Computers and Education: Artificial Intelligence*, *5*:100151. http://doi.org/10.1016/j.caeai.2023.100151.

Kulik, J. A. and Fletcher, J. D. (2016). Effectiveness of intelligent tutoring systems: A meta-analytic review. *Review of Educational Research*, *86*(1):42–78. http://doi.org/10.3102/0034654315581420.

Liu, Y., Han, T., Ma, S., Zhang, J., Yang, Y., Tian, J., He, H., Li, A., He, M., Liu, Z., Wu, Z., Zhao, L., Zhu, D., Li, X., Qiang, N., Shen, D., Liu, T., and Ge, B. (2023). Summary of ChatGPT-related research and perspective towards the future of large language models. *Meta-Radiology*, *1*(2):100017. http://doi.org/10.1016/j.metrad.2023.100017.

Lu, Q., Yao, Y., Xiao, L., Yuan, M., Wang, J., and Zhu, X. (2024). Can ChatGPT effectively complement teacher assessment of undergraduate students' academic writing? *Assessment & Evaluation in Higher Education*, *49*(5):616–633.

Maitland, A., Fowkes, R., and Maitland, S. (2024). Can ChatGPT pass the MRCP (UK) written examinations? Analysis of performance and errors using a clinical decision-reasoning framework. *BMJ Open*, 14(3):e080558.

Mann, B., Ryder, N., Subbiah, M., Kaplan, J., Dhariwal, P., Neelakantan, A., et al. (2020). Language models are few-shot learners. *arXiv preprint*, arXiv:2005.*14165*:1. Available at https://arxiv.org/abs/2005.14165.

Mansour, W., Albatarni, S., Eltanbouly, S., and Elsayed, T. (2024). Can large language models automatically score proficiency of written essays? *arXiv preprint arXiv:2403.06149.*

Markauskaite, L., Marrone, R., Poquet, O., Knight, S., Martinez-Maldonado, R., Howard, S., et al. (2022). Rethinking the entwinement between artificial intelligence and human learning: What capabilities do learners need for a world with AI? *Computers and Education: Artificial Intelligence*, *3*:100056. http://doi.org/10.1016/j.caeai.2022.100056.

Nguyen, A., Hong, Y., Dang, B., and Huang, X. (2024). Human-AI collaboration patterns in AI-assisted academic writing. *Studies in Higher Education*, *49* (5): 847–864.

Niloy, A. C., Akter, S., Sultana, N., Sultana, J., and Rahman, S. I. U. (2024). Is ChatGPT a menace for creative writing ability? An experiment. *Journal of Computer Assisted Learning*, *40*(2):919–930.

OpenAI (2022). How ChatGPT and our language models are developed. OpenAI Help Center.

Papert, S. (1980). Personal computing and its impact on education. In Taylor, R. P., editor, *The Computer in the School: Tutor, Tool, Tutee*, pp. 197–202. Teachers College Press, New York.

Pappano, L. (2012). The year of the MOOC. *The New York Times*. Retrieved from https://www.nytimes.com.

Partnership for 21st Century Skills (2009). P21 framework definitions. Retrieved from https://eric.ed.gov.

Phung, T., Pădurean, V.-A., Cambronero, J., Gulwani, S., Kohn, T., Majumdar, R., Singla, A., and Soares, G. (2023). Generative AI for programming education: Benchmarking ChatGPT, GPT-4, and human tutors. In *Proceedings of the 2023 ACM Conference on International Computing Education Research-Volume 2*, pp. 41–42, Chicago, Illinois, USA.

Pinargote, A., Calderón, E., Cevallos, K., Carrillo, G., Chiluiza, K., and Echeverría, V. (2024). Automating data narratives in learning analytics dashboards using GenAI. In *LAK Workshops*, pp. 150–161.

Putjorn, T. and Putjorn, P. (2023). Augmented imagination: Exploring generative AI from the perspectives of young learners. In *2023 15th International Conference on Information Technology and Electrical Engineering (ICITEE)*, pp. 353–358. IEEE.

Rezwana, J. and Maher, M. L. (2023). Designing creative AI partners with COFI: A framework for modeling interaction in human-AI co-creative systems. *ACM Transactions on Computer-Human Interaction*, *30*(5):1–28. http://doi.org/10.1145/3592425.

Seo, K., Tang, J., Roll, I., Fels, S., and Yoon, D. (2021). The impact of artificial intelligence on learner–instructor interaction in online learning. *International Journal of Educational Technology in Higher Education*, *18*:1–23. https://doi.org/10.1186/s41239-021-00292-9.

Song, C. and Song, Y. (2023). Enhancing academic writing skills and motivation: Assessing the efficacy of ChatGPT in AI-assisted language learning for EFL students. *Frontiers in Psychology*, *14*:1260843.

Starostin, E. L. and van der Heijden, G. H. M. (2007). The shape of a Möbius strip. *Nature Materials*, *6*(8):563–567. http://doi.org/10.1038/nmat1929.

Traxler, J. (2009). Current state of mobile learning. In Ally, M., editor, *Mobile Learning: Transforming the Delivery of Education and Training*, volume 1, pp. 9–24. Athabasca University Press, Edmonton, Canada.

Urban, M., Děchtěrenko, F., Lukavskỳ, J., Hrabalová, V., Svacha, F., Brom, C., and Urban, K. (2024). ChatGPT improves creative problem-solving performance in university students: An experimental study. *Computers & Education, 215*:105031.

van den Berg, G. and du Plessis, E. (2023). ChatGPT and generative AI: Possibilities for its contribution to lesson planning, critical thinking and openness in teacher education. *Education Sciences, 13*(10):998. http://doi.org/10.3390/educsci13100998.

Van Dijk, J. A. G. M. (2020). Closing the digital divide: The role of digital technologies on social development, well-being of all and the approach of the COVID-19 pandemic. In *Virtual Expert Group UN Meeting on "Socially Just Transition Towards Sustainable Development: The Role of Digital Technologies on Social Development and Well-Being of All"*. Virtual Expert Group UN Meeting.

Villan, F. and Santos, R. P. D. (2023). ChatGPT as co-advisor in scientific initiation: Action research with project-based learning in elementary education. *arXiv preprint arXiv:2311.14701.*

Vygotsky, L. S. and Cole, M. (1978). *Mind in Society: Development of Higher Psychological Processes.* Harvard University Press, Cambridge, MA.

Wan, Q., Hu, S., Zhang, Y., Wang, P., Wen, B., and Lu, Z. (2024). "It felt like having a second mind": Investigating human-AI co-creativity in prewriting with large language models. *Proceedings of the ACM on Human-Computer Interaction, 8*(CSCW1):1–26.

Williamson, B. and Eynon, R. (2020). Historical threads, missing links, and future directions in AI in education. *Learning, Media and Technology, 45*(3):223–235. http://doi.org/10.1080/17439884.2020.1798995.

Woolf, B. P. (2010). *Building Intelligent Interactive Tutors: Student-Centered Strategies for Revolutionizing E-Learning.* Morgan Kaufmann, Burlington, MA.

Yan, D. (2023). Impact of ChatGPT on learners in a L2 writing practicum: An exploratory investigation. *Education and Information Technologies, 28*(11):13943–13967.

Yan, L., Greiff, S., Teuber, Z., and Gašević, D. (2024). Promises and challenges of generative artificial intelligence for human learning. *Nature Human Behaviour*, *8*(10):1839–1850. https://doi.org/10.1038/s41562-024-02004-5.

Yeh, H.-C. (2024). The synergy of generative AI and inquiry-based learning: Transforming the landscape of english teaching and learning. *Interactive Learning Environments,33*(1): 88–102.

Zhang, L., Lin, J., Kuang, Z., Xu, S., Yeasin, M., and Hu, X. (2024a). SPL: A socratic playground for learning powered by large language models. *arXiv preprint*, arXiv:2406.13919. Available at https://arxiv.org/abs/2406.13919.

Zhang, X., Zhang, P., Shen, Y., Liu, M., Wang, Q., Gašević, D., and Fan, Y. (2024b). A systematic literature review of empirical research on applying generative artificial intelligence in education. *Frontiers of Digital Education*, *1*(3):223–245.

Zheng, N., Liu, Z., Ren, P., Ma, Y., Chen, S., Yu, S., et al. (2017). Hybrid-augmented intelligence: Collaboration and cognition. *Frontiers of Information Technology & Electronic Engineering*, *18*(2):153–179. http://doi.org/10.1631/FITEE.1601885.

CHAPTER 2

Empirical Research Design That Linking Theoretical Concepts and Empirical Data: Learning with GenAI or Human Teacher

Yizhou Fan, Peng Zhang, Luzhen Tang, and Xinyu Li

To fully understand the impact of Generative Artificial Intelligence (GenAI) on learning, solid empirical research is required. In the past two years, a wave of research has emerged around GenAI and its teaching and learning applications, employing a wide variety of research designs, methods, and analytical paths. However, which research designs are suitable for answering different types of research questions? What are the unique research methods in educational technology studies in the era of GenAI? How do different methods use specific learning processes and different data channels to measure learning theories and concepts? These questions are not only important for researchers in the field but also valuable for educators and scholars who are interested in related research. In particular, the following chapters in this book will present

DOI: 10.4324/9781003632146-2

research findings based on the same empirical research design. Therefore, the core purpose of this chapter is to review previous research designs for their strengths and weaknesses and to detail the research design, learning task, and data collection of the core empirical study in this book. The empirical research design introduced in this chapter runs through Chapters 3–8, aiming at comparing different learning conditions, such as GenAI and human experts, through a lab-based and multi-modal experimental study, thereby analysing the multifaceted impact of GenAI on learning.

2.1 INTRODUCTION: RESEARCH DESIGN OF PREVIOUS EMPIRICAL STUDIES IN LEARNING WITH GENAI

In recent years, the application of Generative Artificial Intelligence (GenAI) in education has become increasingly prevalent, drawing widespread attention for its potential to transform learning processes and enhance learning outcomes (Montenegro-Rueda et al., 2023; Lo, 2023). To fully understand the actual effects of GenAI in education, empirical research is crucial (Albadarin et al., 2024). Rigorous empirical studies combine theoretical concepts with real-world data, providing concrete evidence regarding the application of GenAI. The design of empirical research can be primarily categorised into three main types: quantitative research, qualitative research, and mixed methods research. Each type has its unique applications and suitability for different research questions.

Firstly, quantitative research methods are prevalent in the study of educational applications of GenAI, including mainly quasi-experimental studies (Niloy et al., 2024; Dasari et al., 2024; Urban et al., 2024) and survey research (Matthews and Volpe, 2023; Lu et al., 2024). Quasi-experimental studies are suitable for educational environments where strict random assignment is not feasible. These studies typically involve one control group and at least one experimental group (mostly using GenAI tools). For instance, Zhang and Huang (2024) evaluated the effectiveness of GenAI in vocabulary learning among English as a Foreign Language (EFL) students by dividing participants by dividing students into an experimental group using large language models (LLMs) as learning aids and a control group using conventional digital resources. This design is apt for assessing the impact of specific interventions, offering flexibility in real-world educational settings. However, the lack of strict random assignment may limit the reliability of causal inferences. Survey research collects quantitative data through questionnaires or scales, making it suitable for exploring participants' attitudes, motivations, and experiences with GenAI (Wan et al., 2024; Matthews and Volpe, 2023; Lu et al., 2024). For example, studies by Wu et al. (2024) collected data on students' motivation, engagement, and self-efficacy in learning with GenAI tools through surveys. The advantage of survey research lies in its ability to collect broad data, making it ideal for identifying group characteristics and trends through large sample sizes. However, results may be influenced by participant subjectivity and response biases. Additionally, survey research can identify commonalities and differences among various user groups (Tossell et al., 2024), providing insights for improving GenAI tools.

Secondly, qualitative research methods have distinct advantages in exploring specific aspects of GenAI's educational applications. Qualitative research provides detailed information through content analysis (Wan et al., 2024; Nguyen et al., 2024), case studies (Tai et al., 2024; Keiper et al., 2023; Villan and Santos, 2023), and observational studies (Liu et al., 2024; Wachira et al., 2023). For instance, Yan et al. (2024) recruited eight participants through a case-by-case observation, conducting three in-depth interview sessions to explore their perceptions of using ChatGPT for writing tasks. Through detailed analysis of individuals, the study provided deep insight into the application details and impacts of GenAI tools in specific contexts. Although qualitative research provides rich detail and profound insight, its findings are often difficult to generalise (Wan et al., 2024).

Lastly, mixed-method research designs combine quantitative and qualitative approaches, capturing the multifaceted impacts of GenAI in educational applications. For example, the study by Song et al. (2022) employed a mixed-method approach, using pre- and post-tests to evaluate the improvement of writing skills and semi-structured interviews to dive into student writing motivations and experiences. Mixed methods are suitable for comprehensively understanding various dimensions of research questions, such as exploring the general effects and specific application experiences of GenAI tools. The strength of this approach lies in its ability to offer comprehensive and multidimensional research perspectives, although its implementation and data analysis are complex and resource-intensive (Song et al., 2022). By integrating quantitative and qualitative data, researchers can achieve a more thorough and multifaceted understanding of GenAI's impact on learning.

Despite the progress made in exploring the educational applications of GenAI, several limitations persist. Several studies employ quasi-experimental designs instead of experimental designs (Matthews and Volpe, 2023; Lu et al., 2024), which may weaken the strength of causal inferences. Furthermore, a significant number of these studies utilise data collection methods, such as questionnaires, scales, and interviews (Wan et al., 2024; Matthews and Volpe, 2023), lacking the collection of multi-dimensional process data that could better inform the understanding of learning with GenAI. Furthermore, much empirical research focuses on comparing GenAI with traditional teaching methods or technologies, often lacking the integration and support of theoretical frameworks, thus limiting the theoretical contributions of these empirical studies.

To address these limitations, the empirical research we aim to introduce in this book adopts a rigorous experimental design to overcome the aforementioned challenges. Firstly, we employ randomised controlled trials (RCTs) to establish clear causal relationships, evaluating the effects of GenAI interventions through pre- and post-tests to ensure the reliability and validity of the results. Secondly, we collect data through various data channels, such as questionnaires, interviews, learning trace data, screen recording, and eye-tracking data, to capture different aspects of the learning process, enhancing the richness and diversity of data. Our research integrates established theories such as self-regulation theory, help-seeking theory, and value-sensitive design to ensure scientific rigour in research design and theoretical depth in result interpretation. These methods and measures aim to overcome the limitations of existing studies and provide more comprehensive empirical evidence about learning with GenAI.

In summary, understanding the impact of GenAI on learning requires carefully designed empirical research that tightly integrates theory with practice. While existing studies have strengths and weaknesses in design and methodology, summarising their contributions and shortcomings can provide valuable references for future research. Our study aims to contribute to this rapidly evolving field through rigorous experimental design, multimodal data collection, and solid theoretical foundations, providing scientific evidence for educational practice.

2.2 THE EMPIRICAL STUDY IN THIS BOOK: BACKGROUND, THEORY, CONTEXT, TECHNIQUE, DATA AND LEARNING ANALYTICS

2.2.1 Research Background and Questions

By the end of 2022, GenAI technologies such as ChatGPT garnered widespread global attention for their ability to generate more coherent, systematic, and information-rich responses (Zhai, 2022). GenAI has demonstrated excellence not only in text generation and information retrieval but also in the educational field, where it shows great potential. For example, ChatGPT can quickly and comprehensively assist learners in solving various complex problems, supporting tasks such as text summarisation, essay generation, code generation, and code debugging (Adeshola and Adepoju, 2023). Thus, learning with GenAI has emerged as a new research direction. Recent studies have primarily focused on how GenAI can act as an effective agent to support and enhance learning (M Alshater, 2022; Terwiesch, 2023; Baidoo-Anu and Ansah, 2023; Noy and Zhang, 2023). For example, ChatGPT can provide timely feedback (Dai et al., 2023) and personalised learning (Limo et al., 2023) during the learning process. However, researchers also point out that GenAI aids learners mainly by generating content from existing data and providing high-quality materials, but it cannot offer context-specific explanations like human teachers nor fully replace their roles (Ausat et al., 2023). The research gap lies in exploring how students interact with human teachers or GenAI, as well as understanding the impact these interactions have on their learning process and performance.

Although GenAI has been applied in various contexts, including programming teaching (Cambaz and Zhang, 2024), art education (Dehouche and Dehouche, 2023), history teaching (Ma, 2023), and medical education (Abd-Alrazaq et al., 2023), we focus on writing instruction in our research. Writing is a higher-order cognitive skill that involves complex processes such as critical thinking, organisation, and argumentation. Moreover, it has a high degree of transferability across different contexts, making it a valuable skill for students in various disciplines. Additionally, the textual output generated during writing provides a rich source of data, allowing for detailed analysis of student progress and interaction patterns with both human teachers and GenAI.

Therefore, we designed a writing task on an online learning platform in our empirical study.

Previous studies have mentioned the role of GenAI in writing instruction. For instance, ChatGPT can generate detailed, fluid, and coherent feedback on student essays (Dai et al., 2023), such as spelling checks, language refinement, and idea suggestions during the writing process (Baskara, 2023; Imran and Almusharraf, 2023). Past research has shown that providing feedback to students during the writing process can help them improve their essays (Paulus, 1999). Traditional writing feedback is given by human teachers (Hyland, 2003) or peer reviews (Huisman et al., 2019). Alternatively, ChatGPT as a generative large language model is able to serve as a new agent to provide automated and instant feedback to learners. However, still there are relatively few empirical studies on the intervention effects of different agents, particularly comparative studies on the impact of GenAI and human teachers in writing instruction. Therefore, by designing a comprehensive reading and writing task and providing feedback from different agents, we hope to explore the impact of different agents from different perspectives of learning.

Our first research question focuses on human–AI interaction, particularly human-AI dialogue. GenAI has the potential to simulate the conversational style of human teachers and generate personalised teaching content and feedback. However, the introduction of GenAI in teaching raises a crucial question: Can human-machine dialogue truly replace traditional learner-teacher dialogue? In other words, how does learner-AI dialogue differ from teacher-led dialogue? The traditional Socratic method of dialogue instruction emphasises deepening knowledge and enhancing skills through teachers' inquiries and students' critical thinking and debate. The effectiveness of this approach depends on dynamic interaction and meaningful communication between teachers and students. In contrast, while GenAI can generate responses quickly and guide student learning, its interaction modes may differ significantly from those of a human teacher, which may affect the student's subsequent behaviour and reflection. Therefore, in Chapter 3, we will explore the following question: **What are the differences between GenAI-led dialogue and teacher-led dialogue? What is the difference between the process of students seeking help from teachers and seeking help from GenAI?** In Chapter 3, we will analyse these differences by combining *Pedagogy of Dialogue Theory* and *Help-seeking Theory*, providing a foundational understanding of the interaction between students and GenAI.

Emotional dynamics in human–computer interaction is also an important topic in our research. Teachers influence students not only by delivering knowledge but also by providing emotional support, such as expressing understanding and encouragement, which enhances students' motivation and confidence in learning. Similarly, when students interact with GenAI, it is crucial for GenAI to provide comparable emotional support effectively. For instance, can GenAI recognise the emotional changes that students may experience, particularly during moments of frustration, and provide timely comfort and positive guidance? Furthermore, how do these emotional changes differ from students' experiences with human teachers? Do students feel less emotional burden, or perhaps more isolated due to the absence of human warmth? These questions about emotional changes not only impact learning outcomes but may also shape students' overall attitudes toward learning. In Chapter 4, we will explore the following question: **What is the difference between students' emotional states and emotional changes when interacting with GenAI versus teachers?** Our research in Chapter 4, based on *Emotion and Empathy Theory*, will examine the emotional differences in students tutored by GenAI and human teachers, providing insights into how GenAI offers more effective teaching strategies to enhance students' emotional engagement.

Building on our previous discussions of GenAI's role in education, it is essential to examine its impact on student learning outcomes, which has become a critical focus in evaluating GenAI's effectiveness. An increasing number of students are turning to GenAI to support their studies. On the one hand, GenAI can quickly provide extensive feedback, helping students complete their tasks more efficiently and ultimately achieve better performance. Additionally, the process of filtering and reflecting on the information provided by GenAI exercises students' higher-order thinking skills, such as critical thinking, problem-solving, and creative thinking. However, this growing reliance on GenAI in education has also raised some concerns. For teachers, it is becoming increasingly challenging to assess students' genuine understanding. When every student can produce high-quality assignments with the help of GenAI, it becomes difficult for teachers to determine whether the student has truly grasped the knowledge. While GenAI can significantly enhance the quality of assignments, it does not necessarily facilitate students' comprehension of concepts or mastery of knowledge. Students might merely use GenAI to generate answers mechanically, without truly engaging in the knowledge construction process, which could hinder their ability to transfer knowledge to new contexts in the future. Therefore, beyond the apparent improvement in performance (e.g. grade, score), it is crucial to consider whether students are genuinely learning. In Chapter 5, we will explore the following question: **What are the differences in learning outcomes when students are supported by GenAI versus human teachers?** Drawing on *Constructivism Learning Theory*, we will specifically analyse the differences in student learning performance, knowledge gains, and the ability to transfer knowledge.

While Chapter 5 focuses on student learning outcomes, we will also explore the learning process, particularly students' cognitive and metacognitive processes. Effective and autonomous learners need to develop strong metacognitive abilities and self-regulated learning (SRL)skills to plan, monitor, and evaluate their learning processes. The strength of GenAI lies in its ability to quickly generate extensive feedback and guidance, offering students diverse perspectives that enhance their critical and creative thinking skills. However, it's important to note that an over-reliance on GenAI for answers might reduce learners' motivation for independent thought and self-reflection. To prevent this, learners should actively consider how to regulate their learning strategies and behaviours with the support of GenAI, aiming for deep learning and long-term knowledge transfer. Within this context, Chapter 6 will address the following question: **What are the impacts of GenAI on learners' metacognitive processes and self-regulated learning?** Based on *Metacognition Theory* and *Self-regulated Learning Theory*, we will particularly examine potential issues of metacognitive laziness in the use of GenAI and propose strategies to encourage active learning and effective use of GenAI.

Furthermore, we also explore the potential applications of GenAI in educational assessment. Assessment, as a crucial component of the educational process, guides teachers in adjusting their teaching methods to meet learners' learning needs and aiding learners in understanding their progress, thereby fostering self-reflection and the adjustment of learning strategies. On one hand, GenAI has the potential to serve as a teacher's assistant by helping grade students' learning outcomes and providing feedback. On the other hand, GenAI can also be involved in students' learning process by assisting them in self-assessing their learning performance. However, there is uncertainty regarding the effects of using GenAI for educational assessment, such as the consistency, objectivity, and stability of assessment results. Therefore, Chapter 7 will explore: **How can GenAI be utilised for assessing both learning outcomes and processes? What are the effects of using GenAI for educational evaluation?** By integrating *Educational Assessment Approaches* and *Self-assessment Theory*, Chapter 7 will reveal the potential of GenAI in future educational assessments.

Finally, we must consider the ethical challenges associated with applying GenAI to education. While GenAI offers numerous conveniences for teaching, its widespread use raises a series of ethical concerns, including privacy breaches, academic misconduct, and over-reliance on the technology. Addressing these challenges effectively requires educators, technology developers, and policymakers to collaborate in establishing clear ethical standards and usage guidelines that balance the innovations GenAI offers with the potential ethical risks. In Chapter 8, we will focus on the following questions: **What ethical challenges might GenAI introduce to education? What values do learners prioritise when interacting with GenAI or teachers? How do GenAI's goals and actions align with learners' values?** By conducting *Value Analysis* within this chapter, we aim to provide a comprehensive framework for understanding and mitigating the ethical challenges associated with integrating GenAI into educational settings.

2.2.2 Research Design and Learning Task

Our study was conducted in a controlled laboratory setting. Figure 2.1 shows our research design. Participants were requested to complete the pre-task stage before entering the laboratory. The subsequent learning task is conducted within the laboratory, including the writing stage and revision stage. After completing the learning task in the laboratory, the participants were asked to complete the post-task stage outside the laboratory within three days.

1. Pre-task stage: The day before entering the formal learning task, learners were asked to complete the pre-test questionnaire in the pre-task stage.

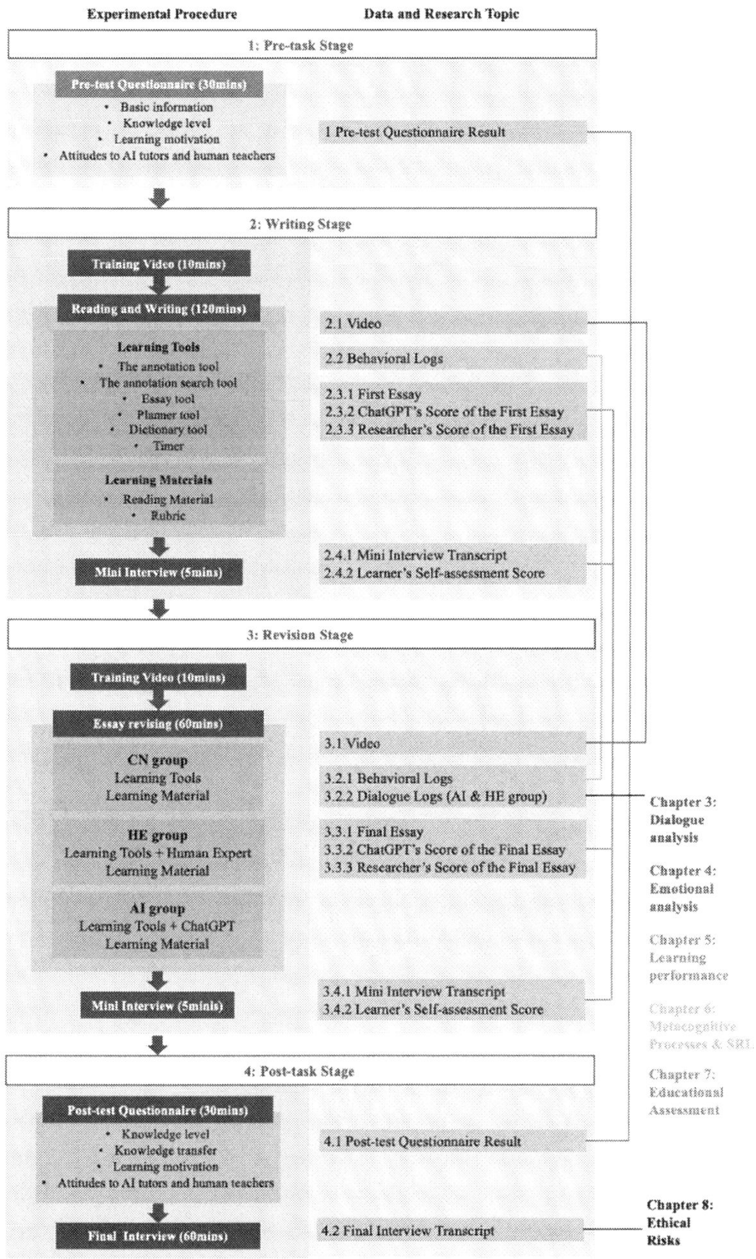

Figure 2.1 Research design and research topic of whole study.

2. Writing stage: Prior to the writing stage, participants were provided with training video to help them understand the operation of the learning platform and the instructions for learning task. The writing stage was a reading and writing task, which required participants to read the reading material on three topics: artificial intelligence, differentiation in the classroom, and scaffolding of learning. Based on these materials, participants were required to write a 200–400 word essay that envisioning the education in 2035. Participants were also provided with the rubric to help them understand the essay scoring rules. The writing stage was limited to 120 minutes. Upon completion, participants were invited to participate in a 5-minute mini-interview to reflect on and assess task performance, after which participants could take a 15-minute break to move on to the revision stage.

3. Revision stage: Participants in this stage were allocated into three groups: control group (CN group), artificial intelligence group (AI group), and human expert group (HE group). The CN group maintained the same learning environment as the writing stage. The AI group had the tool to communicate with ChatGPT4. The HE group had the tool to communicate with a human expert, who is an academic writing teacher, has extensive experience in academic writing, and is familiar with our task topic. Prior to the revision stage, participants were provided with training videos to help them understand the operation of the learning platform and the instructions for learning task. The revision stage was the essay revision task, which required participants to revise their first essay in the writing stage. The CN group completes the revision independently, the AI group communicates with ChatGPT4 to receive feedback, and the HE group communicates with a human expert to receive feedback. The revision stage was limited to 60 minutes. Upon completion, participants were invited to participate in a 5-minute mini-interview to reflect on and assess task performance.

4. Post-task stage: After completing the learning task, the researchers and ChatGPT4 scored participants' first and final essays and provided feedback independently. We sent both researchers and ChatGPT4 scores and feedback to participants. Within three days of completing the learning task, participants were required to complete a post-test questionnaire and participate in semi-structured interviews of up to one hour.

2.2.3 Participants

We recruited participants through a web bulletin. All participants participated voluntarily and received a fee after completing all tasks. A total of 100 learners (average age 22.42, SD = 3.48, with 63% female and 53% undergraduate) from Peking University participated in the experiment from May to September 2023. Peking University is a first-class university in China, so the knowledge and competence of the participants are relatively high compared to their peers across the country. These learners are not native English speakers. 73% of these learners have used GenAI, including searching for information, processing data, polishing essays, and translating foreign languages. These learners come from a diverse array of disciplines, including science (24%), medicine (16%), law (12%), management (12%), literature (10%), education (6%), engineering (4%), economics (4%), history (4%), philosophy (4%), interdiscipline(3%), and art (1%).

These 100 learners were randomly divided into three groups, and all sets completed the English writing task within the same learning environment in stage one. However, during stage two, one group had the support of ChatGPT (AI group, 36 participants), one group had the support of a human expert (HE group, 31 participants), while the control group did not (CN group, 33 participants). In particular, due to the different data types used in each chapter, the number of participants retained in each chapter may be different in order to ensure data integrity.

2.2.4 Learning Environment and Learning Tools

The learning environment utilised in our studies is known as FLoRA (https://github.com/Xinyu-Li/FLoRA) (Figure 2.2), an advanced, web-based, micro-service architectural learning and data analysis engine designed to enhance SRL among learners. The FLoRA learning environment is the product of the FLoRA project[1], which is led by Maria Bannert, Inge Molenaar, Dragan Gasevic and Johanna D. Moore. This innovative tool is grounded in decades of research in SRL theory and empirical studies (Li et al., 2024). The engine leverages contemporary advancements in learning analytics (LA), artificial intelligence (AI),

[1] https://floraproject.org/website/.

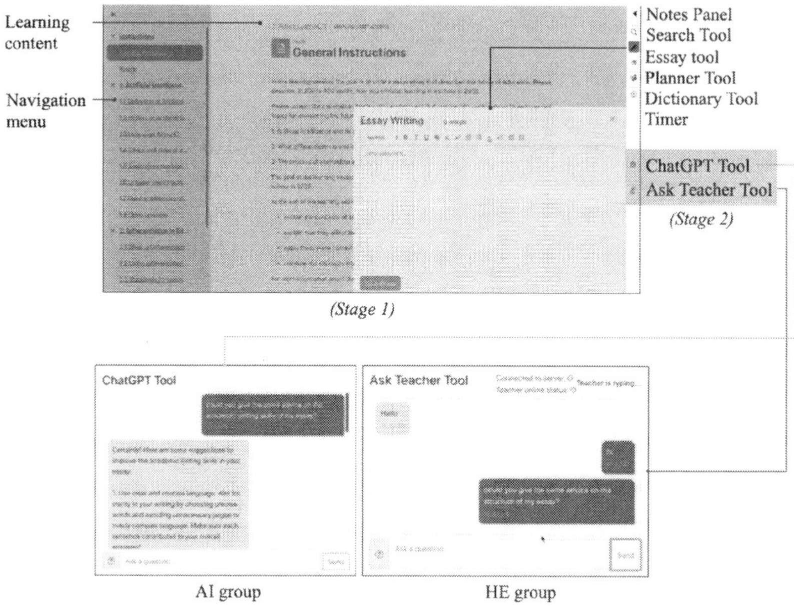

Figure 2.2 Learning environment and learning tools of FLoRA.

and data analytics to provide a comprehensive solution for detecting, measuring, and facilitating SRL processes across diverse educational contexts. The FLoRA engine comprises a suite of instrumentation tools designed to support a variety of learning tasks, including text annotation, essay writing, problem-solving, and more. These tools are not only functional but also unobtrusively collect fine-grained trace data as learners engage with their tasks. This data includes detailed records of interactions such as mouse movements, clicks, keystrokes, and page navigations, which are essential for understanding and analysing learners' behaviours and strategies. The instrumentation tools are customisable, enabling educators and researchers to tailor them to specific learning environments and tasks.

Our study selected several instrumentation tools from FLoRA, including the annotation tool, annotation search tool, essay tool, planner tool, dictionary tool, timer, chatbot tool, and chathuman tool. *The annotation tool* enables users to highlight text, write notes associated with the highlighted text, and assign labels. Additionally, *the annotation search tool* allows learners to search their annotations across different pages within the learning environment. *The essay tool*, a rich text editor, permits users to compose task content. Furthermore, *the planner tool* facilitates users in creating a plan for their learning by offering a predefined step-by-step guide to help learners complete the plan efficiently. *The dictionary tool* allows learners to translate English words into Chinese. *Timer* displays the remaining time until the completion of the task. *The ChatGPT tool*, based on the OpenAI GPT-4 API, allows learners to interact by sending their essay and background text material along with their questions to OpenAI to receive a response. Consequently, the GPT-4 LLM is aware of the context of the question asked. Regarding *the ask teacher tool*, a separate chat portal is provided to an experienced human teacher. Learners can engage in real-time chats with the human teacher to receive instant feedback. The human teacher can view learners' essays in the backend as learners apply the feedback updates.

In our task, learners are required to revise their essays using the provided tools. All learners are randomly divided into three groups: Control group (CN group), ChatGPT group (AI group) and Human Expert group (HE group). Except for the CN group, each group is assigned a feedback tool. The CN group does not have any feedback tool and must revise their essays independently. The AI group uses the ChatGPT tool and the HE group uses the Ask Teacher tool.

2.2.5 Quantitative and Qualitative Multi-Channel Data

Our experiment consists of four parts: pre-task stage, writing stage, revision stage, and post-task stage. We collect different types of data during these four parts:

1. **Pre-task stage:** In the pre-test, we used a questionnaire to gather data on the participants' basic information, knowledge levels, learning motivation, and attitudes to AI tutors and human teachers.

2. **Writing stage:** During the writing stage, participants watched a training video and completed a reading and writing task. We collected log data from the learning platform (including behavioural logs such as mouse and keyboard data) and video data during the task (including facial data from the front-facing camera, body

posture data from the rear-facing camera, and screen activity from the screen recording camera). After the writing stage, we collected the participants' first essays and their self-assessment scores of their essays. Table 2.1 shows different types of our data during the writing stage.

3. **Revision stage:** During the revision stage, participants watched a training video and completed a revision task. We collected log data (including behavioural logs, dialogue logs of AI group and HE group) and video data (including facial data from the front-facing camera, body posture data from the rear-facing camera, and screen activity from the screen recording camera). After revision stage, we collected the participants' final essay and their self-assessment scores of their essays. Table 2.1 shows different types of our data during revision stage.

4. **Post-task stage:** In the post-test, we used a questionnaire to gather data on the participants' knowledge levels, knowledge transfer results, learning motivation, and attitudes to AI tutors and human teachers. Additionally, we conducted interviews with participants and provided them with essay scores and feedback (including scores from ChatGPT4 and researchers). We also collected feedback on these scores through a questionnaire.

2.3 OVERVIEW OF EMPIRICAL STUDIES IN THE FOLLOWING CHAPTERS

As the integration of GenAI tools such as ChatGPT in educational settings continues to expand, researchers are increasingly exploring their effects on various aspects of the learning process, from cognitive and metacognitive engagement to emotional responses and performance outcomes. In the following chapters, we delve into a series of empirical studies that examine how learners interact with AI in different educational contexts, particularly in the realm of English language learning. These studies shed light on the nuanced ways in which students engage with GenAI tools, comparing them to traditional human interactions, and provide insights into both the potential benefits and challenges of incorporating GenAI in educational practices. Specifically, we will

TABLE 2.1 Types of Data (Writing Stage & Revision Stage)

	Writing Stage	**Revision Stage**
Questionnaire	Self-assessment score: after writing stage, learners scored their essays according to the rubric	Self-assessment score: after revision stage, learners scored their essays according to the rubric
Interview	Mini interview1: After writing stage. Collect learner's reflection of their performance	Mini interview2: After revision stage. Collect learner's reflection of their performance
Video	(1) Front video: collect facial data, (2) rear video: collect body posture data, (3) screen video: collect screen activity from the screen recording camera	(1) Front video: collect facial data, (2) Rear video: collect body posture data, (3) Screen video: collect screen activity from the screen recording camera
Log data	Behavioural logs: collect behavioural logs such as mouse and keyboard data	(1) Behavioural logs: collect behavioural logs such as mouse and keyboard data. (2) Dialogue logs: collect dialogue logs of AI group and HE group
Essay	First essay	Final essay
Essay score and feedback	(1) ChatGPT score, (2) researcher score	(1) ChatGPT score, (2) researcher score, (3) ChatGPT feedback, (4) Researcher feedback

explore learner behaviours such as help-seeking, emotional responses to feedback, writing performance, and the implications of over-reliance on AI tools. Each study offers valuable perspectives on the intersection of AI technology and educational theory, ultimately contributing to a deeper understanding of how GenAI can enhance or hinder the learning experience.

The first study in Chapter 3 investigates the authentic process of learner-AI interaction, focusing on how non-native English speakers engage with ChatGPT during English reading and writing tasks. Participants were asked to compose essays envisioning the state of education in 2035, guided by a rubric and prompts related to artificial intelligence, classroom differentiation, and learning scaffolding. To analyse these interactions, the researchers developed a coding framework to classify learners' questions into categories such as task-relevant (e.g., theme-related queries, writing improvement, and meta cognition) and task-irrelevant (e.g., greetings, off-topic remarks). Findings revealed that most interactions centred on writing enhancement and theme-related inquiries, with students frequently asking for content polishing, grammar corrections, and translations. However, the data also highlighted a subset of irrelevant or trivial questions, indicating varying levels of engagement and task focus. The researchers further identified four questioning strategies—off-topic, topic-focused, writing enhancement, and balanced questioning—offering a nuanced understanding of how students utilise AI tools in learning. These insights suggest that while students actively seek help in improving their work, they may require scaffolding to optimise their engagement and task-oriented interactions with ChatGPT.

The second study in Chapter 3 examines the differences in help-seeking behaviours between students interacting with ChatGPT and those consulting a human expert during essay revision tasks. Participants were divided into two groups: the AI group, supported by ChatGPT, and the HE group, guided by a human expert. Using a coding framework for help-seeking stages—diagnosing questions, asking help, evaluating help, and processing help—the study uncovered distinct patterns. Help-seeking with human experts followed a more linear and systematic process, beginning with identifying problems and progressing sequentially through stages. Conversely, interactions with ChatGPT were more flexible and nonlinear, with students often skipping stages or revisiting earlier ones, reflecting a dynamic but less structured approach. Notably, students in the AI group tended to engage in iterative questioning and direct application of help, while those in the HE group prioritised evaluation and reflection before accepting assistance. These findings highlight differences in cognitive and metacognitive self-regulation when seeking help from AI versus human experts, suggesting that while

ChatGPT supports task completion, human experts may better facilitate deeper learning and adaptive help-seeking behaviours.

The empirical study in Chapter 4 compares learners' emotional responses to feedback from GenAI (ChatGPT) versus a human teacher in the context of English writing tutoring. Using data-driven methods such as facial expression analysis and process mining, the study reveals that learners show more frequent boredom when using ChatGPT, but they are also able to regain focus more effectively, likely due to the immediate and on-demand nature of GenAI feedback. In contrast, teacher-led sessions lead to less boredom but may present greater challenges in maintaining sustained focus, possibly due to the more dynamic nature of teacher-student interactions. The study also finds that **guided feedback** from GenAI, which involves prompts and suggestions, is associated with **negative emotions** such as confusion and boredom, likely because it requires learners to engage in more independent problem-solving without clear answers. In contrast, **concise feedback** from teachers, which provides direct and clear answers, tends to evoke **stronger emotional reactions**—both positive and negative—suggesting that learners find such feedback more engaging or motivating. Overall, the study highlights the emotional dynamics of learning with GenAI versus a teacher, emphasising that while GenAI helps learners regain focus quickly, the clarity and immediacy of teacher feedback lead to more intense emotional engagement, providing valuable insights for integrating AI in education effectively.

The empirical study in Chapter 5 explores the impact of GenAI, specifically ChatGPT, on university students' writing performance, knowledge gain, and algorithm aversion, comparing it with human tutors. The study involved 60 ESL learners, who first completed a writing task and then revised their essays either with ChatGPT (AI group) or under human expert guidance (HE group). The results revealed that while both groups performed similarly before revision, the AI group showed significantly greater improvement in essay scores post-revision, indicating that GenAI can enhance writing performance, sometimes surpassing human tutors. However, there were no significant differences between the groups in terms of knowledge gain or transfer, as both groups demonstrated similar pre- and post-test scores on AI-related topics. Observations indicated that many students in the AI group merely copied and pasted content generated by ChatGPT, rather than engaging with the material to deepen their understanding. In terms of algorithm aversion, most participants initially preferred human tutors, but the AI group showed a marginal shift toward accepting AI after the task, suggesting that positive experiences with GenAI may reduce algorithm aversion. This study highlights GenAI's potential to improve specific aspects of learning, such as writing performance, but also emphasises that its effects on knowledge acquisition and long-term learning outcomes remain inconclusive and warrant further research.

The empirical study in Chapter 6 focuses on over-reliance on GenAI utilisation from a metacognitive perspective, the authors empirically investigate how excessive dependence on ChatGPT affects learners' cognitive and metacognitive processes. While previous research has identified the issue of over-reliance, few studies have examined the specific behaviors associated with this phenomenon, especially from a metacognitive standpoint. The study builds on the concept of cognitive offloading, where learners delegate part of their cognitive load to external tools like GenAI, thus potentially reducing cognitive strain but also impacting metacognitive skills. The authors argue that over-reliance may weaken learners' confidence in their abilities, as frequent use of AI tools for answers may diminish their self-regulation skills and judgment of task difficulty. This shift, when unaddressed, could reinforce a cycle of dependency on AI, leading to poorer problem-solving and metacognitive skills. The study utilised a two-stage English reading and writing task, where participants from diverse disciplines were divided into three groups: a control group with no external support, an AI group using ChatGPT, a human expert (HE) group. The participants' interactions with the tasks were tracked using learning trace data, including page views, clickstreams, and mouse movements, which were analysed with process mining methods to uncover the learners' behavior patterns. The findings revealed that learners in the AI group exhibited significantly higher engagement with ChatGPT, particularly during the revision phase. This indicated that they were relying on the AI tool to offload cognitive tasks, such as essay refinement, rather than revisiting the reading materials or independently organising their thoughts. This process of cognitive offloading, termed **metacognitive laziness**, was particularly prominent in the AI group, suggesting that the excessive use of ChatGPT may hinder learners from fully engaging with the learning process and developing independent metacognitive skills.

The study highlights the importance of addressing this over-reliance by encouraging more balanced and active engagement with learning tasks.

The first empirical study in Chapter 7 explores the use of ChatGPT for assessing learners' essay performance, specifically comparing its scoring and feedback to that of human teachers. The study aimed to determine the consistency of ChatGPT's assessments and the characteristics of its feedback. Participants, all non-native English speakers, were tasked with writing an essay based on reading materials on topics such as artificial intelligence and differentiated instruction. After completing the essays, participants received feedback from both ChatGPT and human researchers, using a detailed rubric for evaluation. The results showed a high correlation between the scores given by ChatGPT and human researchers, particularly in areas such as basic writing skills and academic writing style, with moderate agreement in more complex aspects like content depth and originality. However, the study highlighted limitations in ChatGPT's ability to assess creativity and critical thinking, as the AI struggled with scoring originality and providing feedback on nuanced content. Furthermore, the analysis of the feedback showed that while both ChatGPT and human feedback were generally neutral, ChatGPT's feedback tended to focus more on the content topics, offering fluid and coherent responses. In contrast, human feedback was more varied and specific, addressing broader issues such as grammar and word count, and utilising a more complex syntactic structure. These findings suggest that while ChatGPT demonstrates strong potential as an automated assessment tool, particularly for basic skills, it may need further refinement to evaluate more sophisticated aspects of student writing effectively, such as originality and deep analysis.

In the second empirical study in Chapter 7, ChatGPT was used to support learners' self-assessment during writing tasks, with a focus on how the AI tool influenced the accuracy and process of self-assessment. The study investigated whether ChatGPT could enhance learners' ability to assess their own writing performance and improve the self-regulated learning process. Participants were tasked with writing essays and revising them based on feedback. Half of the learners received feedback from ChatGPT, while the other half worked without AI assistance. The study examined the accuracy of learners' self-assessments and the overall impact of the feedback on their revision process. Results indicated that ChatGPT's feedback helped learners more accurately assess their writing, providing specific suggestions for improvement, particularly in areas like grammar and style. The AI also seemed to enhance learners' engagement in the revision process, with participants revising their essays more thoroughly after receiving feedback. However, the study also noted that while ChatGPT facilitated more accurate self-assessment in some cases, learners sometimes became overly reliant on the AI, potentially undermining their own critical thinking and reflection. Overall, the study highlighted ChatGPT's potential as a tool for supporting self-assessment and self-regulated learning, although it also cautioned against the risk of over-reliance on AI feedback in the writing process.

The empirical study in Chapter 8 focuses on value-sensitive design (VSD) in online learning environments, which seeks to understand the ethical values that learners prioritise during AI-assisted and human-assisted learning. Grounded in the VSD framework, which integrates social, cultural, and ethical considerations into technology design, the research investigates how stakeholders' values—such as autonomy, privacy, and freedom from bias—are embedded in educational technology. The study emphasises the need for a more empirical approach to VSD, particularly in the context of GenAI tools like ChatGPT, which have raised ethical concerns in educational settings. While previous research has identified various ethical issues, such as privacy violations and academic misconduct, there has been limited exploration of the value tensions that arise when these issues intersect with online learning environments. The empirical study involved 59 participants who were interviewed after completing tasks with either GenAI or human facilitators. These semi-structured interviews focused on three core research questions: (1) what values learners prioritise during online learning, (2) how GenAI and human facilitators differ in embodying these values, and (3) what value tensions arise when GenAI is involved. The data were analysed using thematic analysis, leading to the identification of eight value themes: responsiveness, social comfort, autonomy, freedom from bias, privacy, efficiency, accuracy, and development. Key findings revealed that learners placed significant importance on the values of responsiveness, social comfort, and autonomy. They expressed a preference for facilitators who could quickly understand and respond to their needs, provide a supportive and non-judgmental environment, and respect their autonomy in the learning process. The study's findings highlight the importance of these values in shaping effective online learning experiences and suggest that AI systems, such as ChatGPT, must be designed to embody these values to foster a supportive and ethical learning environment. The research contributes to the broader conversation on the ethical implications of AI in education, providing insights into how value tensions can be addressed through thoughtful design and stakeholder engagement.

In summary, the studies presented in these chapters collectively highlight the diverse ways in which generative AI, particularly ChatGPT, influences learning. From enhancing writing performance and supporting self-assessment to shaping emotional responses and help-seeking behaviours, these studies reveal both the strengths and limitations of AI tools in educational contexts. While AI can foster increased engagement, improve task-specific skills, and facilitate personalised feedback, it also introduces challenges such as the potential for over-reliance and limited capacity for assessing higher-order cognitive skills like creativity and critical thinking. Moreover, the emotional dynamics of learning with AI—ranging from increased focus to heightened boredom—underscore the complex interplay between technology and learner motivation. Ultimately, these findings emphasise the need for a balanced approach that integrates AI tools thoughtfully, ensuring that they complement, rather than replace, the essential role of human instructors in fostering deep learning, critical thinking, and metacognitive growth.

2.4 HOW DO WE LINK THEORETICAL CONCEPTS TO EMPIRICAL DATA IN THE RESEARCH DESIGN?

In educational research, particularly in the context of evolving technologies like GenAI and their impact on learning environments, the connection between theoretical frameworks and empirical research is both essential and complex.

The studies presented in this book illustrate how theoretical concepts, often drawn from well-established frameworks, can be translated into research designs that generate meaningful empirical data. By examining specific research designs and findings, we can gain insights into how educational theories inform real-world investigations while also highlighting the challenges of addressing these theoretical concepts within actual learning settings.

For example, in Chapter 8, the theoretical framework of VSD plays a central role in guiding the empirical investigation of learners' values and ethical concerns during interactions with AI systems. VSD is grounded in the idea that technology should be developed in a way that aligns with human values and ethical principles, ensuring that technologies like GenAI not only enhance functionality but also foster human welfare and societal good. The study specifically explores how learners prioritise and perceive key values—such as responsiveness, social comfort, and autonomy—during online learning facilitated by ChatGPT and human experts. These values are part of the VSD framework's ethical considerations, including autonomy and freedom from bias, which are often critical in educational contexts.

The study employs VSD's three-part framework (conceptual, empirical, and technical investigations) to gather data through semi-structured interviews, allowing for a deeper exploration of the ethical values learners find most important. For instance, participants highlighted responsiveness as a vital value, expecting facilitators (AI or human) to promptly and empathetically address their needs. This aligns with VSD's emphasis on human welfare and autonomy, where learners want the freedom to express themselves and receive appropriate feedback without bias. Another significant value that emerged was social comfort, wherein learners expressed the need for a non-judgmental, supportive environment, especially during interactions with AI. These findings directly relate to VSD's focus on ensuring technologies foster social well-being and privacy, creating a space where learners feel comfortable and respected.

Through this empirical study, the authors use VSD to uncover value tensions in AI-assisted learning environments, such as the balance between efficiency (a strength of AI) and the emotional support typically offered by human facilitators. By systematically exploring how learners' values are reflected in their interactions with both AI and human facilitators, this research bridges theoretical frameworks with empirical data, highlighting the complexities and ethical considerations involved in designing educational technologies that respect and support human values.

For example, in Chapter 7, theoretical frameworks related to assessment, feedback, and self-regulated learning (SRL) were used to design and analyse the role of ChatGPT in evaluating student writing. The research focused on two key areas: (1) the consistency of ChatGPT's assessment with human ratings, and (2) the characteristics of feedback provided by ChatGPT compared to human teachers. The study draws upon theories of assessment, particularly those related to validity and reliability, as well as feedback theories that emphasise the importance of clear, actionable information for student improvement. By using a rubric as the assessment criterion, the study ensured that both ChatGPT and human raters evaluated the essays consistently. For example, the high correlation between ChatGPT's and human raters' scores on basic writing skills and academic writing abilities supports the validity of ChatGPT as an automated assessment tool.

The use of natural language processing (NLP) to analyse feedback allowed for a comparison of the types of comments given by both raters, revealing distinct patterns in feedback styles. While both sources provided helpful insights, human feedback was more nuanced and comprehensive, using more complex sentence structures and addressing a wider range of writing issues. Additionally, the study explored self-assessment, an essential aspect of self-regulated learning, showing how ChatGPT could enhance learners' ability to assess their own work. Drawing on SRL theories, which emphasise learner agency and reflection, the research highlighted how learners, supported by ChatGPT feedback, could improve their writing skills through iterative self-assessment. By integrating these theoretical frameworks with empirical data, the study demonstrates how emerging technologies like ChatGPT can be effectively employed in educational settings to enhance both assessment and learning processes.

For another example, in Chapter 6, the theoretical frameworks of cognitive offloading and metacognition were pivotal in understanding the learners' over-reliance on GenAI tools like ChatGPT. Cognitive offloading, a concept where learners offload cognitive tasks to external tools to alleviate mental load, is a foundational theory explored here. This framework posits that while offloading can enhance short-term cognitive efficiency, excessive reliance on external resources, like ChatGPT, can have detrimental long-term effects on learners' cognitive and metacognitive development. The study operationalises this theory by examining the specific behaviours associated with this offloading, framing them as "metacognitive laziness," where learners overly depend on GenAI for tasks that typically engage higher-order thinking, such as problem-solving and task evaluation. For instance, in analysing learner interactions with ChatGPT, the study uses process mining and data from learning traces to capture real-time behaviours. These include how often learners interact with ChatGPT versus performing cognitive tasks independently. The findings link back to cognitive offloading by showing that students in the AI group exhibited more frequent "Other" node transitions, reflecting their over-dependence on ChatGPT for feedback and revision tasks, rather than engaging in self-monitoring or evaluation.

Thus, this study bridges theory and empirical data by mapping learners' cognitive behaviors in response to varying levels of GenAI support. By linking metacognitive theories to observable actions—such as returning repeatedly to ChatGPT for revisions or relying on it for task evaluation—the study provides concrete evidence of how cognitive offloading, when taken to an extreme, can lead to impaired metacognitive processes. These findings underscore the importance of designing interventions that can help learners regain metacognitive control and encourage more balanced use of GenAI in educational settings.

Bibliography

Abd-Alrazaq, A., AlSaad, R., Alhuwail, D., Ahmed, A., Healy, P. M., Latifi, S., et al. (2023). Large language models in medical education: Opportunities, challenges, and future directions. *JMIR Medical Education*, *9*(1):e48291.

Adeshola, I. and Adepoju, A. P. (2023). The opportunities and challenges of ChatGPT in education. *Interactive Learning Environments*, *10* (10):6159—6172. https://doi.org/10.1080/10494820.2023.2253858

Albadarin, Y., Saqr, M., Pope, N., and Tukiainen, M. (2024). A systematic literature review of empirical research on ChatGPT in education. *Discover Education*, *3*(1):60.

Alshater, M. M. (2022). Exploring the role of artificial intelligence in enhancing academic performance: A case study of ChatGPT. *Available at SSRN*.

Ausat, A. M. A., Massang, B., Efendi, M., Nofirman, N., and Riady, Y. (2023). Can ChatGPT replace the role of the teacher in the classroom: A fundamental analysis. *Journal on Education*, *5*(4):16100–16106.

Baidoo-Anu, D. and Ansah, L. O. (2023). Education in the era of generative artificial intelligence (AI): Understanding the potential benefits of ChatGPT in promoting teaching and learning. *Journal of AI*, *7*(1):52–62.

Baskara, F. (2023). Integrating ChatGPT into EFL writing instruction: Benefits and challenges. *International Journal of Education and Learning*, *5*(1):44–55.

Cambaz, D. and Zhang, X. (2024). Use of AI-driven code generation models in teaching and learning programming: A systematic literature review. In *Proceedings of the 55th ACM Technical Symposium on Computer Science Education Volume 1*, pp. 172–178, New York, NY, USA.

Dai, W., Lin, J., Jin, H., Li, T., Tsai, Y.-S., Gašević, D., and Chen, G. (2023). Can large language models provide feedback to students? A case study on ChatGPT. In *2023 IEEE International Conference on Advanced Learning Technologies (ICALT)*, pp. 323–325, Orem, UT, USA.

Dasari, D., Hendriyanto, A., Sahara, S., Suryadi, D., Muhaimin, L. H., Chao, T., and Fitriana, L. (2024). ChatGPT in didactical tetrahedron, does it make an exception? A case study in mathematics teaching and learning. *Frontiers in Education*, *8*:1295413.

Dehouche, N. and Dehouche, K. (2023). What's in a text-to-image prompt? The potential of stable diffusion in visual arts education. *Heliyon*, *9*(6):e16757.

Huisman, B., Saab, N., Van Den Broek, P., and Van Driel, J. (2019). The impact of formative peer feedback on higher education students' academic writing: A meta-analysis. *Assessment & Evaluation in Higher Education*, *44*(6):863–880.

Hyland, F. (2003). Focusing on form: Student engagement with teacher feedback. *System*, *31*(2):217–230.

Imran, M. and Almusharraf, N. (2023). Analyzing the role of ChatGPT as a writing assistant at higher education level: A systematic review of the literature. *Contemporary Educational Technology*, *15*(4):ep464.

Keiper, M. C., Fried, G., Lupinek, J., and Nordstrom, H. (2023). Artificial intelligence in sport management education: Playing the AI game with ChatGPT. *Journal of Hospitality, Leisure, Sport & Tourism Education*, *33*:100456.

Li, X., Li, T., Raković, M., Singh, S., van der Graaf, J., Lim, L., Moore, J., Molenaar, I., Bannert, M., Gašević, D., and Fan, Y. (2024). FLoRA engine: Facilitating learners' own regulation activities. *Journal of Learning Analytics*, 1–24. https://doi.org/10.18608/jla.2025.8349

Limo, F. A. F., Tiza, D. R. H., Roque, M. M., Herrera, E. E., Murillo, J. P. M., Huallpa, J. J., et al. (2023). Personalized tutoring: ChatGPT as a virtual tutor for personalized learning experiences. *Przestrzeń Społeczna (Social Space)*, *23*(1):293–312.

Liu, M., Zhang, L. J., and Biebricher, C. (2024). Investigating students' cognitive processes in generative AI-assisted digital multimodal composing and traditional writing. *Computers & Education*, *211*:104977.

Lo, C. K. (2023). What is the impact of ChatGPT on education? A rapid review of the literature. *Education Sciences*, *13*(4):410.

Lu, Q., Yao, Y., Xiao, L., Yuan, M., Wang, J., and Zhu, X. (2024). Can ChatGPT effectively complement teacher assessment of undergraduate students' academic writing? *Assessment & Evaluation in Higher Education*, *49*(5):616–633.

Ma, G. (2023). Chance or challenge: The role of ChatGPT in history teaching and historical research in higher education. In *2023 3rd International Conference on Education, Information Management and Service Science (EIMSS 2023)*, pp. 869–874. Atlantis Press, Qingdao, China.

Matthews, J. A. and Volpe, C. R. (2023). Academics' perceptions of ChatGPT-generated written outputs: A practical application of turing's imitation game. *Australasian Journal of Educational Technology*, *39*(5):82–100.

Montenegro-Rueda, M., Fernández-Cerero, J., Fernández-Batanero, J. M., and López-Meneses, E. (2023). Impact of the implementation of ChatGPT in education: A systematic review. *Computers*, *12*(8):153.

Nguyen, A., Hong, Y., Dang, B., and Huang, X. (2024). Human-AI collaboration patterns in AI-assisted academic writing. *Studies in Higher Education, 49*:1–18.

Niloy, A. C., Akter, S., Sultana, N., Sultana, J., and Rahman, S. I. U. (2024). Is ChatGPT a menace for creative writing ability? An experiment. *Journal of Computer Assisted Learning, 40*(2):919–930.

Noy, S. and Zhang, W. (2023). Experimental evidence on the productivity effects of generative artificial intelligence. *Science, 381*(6654):187–192.

Paulus, T. M. (1999). The effect of peer and teacher feedback on student writing. *Journal of Second Language Writing, 8*(3):265–289.

Song, W., Hou, X., Li, S., Chen, C., Gao, D., Sun, Y., et al. (2022). An intelligent virtual standard patient for medical students training based on oral knowledge graph. *IEEE Transactions on Multimedia, 25*:6132–6145.

Tai, R. H., Bentley, L. R., Xia, X., Sitt, J. M., Fankhauser, S. C., Chicas-Mosier, A. M., and Monteith, B. G. (2024). An examination of the use of large language models to AID analysis of textual data. *International Journal of Qualitative Methods, 23*:16094069241231168.

Terwiesch, C. (2023). Would Chat GPT3 get a Wharton MBA? A prediction based on its performance in the operations management course. Mack Institute for Innovation Management at the Wharton School, University of Pennsylvania.

Tossell, C. C., Tenhundfeld, N. L., Momen, A., Cooley, K., and de Visser, E. J. (2024). Student perceptions of ChatGPT use in a college essay assignment: Implications for learning, grading, and trust in artificial intelligence. *IEEE Transactions on Learning Technologies, 17*:1069–1081.

Urban, M., Děchtěrenko, F., Lukavskỳ, J., Hrabalová, V., Svacha, F., Brom, C., and Urban, K. (2024). ChatGPT improves creative problem-solving performance in university students: An experimental study. *Computers & Education, 215*:105031.

Villan, F. and Santos, R. P. D. (2023). ChatGPT as co-advisor in scientific initiation: Action research with project-based learning in elementary education. *arXiv preprint arXiv:2311.14701.*

Wachira, K., Wachira, L. N., Mwangi, E., Absaloms, H. O., and Jeon, G. (2023). Tertiary education integrity in a ChatGPT conscious world: Preliminary Kenyan observations. In *2023 IEEE AFRICON*, pp. 1–6. IEEE, Nairobi, Kenya.

Wan, Q., Hu, S., Zhang, Y., Wang, P., Wen, B., and Lu, Z. (2024). "It felt like having a second mind": Investigating human-AI co-creativity in prewriting with large language models. *Proceedings of the ACM on Human-Computer Interaction, 8*(CSCW1):1–26.

Wu, T.-T., Lee, H.-Y., Li, P.-H., Huang, C.-N., and Huang, Y.-M. (2024). Promoting self-regulation progress and knowledge construction in blended learning via ChatGPT-based learning AID. *Journal of Educational Computing Research, 61*(8):3–31.

Yan, W., Nakajima, T., and Sawada, R. (2024). Benefits and challenges of collaboration between students and conversational generative artificial intelligence in programming learning: An empirical case study. *Education Sciences, 14*(4):433.

Zhai, X. (2022). ChatGPT user experience: Implications for education. *Available at SSRN 4312418.*

Zhang, Z. and Huang, X. (2024). The impact of chatbots based on large language models on second language vocabulary acquisition. *Heliyon, 10*(3):e25370.

CHAPTER 3

Enhancing Learning Through Interaction with GenAI: Opportunities, Challenges and Future Directions

Zixian Yu, Mengtong Xiang, and Yizhou Fan

As artificial intelligence advances rapidly, learner–AI interaction emerges as a crucial link between human needs and machine capabilities. Within the educational domain, the integration of Generative Artificial Intelligence (GenAI), exemplified by ChatGPT, has markedly influenced teaching and learning process. This chapter endeavours to investigate the genuine interaction between learners and GenAI from a learner–AI interaction perspective through the examination of practical application scenarios. Such an exploration is vital for comprehending the learning process in novel educational settings and for refining associated educational tools. This chapter commences with a review of the theoretical foundations and technological advancements in learner–AI interaction. It subsequently delves into the educational applications of GenAI, elucidating the research process and methodologies with two case studies. The first empirical study shows that students primarily use

DOI: 10.4324/9781003632146-3

ChatGPT to enhance their writing skills and seek information related to the task's theme, but there is room for improvement in meta-cognition and the effective use of the language model. The second empirical study shows that when students know they are seeking help from a teacher, they tend to prioritise knowledge acquisition and learning. And when students know they are seeking help from ChatGPT, their initial goal may be completing tasks. In conclusion, this chapter summarises the research significance and outlines prospective avenues for future inquiry. It primarily focuses on the analysis of learners' questions and strategies when interacting with ChatGPT. Serving as a continuation of the empirical research on GenAI introduced in the preceding chapter, this chapter provides a foundational understanding for readers to engage with subsequent chapters.

3.1 INTRODUCTION: HUMAN-COMPUTER INTERACTION IN THE ERA OF GENAI

Since the era of oral tradition, interaction has played a crucial role in education, encompassing both teacher-student and student-student exchanges (Miao et al., 2022). The nature and forms of educational interaction have evolved with advancements in information technology (Mahapatra, 2005). During oral tradition, interaction was primarily through spoken dialogue, facilitating the exchange of ideas (Finnegan, 2003). The Socratic method exemplified this era, fostering critical thinking by questioning students and highlighting inconsistencies in their beliefs, thereby seeking clarity and truth (Boghossian, 2004). This pedagogical approach not only emphasised interaction between teachers and students but also encouraged inner reflection and self-exploration among students. The legacy of Socratic teaching profoundly influenced subsequent educational practices, and traditional classrooms often employ questioning to stimulate student thought (Cotton, 1988).

In modern education, traditional classroom settings have incorporated additional interactive elements, such as group discussions (Murphy, 2018) and role-playing (Chesler and Fox, 1966), to enhance students' engagement and practical skills. These methods deviate from the conventional teacher-centric model, promoting student-to-student dialogue (Maziani, 2021; Westrup and Planander, 2013). With the development of information technology, new forms of interaction are emerging. Activities such as voting (Cline and Zullo, 2011), using online discussion boards (Blackmon, 2012) and conferencing systems (Labrie et al., 2022), and scanning QR codes (Saprudin et al., 2014) are gradually being incorporated into classroom teaching. These activities digitise test content and results, allowing for their tracking and analysis, which is beneficial for understanding the actual learning situation of students.

The invention of computers have brought up a new form of interaction, which transfers from the traditional human–human interaction to human-computer interaction (HCI). The advent of graphical user interfaces in the 1960s marked a pivotal moment, with pioneers like Douglas Engelbart (Engelbart, 1962) directing their attention towards the democratisation of interactive technologies. They posited that computer technology could significantly increase human cognitive capacities and communication efficiency, leading to the development of innovative tools such as the mouse, graphical user interfaces, and collaborative online platforms. This field is not solely preoccupied with the utility of technology; it also delves into the nuanced experiences that technological features afford to users.

The emergence of the World Wide Web propelled the rapid progression of HCI technologies, epitomised by web user interfaces. This era witnessed the proliferation of groundbreaking technologies such as search engines, chat tools, and multimedia animations, which facilitated the extensive production and dissemination of information for learners in cyberspace through HCI. The advancement of the internet has led to the rise of video-based course instruction, enabling students to engage with teachers synchronously or asynchronously at any time and place (Belt and Lowenthal, 2021). It indicates that, to some extent, the internet can still realise human–human interaction without time or place limitation. Through online courses, MOOCs, and other formats, the internet facilitates remote education, allowing for the global sharing of learning resources, promoting the globalisation and diversification of education (McLoughlin, 2014). Additionally, the internet provides an abundance of information resources, lowering the threshold for accessing knowledge and enabling more people to access advanced knowledge and technology. Moreover, the internet has changed the traditional "one-to-many" educational model, making personalised learning possible and improving learning outcomes and teaching quality (Ward et al., 2021). Despite these advantages brought by internet to learners, there are still some challenges. For instance, the quality of educational resources on the internet varies, requiring learners to have the ability to screen and discern. In addition, the rapid development of information technology requires that learners continuously update their knowledge and skills to adapt to the new educational environment.

As artificial intelligence technologies including multi-sensory perception technologies and virtual reality have advanced, computer systems have evolved towards anthropomorphism and intelligence, enabling learners to engage with the digital environment through an array of sensory and motor channels, including voice, gaze, and facial expressions. Especially for the new era of GenAI (which is capable of interacting with humans using human language), the focus of HCI research has shifted towards the collaborative dynamics between humans and intelligent systems. We need to change the "human-computer interaction" to learner–AI interaction because GenAI is quite different from the traditional computers. The objects we interact with are no longer the cold mouse, stiff web pages, or boring pre-set interfaces, but a GenAI tool with a vast amount of knowledge. For example, interaction with chatbots not only enhances learning flexibility and supports personalised education, but also prompts a reconsideration of human subjectivity and creativity. Traditional intelligent tutoring systems are constrained in their ability to provide feedback based solely on learners' responses, whereas GenAI exhibits more human-like characteristics, capable of generating comprehensive content and suggestions through large language models (Foung et al., 2024).

Across historical teaching methods, from the dialogues of oral tradition to modern classroom and HCI, and now to learner–AI interaction, interaction remains a vital educational strategy. It shapes the structure of teaching, and more fundamentally, provokes contemplation of the essence of education (Sharp, 1986). The form of interaction has changed, but its vital educational role for learners has never changed. It's an important and eternal way for learners to learn. At the same time, we can not view it as just a learning tool, it's also the aim of learning (Mwakalinga, 2012). As Wegerif (Wegerif, 2013) asserts, "One important aim of dialogic education is dialogue itself". It is imperative to prioritise the quality of interaction, ensuring that every exchange is characterised by openness, equality, and respect to truly fulfil educational objectives and cultivate well-rounded individuals capable of meeting societal demands.

As mentioned above, interaction is quite important for learners. However, since our understanding of learner–AI interaction is limited, there are concerns about issues such as over-reliance (Nguyen, 2024). Nevertheless, it is incorrect to make arbitrary judgements about the quality of the learner–AI interaction without examining how it occurs. Therefore, we need to explore the actual process of it and figure out how learning happens in the context. Although GenAI technologies, exemplified by ChatGPT, have existed for over a year, research on the process of learner–AI interaction is still scarce. Hence, we need to reveal the true nature of learner–AI interaction and explore how learning happens through this interaction.

To reveal the actual process and particulars of learner–AI interaction, this chapter will explore the following issues: (1) From the perspective of interaction, what are the similarities and differences, in terms of form, content and outcome, between learner–AI interaction and learner–teacher interaction? (2) What unique advantages does GenAI possess in its interactions with learners, as compared to learner–teacher interaction? (3) What challenges might arise from interactions between learners and GenAI? To address these questions, this chapter will first review articles related to learner–AI interaction. then we will also introduce two empirical studies related to learner–AI interaction, which reflect our own theoretical perspectives and analytical methods.

3.2 REVIEW OF LEARNERS' INTERACTION WITH GENAI

We conducted a literature search in the Google Scholar database, using search terms such as "interaction, ChatGPT, large language model, challenge, dialogue, GenAI and generative artificial intelligence" to swiftly identify studies relevant to the theme of interaction. We will discuss the research from three aspects. First we will explore the similarities and differences between learner–AI interaction and learner–teacher interaction. Then, we discuss the advantages of learners' interaction with GenAI. Finally, we posed a few challenges that may arise from learner–AI interaction.

3.2.1 The Similarities and Differences between **Learner–AI Interaction** and Learner–Teacher Interaction

According to the previous research, there are similarities and differences between learner–AI interaction and learner–teacher interaction. Through analysing the articles, our discussion mainly focus on the form, the content and the outcome of interaction.

As for the interactive form, the similarity is reflected in that both learner–AI interaction and learner–teacher interaction are Q and A style interactions. When learners pose a question, both GenAI and teachers will answer their puzzles (Kloos et al., 2024). According to Piaget's (Piaget and Inhelder, 2008) theory of cognitive development, interaction is a process through which learners internalise knowledge by continuously adjusting their cognitive structures through communication with others. And researches have shown that this style can effectively improve learners' cognitive level and participation (Ouyang and Chang, 2019). However, there are also differences between learner–AI interaction and learner–teacher interaction. They have different dialogue subjects. The dialogue between learners and teachers is with humans who possess rich educational experience and emotional cognition, whereas GenAI is based on algorithmic and big data-driven programs (Chaccour et al., 2024). This discrepancy leads to fundamental differences in the dialogue process. Samala et al. (2024) have pointed out that ChatGPT lacks personalisation, and its replies may be confined and not always effective, leading to interactions that seem less intimate. At the same time, teachers are more familiar with learners' abilities and habits, often able to delve deeper into learners' needs, interests, and potentials through dialogue. In contrast, GenAI has limitations in understanding human emotions and values (Salvagno et al., 2023; Kooli, 2023), because it does not possess profound comprehension of emotions or social nuances, which can be essential in scenarios that call for empathy and a more intimate grasp of a person's emotional condition (Samala et al., 2024).

In terms of interactive content, learner–AI interaction has certain similarities and differences with learner–teacher interaction. As for the similarity, whether it is learner–AI interaction or learner–teacher interaction, the core purpose is the transmission of knowledge and learners' understanding (Nyaaba et al., 2024; Çelik et al., 2023; Wang, 2008). During the interactive process, both GenAI and teachers will provide corresponding knowledge points and explanations based on students' needs. However, there are also certain differences between the two. In learner–AI interaction, interactive content often focuses on factual knowledge, procedural knowledge, and some problems that can be processed through algorithms (Nelles et al., 2024). Learner–teacher interaction, on the other hand, places more emphasis on cultivating conceptual knowledge (Bossér and Lindahl, 2019), critical thinking (Cui and Teo, 2023; Talebinejad and Matou, 2012), and emotional values (Pöysä et al., 2019). For example, when a teacher is explaining a problem, they may guide students to think deeply (Van Zee and Minstrell, 1997) and explore the essence of the problem, while GenAI may focus more on providing direct answers (Opara et al., 2023). In terms of emotional communication, the difference between learner-AI interaction and learner–teacher interaction is particularly evident. Teachers can interact emotionally with students through language, body movements, and facial expressions (Kucuk, 2023), providing them with encouragement and support. However, GenAI still has shortcomings in emotional communication, making it difficult for it to truly understand and respond to students' emotional needs like human teachers. Teachers have obvious advantages in guiding values (Zhang, 2024). They can provide targeted values education based on the actual situation of students. However, GenAI often falls short in dealing with ethical, moral, and value issues (Dobrin, 2023; Law, 2024).

As for the interactive outcome, they are different in feedback methods. When students pose questions to teachers, the teachers are often able to provide concise and targeted answers. In contrast, GenAI offers comprehensive, rich and general feedback (Samala et al., 2024), requiring learners to select and refine the information themselves. Compared to learner–teacher interaction, learner–AI interaction may lead to better learning outcomes. For example, an article by (Essel et al., 2022) introducing the application of the virtual chatbot KNUSTbot in a multimedia programming course compared the differences in learning outcomes between students interacting with the bot and those interacting with instructors. The research findings indicate that students who interacted with the chatbot achieved better learning outcomes compared to those who interacted with course lecturers. This can be attributed to the immediate feedback they received from the chatbot, as well as the significant contribution to the learning process through more interactions with the chatbot at different times without encountering any delays. Additionally, by observing the number of student interactions with KNUSTbot per hour, it was found that most interactions occurred between 20:00 and 22:00, times when instructors were typically not available and unresponsive. However, it is important to note that while GenAI can provide immediate feedback and increased interaction opportunities, the quality of these interactions and the depth of learning they facilitate may vary. More empirical research is needed to fully understand the long-term impact of learner–AI interaction on learning outcomes compared to learner–teacher interaction (Jadhav et al., 2024).

Although there are similarities and differences between learner–AI interaction and learner–teacher interaction, the future of education may engage in the synergistic combination of both (Al Yakin et al., 2024). Teachers should explore ways to integrate GenAI into their teaching practices, leveraging its strengths in providing immediate feedback and engaging students in out-of-class hours. At the same time, teachers can focus on areas where GenAI falls short, such as providing emotional support, fostering critical thinking, and guiding students through complex problem-solving. Jeon and Lee (2023) have provided a framework for this collaboration. They focused on the complementary relationship between human teachers and ChatGPT, integrating interaction logs of teachers using ChatGPT with personal interviews to explore this relationship. Through qualitative data analysis, four ChatGPT roles (interlocutor, content provider, teaching assistant, and evaluator) and three teacher roles (orchestrating different resources with quality pedagogical decisions, making learners active investigators, and raising AI ethical awareness) were identified, and further research should aim to develop practical strategies for implementing these roles in the classroom.

3.2.2 Advantages of Learners' Interaction with GenAI

Compared to traditional teaching methods, interactions between learners and GenAI offer several advantages, which include enhancing learners' learning efficiency, achieving personalised learning and cultivating learners' learning independence.

First, GenAI is beneficial to enhance learning efficiency (Lv, 2023). Learner–AI interaction represents a transformative shift in the landscape of education, offering a range of benefits that significantly enhance the learning experience when compared to traditional teaching methods. One of the most pronounced advantages is the enhancement of learning efficiency (Bahrini et al., 2023). Unlike human teachers who are limited by the constraints of time and physical presence, GenAI facilitates communication that transcends these barriers, allowing students to receive timely answers to their queries regardless of the hour or their location (Thway et al., 2024). This immediate access to knowledge not only accelerates the learning process but also encourages continuous learning beyond the confines of a classroom. Researchers have found that ChatGPT can help by breaking down complex medical concepts into simple language, thus helping medical students learn more efficiently, potentially leading to improved patient care (Bhattacharya et al., 2023). The real-time feedback provided by GenAI systems is both swift and objective, often surpassing the capabilities of human teachers in terms of consistency and fairness (Choudhuri et al., 2024; Hota and Jokinen, 2024). For instance, in the realm of argumentation and debate (Guo et al., 2023), GenAI chatbots have been instrumental in delivering immediate and constructive feedback on the strengths and weaknesses of students' arguments, thereby refining their skills and improving their performance. Moreover, GenAI's extensive knowledge base and advanced language comprehension abilities enable it to address a wide spectrum of questions with clarity and precision, offering explanations that can sometimes be more coherent and accessible than those provided by human educators (Aktay et al., 2023).

Therefore, it is not surprising that GenAI has found its way into a multitude of educational domains, seamlessly integrating with various fields to enhance the learning experience even further. In academic research and language learning, AI tools are commonly used as writing aids (Imran and Almusharraf, 2023). Quillbot, for instance, is often employed to refine language expression, while other tools assist in evaluating vocabulary choices, sentence structures, and writing styles (Agustini, 2023; Schmidt-Fajlik, 2023). In the domain of knowledge construction, learners can pose specific questions to ChatGPT and utilise additional tools to verify the accuracy of ChatGPT's responses (Chen et al., 2023). In the field of learning analytics, GenAI aids in the analysis of unstructured data, generation of learner data, enrichment of multi-modal learner interactions, advancement of interactive and interpretive analyses, and facilitation of personalised and adaptive interventions (Yan et al., 2024). In computer science, learners can improve their coding abilities through interactions with GenAI. For example, Harvard's CS50 course has developed an AI tool named "CS50.ai" to assist students in resolving coding challenges (Liu et al., 2024). Furthermore, students can engage in role-playing exercises with GenAI, such as simulated interviews, speeches, or dialogues with historical figures, thereby enhancing their communication and expressive skills. GenAI also provides career planning advice and can monitor students' emotional states (Keerthika et al., 2024). Learners can also prompt GenAI to devise marketing strategies or craft research articles by providing specific prompts (Celiktutan et al., 2024).

In addition to enhancing learning efficiency, GenAI plays a pivotal role in achieving personalised learning experiences for learners (Hong, 2023; Tafazoli, 2024; Owoseni et al., 2024). A study suggests that ChatGPT may be used to provide virtual intelligent tutoring services, where students can ask questions and receive personalised responses and feedback. As demonstrated by the Two Sigma effect, this personalised feedback supports iterative learning and leads to significant learning benefits (Qadir, 2023). The adaptability of GenAI systems allows them to cater to the unique learning needs, and interests of each individual. This customisation is facilitated by GenAI's ability to analyse learners' interactions and adapt its responses accordingly, creating a learning environment that is tailored to the specific requirements of each learner. For example, in the field of language learning, GenAI tools can be employed to refine language expression, evaluate vocabulary choices, and offer feedback on sentence structures and writing styles (Kohnke, 2024; Law, 2024), all according to the learner's proficiency level. This level of personalisation not only accelerates learning but also fosters a deeper engagement with the material, as students are able to interact with content that resonates with their personal interests and talents. For teachers, they can use GenAI to design custom exams for different students (Cotton et al., 2023). However, it is crucial to be mindful of the potential for over-standardisation that could arise from the widespread use of GenAI, which might inadvertently limit the exploration of students' latent talents and imaginative expression (Laak et al., 2024).

Furthermore, GenAI is instrumental in cultivating learners' independence in their educational journey. By engaging in interactive question-and-answer sessions with GenAI, learners are encouraged to develop their critical thinking and questioning skills in a stress-free environment (Lee and Moore, 2024; Zadorozhnyy and Lai, 2023). The absence of social pressures or fear of judgment when interacting with GenAI promotes a culture of curiosity and inquiry among learners, who are more likely to ask questions and explore topics of interest without the anxiety of being criticised. Research (Rawas, 2024) has found that ChatGPT may function as a facilitative intermediary, particularly for learners who exhibit reticence or hesitancy in classroom inquiry contexts, as well as for those with disabilities that might impede traditional modes of engagement. GenAI's ability to provide timely and accurate feedback also supports students in correcting their mistakes and refining their learning approach, thereby empowering them to take control of their education. Research has shown that GenAI can significantly increase students' desire to explore new areas of knowledge. After using GenAI, learners have noted that: "With AI, we can research things we don't know, even in our classes or in school, and find the meaning or something else" (Aktay et al., 2023). This autonomy in learning is particularly evident in fields such as English language learning, where GenAI has been found to enhance students' self-directed learning capabilities (Agustini, 2023; Ali et al., 2023; Forrester, 2023). Overall, the integration of GenAI in education promises to not only make learning more efficient and personalised but also to nurture a generation of independent and self-motivated learners.

3.2.3 Challenges That May Arise from Learners' Interaction with GenAI

While GenAI can bring many conveniences to students' learning, there are still many challenges that need to be considered due to our limited understanding of the application of this technology. According to the research, there are challenges that may arise from learners' interaction with GenAI.

First, GenAI may lead to information overload (Kim et al., 2023), as it can rapidly produce a vast amount of content. This rapid production can lead to learners' information overload. As GenAI spews out a deluge of data, students must develop sophisticated filtering skills to separate the wheat from the chaff. They need to discern valuable, accurate, and relevant information from a large amount of information. Moreover, the constant evolution of GenAI technology demands that learners remain in a state of perpetual learning, constantly updating their knowledge and skills to keep pace with the latest advancements.

This need for continuous adaptation can be particularly stressful for those who are not technologically inclined or who lack access to the necessary resources.

Second, the convenience offered by GenAI can foster a reliance (Kohnke, 2024) that may hinder the development of critical thinking and problem-solving abilities. Learners might become excessively dependent on GenAI for tasks that require deep cognitive engagement, such as writing essays or solving complex problems. This dependency can lead to a decline in academic integrity (Rasul et al., 2024a,b; Rahman and Watanobe, 2023), as students might be tempted to use GenAI to cheat or to produce work that is not their own. In the realm of EFL, concerns have been raised about the potential of GenAI, like ChatGPT, to impede the acquisition of language skills and critical research abilities. The risk of biases being reinforced and the dissemination of misinformation is also a significant concern (Yuan et al., 2024; Korucu-Kiş, 2024). Some researchers have pointed out the risk of plagiarism (Su and Yang, 2023; Ray, 2023; Teel et al., 2023). Over-reliance on GenAI could thus have far-reaching implications for the quality of education and the ethical conduct of students.

Third, the information generated by GenAI may not be entirely accurate. It is constrained by the data it has been trained on and the scope of questions it has encountered. Consequently, the content produced may be outdated or inaccurate, leading to potential misdirection for learners. The accountability for such inaccuracies is often blurred (Beltran et al., 2024), as it is not always clear whether the fault lies with the AI or the user. This necessitates a critical approach from learners, who must independently verify the information provided by GenAI to ensure its reliability and correctness (Johinke et al., 2023). Users have the responsibility to develop a healthy skepticism towards the outputs of GenAI and to cross-reference information with credible sources.

Fourth, the use of GenAI raises significant concerns about information security and privacy. Some research indicates that GenAI systems may collect personal data (Montenegro et al., 2021), which could be misused if not properly safeguarded. The current regulatory landscape for GenAI is nascent, leaving potential loopholes for data breaches and privacy violations (Su and Yang, 2023; Miao et al., 2021; Chan, 2023; Shailendra et al., 2024). This lack of regulation is a cause for concern, as it leaves users vulnerable to exploitation. Additionally, the evaluation of GenAI systems poses its own set of challenges (Bahrini et al., 2023; Su and Yang, 2023; Sabzalieva and Valentini, 2023), including ensuring that the AI is performing as intended and that it adheres to ethical standards.

Finally, the introduction of GenAI has the potential to exacerbate the digital divide (Aksoy and Kursun, 2024). Unequal access to advanced AI technologies can widen the gap between those who can leverage GenAI for educational purposes and those who cannot. Factors such as social exclusion, gender imbalances, and accessibility for individuals with disabilities can all contribute to this divide. Without a concerted effort to promote equitable access and the embrace of AI technologies, the existing disparities in educational opportunities could deepen (Efe, 2022; Wu, 2022). This digital divide not only affects individuals but also has broader implications for society, as it can perpetuate inequalities and limit social mobility. Aktay et al. (2023) have highlighted that the negative aspects of using GenAI include limited access for many learners, which can prevent them from benefiting from its potential. Moreover, there is a question of the effectiveness of AI-assisted instruction compared to traditional methods. If there is no significant difference in outcomes, the hype around GenAI might be misplaced. It is crucial to conduct rigorous evaluations to determine the true value of GenAI in education and to ensure that its integration into learning environments is justified and beneficial.

In this review, we have delved into the key aspects of learner–AI interaction. We began by examining the similarities and differences between interactions with GenAI and learner–teacher interaction, analysing the nuances in form, content, and outcomes. We then highlighted the advantages of learners' engagement with GenAI, which include enhanced learning efficiency, personalised learning experiences, and the cultivation of learner independence. Then, we also identified several challenges that arise from this interaction, such as information overload, over-reliance on AI, concerns about the accuracy of information generated, privacy and security issues, and the potential exacerbation of the digital divide. Moving forward, this review will transition into the presentation of two empirical studies that focus on the analysis of the content and process of learners' interaction with GenAI. These studies aim to provide a more granular understanding of the practical application of GenAI in educational settings.

3.3 EMPIRICAL STUDY: EXPLORE THE AUTHENTIC PROCESS OF **LEARNER–AI INTERACTION**

3.3.1 Analysis of Learners' Questions and Strategies in **Learner–AI Interaction**

With the development of the new generation of artificial intelligence technology represented by GenAI, more and more researchers are paying attention to the application of GenAI in learning. However, at present, most research topics are still limited to general discussions on the impact of GenAI on learning, and few studies have truly put it into practice, exploring the use of GenAI in real learning contexts, let alone its effects. The overall goal of this study is to embed GenAI represented by ChatGPT into English reading and writing platforms, collect and analyse the content of learner–AI interaction, and explore the implicit interaction strategies between learners and ChatGPT. Our study is guided by the following question:

> **RQ1**: What interactive content will occur between students and GenAI in the context of English reading and writing tasks?
>
> **RQ2**: What interactive strategies will students use with GenAI in the context of English reading and writing tasks?

In the study involving non-native English speakers, participants were tasked with crafting a concise essay, ranging from 200 to 400 words, forecasting the state of school education in 2035. The essay was to synthesise concepts from three provided topics: artificial intelligence, classroom differentiation, and learning scaffolding. Accompanying the topics were comprehensive instructions and a scoring rubric, which not only guided essay construction but also served as an evaluation tool for both researchers and ChatGPT. Post-submission, essays were submitted to ChatGPT for assessment against the rubric, with the AI also assuming the role of an educator to furnish approximately 200-word feedback. In order to investigate the content and strategies of students' interactions with ChatGPT, we collected data on the dialogues between students and ChatGPT during the writing process and conducted the research procedure as follows.

Firstly, we gained an understanding of the basic content of the dialogues between students and ChatGPT by examining the raw data.

Based on this, we developed a coding framework of learners' questions to ChatGPT, as shown in Table 3.1. We categorised the content of students' questions to ChatGPT into two broad categories: Task-relevant and Task-irrelevant. The Task-relevant category includes Theme-relevant (general-theme, example-ask, material-specific, concept-explain, and translate), Improve-writing (general, polish, grammar-spelling, structure, and logic), and Meta-cognition (planning, question, and evaluate). The Task-irrelevant category includes Greetings and Off-topic. We coded the raw data according to the coding scheme. Subsequently, we conducted general descriptive statistical analyses on the coded data. Then, we drew each individual's question process map and obtained transition matrices of each individual. After that, we performed cluster analysis based on these matrices. Finally, we conducted a sequence analysis on each category within the clusters to derive students' question strategies.

To address RQ1, we conducted a general descriptive statistical analysis of the coded data. The results are presented in Figure 3.1. The findings indicate that the interaction between students and ChatGPT covers a wide range of categories. Among them, there are more questions related to Improve-writing and Theme-relevant, and relatively less Meta-cognition and Greetings, but some meaningless questions may also be found. In the Theme-relevant questions, students mainly ask ChatGPT questions related to the content of the article and often ask for a translation, with fewer requests for examples. In the Improve-writing questions, students mainly ask ChatGPT to polish the article, but there are also some grammar and structural issues, with less logical issues. In the Meta-cognition questions, students often ask ChatGPT to evaluate their articles, question ChatGPT's responses, and ask them to help develop task plans. It is worth noting that students instil a lot of meaningless words into ChatGPT.

To address RQ2, we drew individuals' process map to obtain transition matrices and conducted cluster analysis based on these matrices. Finally, we performed a process mining instil category within the clusters to identify four types of questioning strategies. **Off-Topic Strategy** means that students primarily engage in trivial conversations with ChatGPT that are unrelated to the writing task. **Topic-Focused Strategy** means that students mainly inquire about content related to the writing theme with ChatGPT. **Writing Enhancement Strategy**

TABLE 3.1 Coding Framework of Learners' Questions to ChatGPT

1st Indices	2nd Indices	3rd Indices	Description
Task-relevant	Theme-relevant	General-theme	General topic-related questions
		Example-ask	Ask GPT for examples
		Material-specific	Questions related to the theme content
		Concept-explain	Question the conceptual explanation of a word or phrase related to the topic
		Translate	Translate
	Improve-writing	General	General questions related to writing
		Polish	Ask GPT to polish the writing
		Grammar-spelling	Grammar and spelling related issues
		Structure	Issues related to article structure
		Logic	Logic related issues in the article
	Meta-cognition	Planning	Ask GPT to provide a task plan
		Question	Inquiring or questioning GPT
		Evaluate	Questions related to rating standards and ratings
Task-irrelevant	Greetings	Greetings	Polite language such as greeting
	off-topic	Off-topic	Other words unrelated to the task

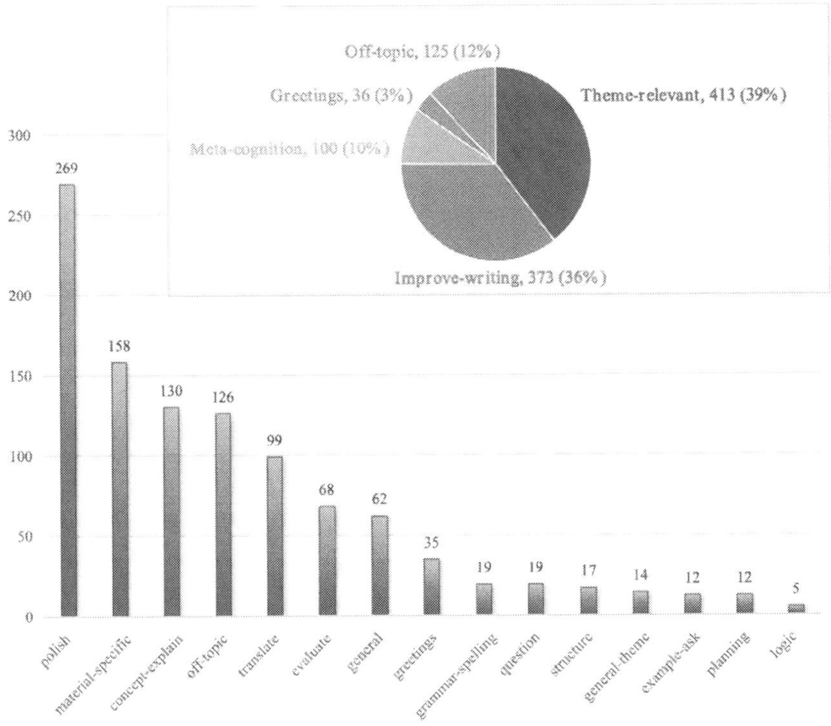

Figure 3.1 Results of the general descriptive statistical analysis.

means that students primarily ask ChatGPT for advice on how to revise and polish their writing. **Balanced Questioning Strategy** means that students are able to allocate their questions across various categories effectively and communicate well with ChatGPT.

The findings of this study provide valuable insights into the interaction patterns between students and ChatGPT. The descriptive statistical analysis and process maps offer a comprehensive understanding of the content categories and questioning strategies employed by students. Firstly, the interaction content between students and ChatGPT covers a wide range of categories, with a focus on improving writing and themes. This suggests that students primarily seek assistance from ChatGPT in areas where they perceive a need for improvement (Javaid et al., 2023). However, the presence of meaningless content indicates that some students may not fully utilise the capabilities of ChatGPT (Desseauve et al., 2024) or may use it for purposes unrelated to the task at hand (Tankelevitch et al., 2024). Secondly, the findings reveal that students predominantly ask questions related to article content and translation, with fewer requests for examples. This could imply that students are more interested in obtaining direct information and solutions rather than exploring different perspectives or seeking in-depth understanding (Pence et al., 2024). Additionally, the focus on polishing articles and addressing grammar and structural issues in the improve-writing category suggests that students value ChatGPT's ability to enhance the quality of their writing (Li et al., 2024; Ironsi and Ironsi, 2024). Thirdly, the meta-cognition category indicates that students seek feedback on their articles and question ChatGPT's responses, which reflects their desire for validation and improvement. However, the limited number of questions related to developing task plans implies that students may not fully recognise the potential of ChatGPT in assisting with task organisation and time management. It suggests that while students primarily use ChatGPT to improve their writing and seek information related to the task's theme, there is room for improvement in task management and the effective utilisation of the language model. In addition, the identification of four questioning strategies offers insights into the varying levels of engagement and utilisation of ChatGPT by students. For students who frequently ask irrelevant and meaningless questions to the ChatGPT, provide them with appropriate scaffolding to remind them to pay attention to the task itself. Future research could explore the factors that contribute to these different strategies and investigate the impact of these strategies on students' learning outcomes.

3.3.2 Exploring Differences in Help-Seeking Process between ChatGPT and Human Expert

GPT could serve as a human-like intelligent tutor to facilitate help-seeking process. Help-seeking (HS) has been considered as an active learning strategy associated with self-regulated learning (SRL), which was defined as seeking assistance from other individuals or other sources when learners face difficulty during learning (Karabenick and Berger, 2013). However, seeking appropriate help is challenging for learners as they fall short in regulating their help-seeking process, such as monitoring whether help is needed, reflecting on how to ask for help, and evaluating whether the help they received is meaningful (Aleven et al., 2003). Help-seeking is a dynamic process with sequential and temporal stages containing interwoven behavioural activities (Fan and Lin, 2023; Finney et al., 2018; Karabenick and Gonida, 2017), it is necessary to unpack the help-seeking process to offer timely support for learners. Nevertheless, little is known about how learners seek help from ChatGPT, especially comparing the process of seeking help from AI and human expert. Therefore, we attempt to investigate the difference in help-seeking process between ChatGPT and human teacher. The focus of our study includes two research questions:

1. What are the differences in the overall help-seeking pattern when learners ask help from ChatGPT and the human expert?
2. What are the differences in the specific help-seeking sequences when learners ask help from ChatGPT and the human expert?

An important limitation of previous studies on help-seeking is that most of them relied on using a self-report method without analysing the specific help-seeking process. We proposed a coding framework (see Table 3.2) to measure help-seeking process using three data sources (eye-tracking, log, and conversation text) in an online essay revision task. The task asked participants to compose a 300–400 word essay under the guidance of learning materials and writing rubric. Then participants were assigned to two groups to revise their essays with the assistance of different help sources:

The *AI Group* received assistance from ChatGPT 4.0. We designed a plugin that utilises the ChatGPT 4.0 API and integrated it into the online learning platform used in our experiment. Participants could ask context-specific inquiries and receive pertinent response. The objective for the participants was to revise their essays utilising the help of ChatGPT while incorporating the instructions and rubric to aim for higher scores.

The *HE Group* participants, on the other hand, were supported by a human expert. In our platform, the human expert could observe participants' essays in real-time through an online tool. Participants were afforded the opportunity to have instant and one-on-one chats with the human expert, thereby facilitating an interactive help-seeking process. Additionally, participants were also requested to follow the provided rubrics to assist them in seeking task-relevant help and achieving higher scores.

To address RQ1, we employed the process mining method using the pMineR package to calculate the transition probabilities between help-seeking stages. The help-seeking process in the HE Group follows a linear and temporal progression, aligning closely with our coding framework. Learners typically begin with diagnostic questioning, followed by seeking help. They then evaluate the help received, which can be either positive or negative, before ultimately accepting or disregarding the help to resolve their problems. In contrast, the help-seeking process in the AI Group exhibits a more dynamic and less structured pattern. Learning sessions often begin directly with help-seeking, with a high transition probability for this stage.

Learners in the AI Group sometimes transition directly from help-seeking to help processing without prior evaluation, reflecting a more immediate approach to handling assistance. Furthermore, it is common for learners to cycle back from help processing to help-seeking, indicating a tendency to request additional help from ChatGPT even after receiving support. These findings suggest that the help-seeking process with ChatGPT is less orderly than the theoretical model, particularly in the sequencing of certain cognitive stages (Mercier and Frederiksen, 2008; Davison et al., 2023).

To answer RQ2, we compared the help-seeking activities of Group AI and Group HE using process mining analysis. The results revealed that learners in Group HE exhibited a significantly higher transition probability from diagnosing questions to subsequent stages compared to Group AI. In contrast, learners in Group AI often bypassed the diagnosing stage and directly sought help, suggesting that seeking help from ChatGPT did not always indicate a genuine difficulty. This finding underscores the role of process analysis in assessing the necessity of help and the context in which it occurs.

The patterns of instrumental help-seeking also differed between the two groups. Learners in Group AI were more likely to seek instrumental help after evaluating help negatively or avoiding help-seeking, reflecting a more exploratory approach where they spent time assessing content before formulating adaptive questions. In comparison, learners in Group HE tended to request instrumental help directly when faced with difficulties, reflecting a more straightforward approach.

TABLE 3.2 Coding Framework of the Help-Seeking Process

Stage	Activities	Definition	Code
Diagnosing question	Diagnosing question	learners need to determine if there is a problem based on their own learning status and decide if they need help	Diag.ques
Asking help	Asking help.instrumental	Instrumental help-seeking (learners ask facilitated hints that can assist them in revising their essays independently afterwards)	Ask.instr
	Asking help.executive	Executive help-seeking (learners tend to look for answers that can be applied directly)	Ask.exec
	Asking help.avoidant	Avoid asking for help (learners try to ask questions but not to send them)	Ask.avo
Evaluating help	Evaluating help.positive	Positive evaluation (learners evaluate the help messages and give positive feedback)	Eva.pos
	Evaluating help.negative	Negative evaluation (learners evaluate the help messages and give negative feedback or not to give any feedback)	Eva.neg
Processing help	Processing help.accepting	Accepting help (learners apply the help directly in revising their essays)	Pro.acc
	Processing help.neglecting	Neglecting help (learners do not apply the help directly in revising their essays)	Pro.neg
	Processing help.returning	Returning to the help (learners look back to some previous help message)	Pro.re

Regarding help evaluation and acceptance, learners in Group HE were more likely to positively evaluate help before accepting it. By contrast, learners in Group AI required additional exploration and intermediate steps before accepting help, suggesting a more iterative process of reflection and judgment.

Executive help-seeking behaviors further highlighted these differences. Learners in Group AI frequently requested executive help after neglecting previous help and often moved directly to accepting help with relatively high transition probabilities. This indicates that ChatGPT's assistance facilitated a more immediate resolution of their queries, contrasting with the more deliberate approach observed in Group HE.

Overall, the help-seeking process in Group AI demonstrated a more complex and dynamic pattern, with more iterative transitions and exploratory behaviors, as opposed to the more linear and goal-oriented approach observed in Group HE. These distinctions highlight the differences in how learners engage with human versus AI assistance during the help-seeking process.

To further illustrate, we present examples of interaction in AI group and HE group. We have collected screenshots of the interaction and provided a detailed explanation of the process. For HE group, the students diagnosed questions by focusing their eyes' point in writing area and then moved their attention to the message box of the helper. After that, they asked the instrumental help directly. They focused on the input box and wrote the question text. Then they clicked the button to send questions. After receiving the help, the students began to evaluate them with their eyes focused on the help message. They evaluated the help as positive, so they sent positive comments, like "Very useful advice" (Figure 3.2). For AI group, learners firstly asked executive help such as automatically deleting some words as shown in screenshot. But they did not send it and revised the questions, which was coded as asking avoidant help. After that, they evaluated the help negatively with eyes' point focusing on the message but not commenting the response message. Finally, they began to ask instrumental help after monitoring and reflecting process such as asking avoidant help and evaluating help negatively (Figure 3.3).

In general, adaptive help-seeking by the AI group occurs after rejecting assistance, followed by directly accepting help. On the other hand, adaptive help-seeking by the HE group happens at the onset

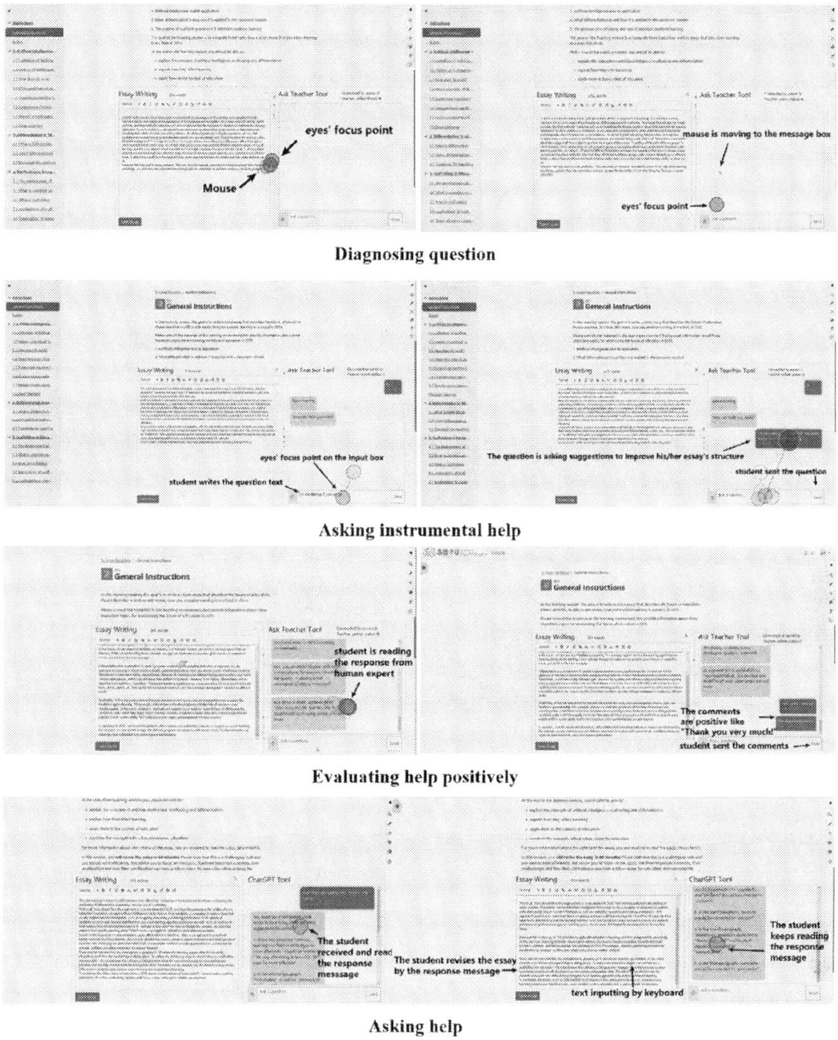

Figure 3.2 Example of interaction in HE group.

of encountering a problem, followed by evaluation after seeking help. Regarding executive help, it tends to occur at the beginning of encountering problems in AI group and then accompanied with directly accepting help. In contrast, the HE group engages in passive evaluation and reflection on the assistance provided after executive seeking. We believe these differences stem from the help object. When students

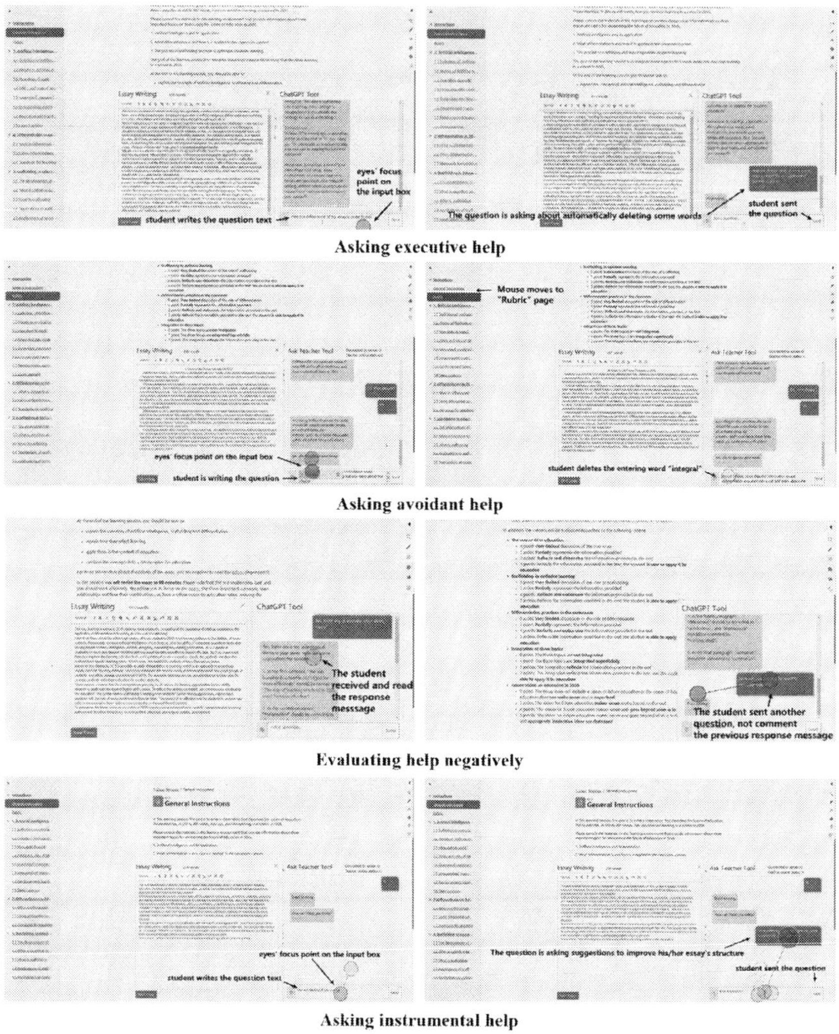

Figure 3.3 Example of interaction in AI group.

know they are seeking help from a teacher, they tend to prioritise knowledge acquisition and learning, thus asking more adaptive questions. Conversely, when students know they are seeking help from ChatGPT, their initial goal may be completing tasks. However, this does not imply a lack of self-regulation. The presence of rejecting assistance indicates that they monitor and reflect on ChatGPT's responses, triggering adaptive seeking rather than blindly accepting them. This reflects the difference of learners' cognitive and meta-cognitive self-regulation during the process of seeking assistance from and interacting with ChatGPT. For more details and findings from this study, see the paper led by Angxuan Chen and Yizhou Fan "Unpacking help-seeking process through multimodal learning analytics: A comparative study of ChatGPT vs Human expert" Chen et al. (2025).

3.4 IMPLICATION AND FUTURE WORKS

This chapter offers valuable insights and has broad implications for various stakeholders in the field of educational technology, and who are interested in the application of GenAI in education. For researchers, they will benefit from the comprehensive review of learner–AI interaction. This chapter's exploration of the theoretical underpinnings and empirical studies provides a solid foundation for designing future studies that can build upon the current understanding of learner–AI interaction. They can also use this chapter's findings on interaction patterns and questioning strategies to design future studies. The empirical research presented in this chapter provides a detailed analysis of the interactive process and content of learner–AI interaction, which may be worth learning from for researchers interested in learner–AI interaction. Educators can leverage the findings of this chapter to integrate GenAI tools like ChatGPT into their teaching practices.

The analysis of interaction patterns and strategies provides teachers with insights into how students engage with AI, which can inform instructional design and enhance the effectiveness of educational technologies in the classroom. Teachers can also use this chapter's findings to develop strategies for fostering critical thinking and self-directed learning among students, as well as to address potential challenges such as information overload and reliance on AI. Software developers working on educational technologies can use the insights from this chapter to refine existing GenAI tools and develop new features that cater to the specific needs of learners.

The discussion on the advantages and challenges of learner–AI interaction can inform the design of more interactive, personalised, and effective learning experiences. Developers can also consider the ethical implications and privacy concerns raised in this chapter to ensure that their products are responsible and respectful of user data. Policymakers can use the information in this chapter to guide the development of educational policies that support the integration of GenAI in education. This chapter's discussion on the potential of GenAI to enhance learning efficiency, personalise education, and foster learner independence can help policymakers understand the benefits and challenges of these technologies. Additionally, this chapter's focus on ethical considerations and the digital divide can inform policies that promote equitable access to technology and ensure ethical use of AI in education. Students can benefit from this chapter's exploration of help-seeking processes with GenAI. Understanding how to effectively interact with AI tools can empower students to take more control over their learning journey, fostering independence and self-directed learning.

The field of GenAI in education is ripe for further research and exploration. Here are some potential directions for future work. Researchers can conduct longitudinal studies to understand the long-term impact of learner–AI interaction on learning outcomes and the development of cognitive and meta-cognitive skills. This can provide insights into the sustainability and effectiveness of GenAI tools in educational settings. In addition, researchers can also compare the effectiveness of learner–AI interaction with learner–teacher interaction across different subjects and learning objectives. This can help identify areas where GenAI can complement or enhance traditional teaching methods. What's more, researchers can establish ethical guidelines for the use of GenAI in education, addressing concerns such as data privacy, academic integrity, and the potential for bias in AI-generated content. Besides, researchers can investigate the need for and develop training programs for teachers to effectively integrate GenAI tools into their teaching practices. This can help teachers maximise the benefits of these tools and address potential challenges. Researchers can also explore the potential of multi-modal interaction (e.g., combining text, voice, and visual input) in learner–AI interaction to create more engaging and intuitive learning experiences. By pursuing these research directions, the research community can continue to harness the potential of GenAI to enhance teaching and learning process, while also addressing the challenges and ethical considerations that arise with these advanced technologies.

3.5 CHAPTER SUMMARY

In this chapter, We explore the interaction between students and GenAI, uncovering the advantages of GenAI compared to human teachers, the challenges associated with the application of GenAI, and recommendations for its use. We begin by reviewing a review of the theoretical foundations and technological advancements in HCI. We traced the manifestations and significance of interaction in teaching from a long-term historical perspective, further transitioning to the impact of GenAI on interaction. Consequently, in the second part, We reviewed an extensive body of literature related to interactions with GenAI and found that there are numerous advantages to students' interactions with GenAI, while there are also certain challenges. Additionally, it was observed that, to some extent, students' dialogues with GenAI can promote learning more effectively than conversations with teachers. In order to deepen our understanding of the content and formal characteristics of students' interactions with GenAI, we present two case studies in the third part from the perspectives of content and help-seeking process. The first study analyses the content of student interaction with ChatGPT and explores the implicit interaction strategies between students and ChatGPT. The second study explored the differences in the overall help-seeking pattern and the specific help-seeking sequences when learners ask help from ChatGPT and human expert. Our findings suggest that differences exist in the content focus of dialogues between various students and ChatGPT. Furthermore, the patterns and sequences of students seeking help from ChatGPT differ from those when seeking assistance from human teachers. In summary, GenAI can play a significant role in the learning process of students. Through interactions with GenAI, students are able to access a richer body of knowledge compared to what is available from human teachers. Additionally, both educators and technology developers ought to exercise prudence in the application of GenAI and prioritise the cultivation of collaborative relationships between humans and AI.

Bibliography

Agustini, N. P. O. (2023). Examining the role of ChatGPT as a learning tool in promoting students' English language learning autonomy relevant to Kurikulum Merdeka Belajar. *Edukasia: Jurnal Pendidikan Dan Pembelajaran*, *4*(2):921–934.

Aksoy, D. A. and Kursun, E. (2024). Behind the scenes: A critical perspective on GenAI and open educational practices. *Open Praxis*, *16*(3):457–470.

Aktay, S., Gök, S., and Uzunoğlu, D. (2023). ChatGPT in education. *Türk Akademik Yayınlar Dergisi (TAY Journal)*, *7*(2):378–406.

Aleven, V., Stahl, E., Schworm, S., Fischer, F., and Wallace, R. (2003). Help seeking and help design in interactive learning environments. *Review of Educational Research*, *73*(3):277–320.

Ali, J. K. M., Shamsan, M. A. A., Hezam, T. A., and Mohammed, A. A. (2023). Impact of ChatGPT on learning motivation: Teachers and students' voices. *Journal of English Studies in Arabia Felix*, *2*(1):41–49.

Al Yakin, A. M., Ramli Rasyid, A., Massyat, M., Muthmainnah, M., Aquino, A. B., Noche, T. H., et al. (2024). The importance of collaboration between human intelligence and GenAI in digitalization of education. In Sanjay Misra & Kamrul Ahsan, editors, In *Impact and Potential of Machine Learning in the Metaverse*, pp. 129–160. IGI Global, Hershey, PA, USA.

Bahrini, A., Khamoshifar, M., Abbasimehr, H., Riggs, R. J., Esmaeili, M., Majdabadkohne, R. M., and Pasehvar, M. (2023). ChatGPT: Applications, opportunities, and threats. In *2023 Systems and Information Engineering Design Symposium (SIEDS)*, pp. 274–279. IEEE, Charlottesville, VA, USA.

Belt, E. S. and Lowenthal, P. R. (2021). Video use in online and blended courses: A qualitative synthesis. *Distance Education*, *42*(3): 410–440.

Beltran, M. A., Ruiz Mondragon, M. I., and Han, S. H. (2024). Comparative analysis of generative AI risks in the public sector. In *Proceedings of the 25th Annual International Conference on Digital Government Research*, Taipei, Taiwan.

Bhattacharya, K., Bhattacharya, A., Bhattacharya, N., Yagnik, V. D., and Garg, P. (2023). ChatGPT in surgical practice: A new kid on the block. *Indian Journal of Surgery, 85*(6):1346–1349.

Blackmon, S. J. (2012). Outcomes of chat and discussion board use in online learning: A research synthesis. *Journal of Educators Online, 9*(2), 2–3.

Boghossian, P. (2004). Socratic pedagogy, critical thinking, moral reasoning and inmate education: An exploratory study. Thesis, Portland State University.

Bossér, U. and Lindahl, M. (2019). Students' positioning in the classroom: A study of teacher-student interactions in a socioscientific issue context. *Research in Science Education, 49*(2):371–390.

Çelik, F., Yangın Ersanlı, C., and Drummond, A. (2023). GPT-pack: Can GenAI act as tpack peer tutor for preservice teachers? A comparative study on objective tpack of humans and ChatGPT 3.5.

Celiktutan, B., Klesse, A.-K., and Tuk, M. A. (2024). Acceptability lies in the eye of the beholder: Self-other biases in GenAI collaborations. *International Journal of Research in Marketing, 41*(3):496–512.

Chaccour, C., Karapantelakis, A., Murphy, T., and Dohler, M. (2024). Telecom's artificial general intelligence (AGI) vision: Beyond the GenAI frontier. *IEEE Network, 38*(5):21–28.

Chan, C. K. Y. (2023). A comprehensive AI policy education framework for university teaching and learning. *International Journal of Educational Technology in Higher Education, 20*(1):1–25.

Chen, A., Xiang, M., Zhou, J., Jia, J., Shang, J., Li, X., Gašević, D., and Fan, Y. (2025). Unpacking help-seeking process through multimodal learning analytics: A comparative study of ChatGPT vs human expert. *Computers & Education, 226*:105198. http://doi.org/10.1016/j.compedu.2024.105198.

Chen, B., Zhu, X., Fernando Díaz del Castillo, H. (2023). Integrating generative AI in knowledge building. *Computers and Education: Artificial Intelligence, 5*:100184.

Chesler, M. and Fox, R. (1966). *Role-Playing Methods in the Classroom.* Science Research Associates, Inc., Chicago, IL.

Choudhuri, R., Trinkenreich, B., Pandita, R., Kalliamvakou, E., Steinmacher, I., Gerosa, M. et al. (2024). What guides our choices? Modeling developers' trust and behavioral intentions towards GenAI. *arXiv preprint arXiv:2409.04099.*

Cline, K. S. and Zullo, H., editors (2011). *Teaching Mathematics with Classroom Voting: With and Without Clickers*, Number 79. MAA, Washington, DC.

Cotton, D. R., Cotton, P. A., and Shipway, J. R. (2023). Chatting and cheating: Ensuring academic integrity in the era of ChatGPT. *Innovations in Education and Teaching International,61* (2):228—239.

Cotton, K. (1988). Classroom questioning. *School Improvement Research Series, 5*:1–22.

Cui, R. and Teo, P. (2023). Thinking through talk: Using dialogue to develop students' critical thinking. *Teaching and Teacher Education, 125*:104068.

Davison, K., Malmberg, L.-E., and Sylva, K. (2023). Academic help-seeking interactions in the classroom: A microlongitudinal study. *British Journal of Educational Psychology, 93*(1):33–55. http://doi.org/10.1111/bjep.12538.

Desseauve, D., Lescar, R., de la Fourniere, B., Ceccaldi, P. F., Dziadzko, M. (2024). AI in obstetrics: Evaluating residents' capabilities and interaction strategies with ChatGPT. *European Journal of Obstetrics & Gynecology and Reproductive Biology, 303*:419–420.

Dobrin, S. I. (2023). *Talking about Generative AI: A Guide for Educators.* Broadview Press, Peterborough, Ontario.

Efe, A. (2022). The impact of artificial intelligence on social problems and solutions: An analysis on the context of digital divide and exploitation. *New Media, 13*:247–264.

Engelbart, D. C. (1962). Program on human effectiveness. *Reprint in: Nyce, James M./Kahn, Paul (1991)(Hg.)(1962)*, pp. 237–244.

Essel, H. B., Vlachopoulos, D., Tachie-Menson, A., Johnson, E. E., and Baah, P. K. (2022). The impact of a virtual teaching assistant (chatbot) on students' learning in ghanaian higher education. *International Journal of Educational Technology in Higher Education, 19*(1):57.

Fan, Y.-H. and Lin, T.-J. (2023). Identifying university students' online academic help-seeking patterns and their role in internet self-efficacy. *The Internet and Higher Education, 56*:100893.

Finnegan, R. (2003). *Oral Traditions and the Verbal Arts: A Guide to Research Practices.* Routledge, London, UK.

Finney, S., Barry, C. L., Horst, S. J., and Johnston, M. M. (2018). Exploring profiles of academic help seeking: A mixture modeling approach. *Learning and Individual Differences, 61*:158–171. http://doi.org/10.1016/J.LINDIF.2017.11.011.

Forrester, A. D. (2023). ChatGPT what does it mean for language centres. *STiLE-Scholarship of Teaching in Language Education, 1*(1):22.

Foung, D., Lin, L., and Chen, J. (2024). Reinventing assessments with ChatGPT and other online tools: Opportunities for GenAI-empowered assessment practices. *Computers and Education: Artificial Intelligence, 6*:100250.

Guo, K., Zhong, Y., Li, D., and Chu, S. K. W. (2023). Effects of chatbot-assisted in-class debates on students' argumentation skills and task motivation. *Computers & Education, 203*:104862.

Hong, W. C. H. (2023). The impact of ChatGPT on foreign language teaching and learning: Opportunities in education and research. *Journal of Educational Technology and Innovation, 5*(1):37–45.

Hota, A. and Jokinen, J. P. (2024). Cognitively informed human-GenAI interaction. *Authorea Preprints.*

Imran, M. and Almusharraf, N. (2023). Analyzing the role of ChatGPT as a writing assistant at higher education level: A systematic review of the literature. *Contemporary Educational Technology, 15*(4): ep464.

Ironsi, C. S. and Ironsi, S. S. (2024). Experimental evidence for the efficacy of generative AI in improving students' writing skills. *Quality Assurance in Education, 33*(2):237–252.

Jadhav, S., Vhatkar, S., and Aalam, Z. (2024). Bridging the gap: Exploring the revolutionary application of GenAI in language teaching and learning. *Journal of Electrical Systems, 20*(4s):2185–2193.

Javaid, M., Haleem, A., Singh, R., Khan, S., & Khan, I. (2023). Unlocking the opportunities through ChatGPT tool towards ameliorating the education system. *BenchCouncil Transactions on Benchmarks, Standards and Evaluations, 3*(2):100115.

Jeon, J. and Lee, S. (2023). Large language models in education: A focus on the complementary relationship between human teachers and ChatGPT. *Education and Information Technologies, 2023*:15873–15892.

Johinke, R., Cummings, R., and Di Lauro, F. (2023). Reclaiming the technology of higher education for teaching digital writing in a post—pandemic world. *Journal of University Teaching & Learning Practice, 20*(2):01.

Karabenick, S. A. and Berger, J.-L. (2013). *Help Seeking as a Self-Regulated learning Strategy*, pp. 237–261. IAP Information Age Publishing, Charlotte, NC.

Karabenick, S. A. and Gonida, E. N. (2017). Academic help seeking as a self-regulated learning strategy: Current issues, future directions. In Schunk, D. H. and Greene, J. A., editors, *Handbook of Self-Regulation of Learning and Performance*, pp. 421–433. Routledge, London, UK.

Keerthika, M., Abilash, K., Vasanth, M. S., Kuralamudhu, M., and Abbirooban, S. (2024). Emotional AI: Computationally intelligent devices for education. In *Emotional AI and Human-AI Interactions in Social Networking*, pp. 87–99. Elsevier.

Kim, J., Kim, J. H., Kim, C., and Park, J. (2023). Decisions with ChatGPT: Reexamining choice overload in ChatGPT recommendations. *Journal of Retailing and Consumer Services, 75*:103494.

Kloos, C. D., Alario-Hoyos, C., Estevez-Ayres, I., Callejo-Pinardo, P., Hombrados-Herrera, M. A., Munoz-Merino, P. J., Moreno-Marcos,

P. M., Munoz-Organero, M. and Ibanez, M. B. (2024). How can generative AI support education? In *2024 IEEE Global Engineering Education Conference (EDUCON)*. IEEE, Kos Island, Greece.

Kohnke, L. (2024). Exploring eap students' perceptions of GenAI and traditional grammar-checking tools for language learning. *Computers and Education: Artificial Intelligence*, *7*:100279.

Kooli, C. (2023). Chatbots in education and research: A critical examination of ethical implications and solutions. *Sustainability*, *15*(7):5614.

Korucu-Kiş, S. (2024). Zone of proximal creativity: An empirical study on EFL teachers' use of ChatGPT for enhanced practice. *Thinking Skills and Creativity*, *54*:101639.

Kucuk, T. (2023). The power of body language in education: A study of teachers' perceptions. *International Journal of Social Sciences & Educational Studies*, *10*(3):275–289.

Laak, K.-J., Abdelghani, R., and Aru, J. (2024). Personalisation is not guaranteed: The challenges of using generative AI for personalised learning. In *International Conference on Innovative Technologies and Learning*. Springer Nature Switzerland, Cham.

Labrie, A., Mok, T., Tang, A., Lui, M., Oehlberg, L., & Poretski, L. (2022). Toward video-conferencing tools for hands-on activities in online teaching. *Proceedings of the ACM on Human-Computer Interaction*, *6*:1–22.

Law, L. (2024). Application of generative artificial intelligence (GenAI) in language teaching and learning: A scoping literature review. *Computers and Education Open*, *6*:100174.

Lee, S. S. and Moore, R. L. (2024). Harnessing generative AI (GenAI) for automated feedback in higher education: A systematic review. *Online Learning*, *28*(3). https://doi.org/10.24059/olj.v28i3.4593.

Li, H. et al. (2024). The influence of GenAI on the effectiveness of argumentative writing in higher education: Evidence from a quasi-experimental study in China. *Journal of Asian Public Policy*, 1–26. https://doi.org/10.1080/17516234.2024.2363128

Liu, R., Zenke, C., Liu, C., Holmes, A., Thornton, P., and Malan, D. J. (2024). Teaching CS50 with AI: Leveraging generative artificial intelligence in computer science education. In *Proceedings of the 55th ACM Technical Symposium on Computer Science Education Volume 1*, Portland, Oregon, pp. 750–756.

Lv, Z. (2023). Generative artificial intelligence in the metaverse era. *Cognitive Robotics*, *3*:208–217.

Mahapatra, B. C. (2005). *Information Technology and Education*. Sarup & Sons, Delhi.

Maziani, A. (2021). Classroom discourse and aspects of conversation analysis: A qualitative study on student-to-student interaction during group discussion in EFL classrooms.

McLoughlin, C. (2014). Open, flexible and participatory pedagogy in the era of globalisation: Technology, open education and international e-learning. In Keefe D., editor, *International Education and the Next-Generation Workforce: Competition in the Global Economy*, pp. 224–239. IGI Global, Hershey, PA.

Mercier, J. and Frederiksen, C. (2008). The structure of the help-seeking process in collaboratively using a computer coach in problem-based learning. *Computers & Education*, *51*(1):17–33.

Miao, F., Holmes, W., Huang, R., and Zhang, H. (2021). *AI and Education: A Guidance for Policymakers*. UNESCO Publishing, Paris, France.

Miao, J., Chang, J., and Ma, L. (2022). Teacher–student interaction, student–student interaction and social presence: Their impacts on learning engagement in online learning environments. *The Journal of Genetic Psychology*, *183*(6):514–526.

Montenegro, H., Silva, W., and Cardoso, J. S. (2021). Privacy-preserving generative adversarial network for case-based explainability in medical image analysis. *IEEE Access*, *9*:148037–148047.

Murphy, P. K., editor (2018). *Classroom Discussions in Education*. Routledge, London, UK.

Mwakalinga, J. (2012). Teaching social interaction for learners with autism: A study of how teachers aim to influence development of social interaction for learners with autism (Master's thesis). University of Oslo, Norway.

Nelles, J., Muller, F. A., Ramnan, K., Blackwell, E., Atre, M. P., De Guzman, C., et al. (2024). Skill awareness framework for learning design–re-focusing experiential learning towards skills that matter most in times of GenAI. In *Conference on Learning Factories*, Cham. Springer Nature Switzerland.

Nguyen, A. N. M. (2024). Leveraging ChatGPT for enhancing english writing skills and critical thinking in University Freshmen. *Journal of Knowledge Learning and Science Technology, 3*(2):51–62.

Nyaaba, M., Shi, L., Nabang, M., Zhai, X., Kyeremeh, P.,and Ayoberd, S. A., et al. (2024). Generative AI as a learning buddy and teaching assistant: Pre-service teachers' uses and attitudes. *arXiv preprint arXiv:2407.11983*.

Opara, E., Theresa, A. M.-E., and Aduke, T. C. (2023). ChatGPT for teaching, learning and research: Prospects and challenges. *Global Academic Journal of Humanities and Social Sciences, 5*:33–40.

Ouyang, F. and Chang, Y.-H. (2019). The relationships between social participatory roles and cognitive engagement levels in online discussions. *British Journal of Educational Technology, 50*(3):1396–1414.

Owoseni, A., Kolade, O., and Egbetokun, A. (2024). Enhancing personalised learning and student engagement using generative AI. In *Generative AI in Higher Education: Innovation Strategies for Teaching and Learning*, pp. 123–150. Springer Nature Switzerland, Cham.

Pence, H. E., Hightower, G., Forlenza, J., Leonard, K., McLellan, A., Suero, A., et al. (2024). Using generative AI systems for critical thinking engagement in an advanced chemistry course: A case study. *Journal of Chemical Education, 101*(9):3789–3794.

Piaget, J. and Inhelder, B. (2008). *The Psychology of the Child.* Basic Books, New York.

Pöysä, S., Vasalampi, K., Muotka, J., Lerkkanen, M. K., Poikkeus, A. M., and Nurmi, J. E. (2019). Teacher–student interaction and lower secondary school students' situational engagement. *British Journal of Educational Psychology, 89*(2):374–392.

Qadir, J. (2023). Engineering education in the era of ChatGPT: Promise and pitfalls of generative AI for education. In *2023 IEEE Global Engineering Education Conference (EDUCON)*, pp. 1–9. IEEE, Kuwait City, Kuwait.

Rahman, M. M. and Watanobe, Y. (2023). ChatGPT for education and research: Opportunities, threats, and strategies. *Applied Sciences, 13*(9):5783.

Rasul, T., Nair, S., Kalendra, D., Balaji, M. S., Santini, F. D. O., Ladeira, W. J., Rather, R. A., Yasin, N., Rodriguez, R. V. and Kokkalis, P. (2024a). Enhancing academic integrity among students in GenAI era: A holistic framework. *The International Journal of Management Education, 22*(3):101041.

Rasul, T., Nair, S., Kalendra, D., Balaji, M., de Oliveira Santini, F., Ladeira, W. J., et al. (2024b). Enhancing academic integrity among students in GenAI era: A holistic framework. *The International Journal of Management Education, 22*(3):101041.

Rawas, S. (2024). ChatGPT: Empowering lifelong learning in the digital age of higher education. *Educational Information Technology, 29*:6895–6908.

Ray, P. P. (2023). ChatGPT: A comprehensive review on background, applications, key challenges, bias, ethics, limitations and future scope. *Internet of Things and Cyber-Physical Systems*, *3*:121–154.

Sabzalieva, E. and Valentini, A. (2023). ChatGPT and artificial intelligence in higher education: Quick start guide. Technical report, International Institute for Higher Education in Latin America and the Caribbean (IESALC).

Salvagno, M., Taccone, F. S., and Gerli, A. G. (2023). Can artificial intelligence help for scientific writing? *Critical Care*, *27*(1):75.

Samala, A. D., Rawas, S., Wang, T., Reed, J. M., Kim, J., Howard, N. J., and Ertz, M. (2024). Unveiling the landscape of generative artificial intelligence in education: A comprehensive taxonomy of applications, challenges, and future prospects. *Education and Information Technologies,20*:1–40.

Saprudin, A. A., Goolamally, N., and Latif, L. A. (2014). Embedding QR codes in the teaching and learning process. In *Proceedings of the Seminar Kebangsaan Pembelajaran Sepanjang Hayat 2014*, Kuala Lumpur, Malaysia.

Schmidt-Fajlik, R. (2023). ChatGPT as a grammar checker for Japanese English language learners: A comparison with grammarly and prowritingaid. *AsiaCALL Online Journal, 14*(1):105–119.

Shailendra, S., Kadel, R., and Sharma, A. (2024). Framework for adoption of generative artificial intelligence (GenAI) in education. *IEEE Transactions on Education, 67*(5):777–785.

Sharp, A. M. (1986). Is there an essence of education? *Journal of Moral Education, 15*(3):189–196.

Su, J. and Yang, W. (2023). Unlocking the power of ChatGPT: A framework for applying generative AI in education. *ECNU Review of Education, 6*(3):355–366.

Tafazoli, D. (2024). Exploring the potential of generative AI in democratizing English language education. *Computers and Education: Artificial Intelligence, 7*:100275.

Talebinejad, M. R. and Matou, Z. (2012). Teacher–student interaction in EFL reading comprehension contexts at university level a critical thinking perspective. *Sage Open, 2*(4):46–50.

Tankelevitch, L., Kewenig, V., Simkute, A., Scott, A. E., Sarkar, A., Sellen, A., and Rintel, S. (2024). The metacognitive demands and opportunities of generative AI. In *Proceedings of the CHI Conference on Human Factors in Computing Systems*, pp. 1–24. ACM, Honolulu, Hawaii, USA.

Teel, Z. A., Wang, T., and Lund, B. (2023). ChatGPT conundrums: Probing plagiarism and parroting problems in higher education practices. *College & Research Libraries News, 84*(6):205–208.

Thway, M., Recatala-Gomez, J., Lim, F. S., Hippalgaonkar, K., and Ng, L. W. (2024). Harnessing GenAI for higher education: A study of a retrieval augmented generation chatbot's impact on human learning. *arXiv preprint arXiv:2406.07796.*

Van Zee, E. and Minstrell, J. (1997). Using questioning to guide student thinking. *The Journal of the Learning Sciences*, *6*(2):227–269.

Wang, T. T. (2008). Instructional strategies and teacher-student interaction in the classrooms of a Chinese immersion school. PhD thesis, University of San Francisco.

Ward, R., Phillips, O., Bowers, D., Crick, T., Davenport, J. H., Hanna, P., Hayes, A., Irons, A., and Prickett, T. (2021). Towards a 21st century personalised learning skills taxonomy. In *2021 IEEE Global Engineering Education Conference (EDUCON)*, pp. 344–354. IEEE, Vienna, Austria.

Wegerif, R. (2013). *Dialogic: Education for the Internet Age.* Routledge, London, UK.

Westrup, U. and Planander, A. (2013). Role-play as a pedagogical method to prepare students for practice: The students' voice. *Högre utbildning*, *3*(3):199–210.

Wu, Y. (2022). An overview analysis of AI divide: Applications and prospects of AI divide in China's society. In *3rd International Conference on Mental Health, Education and Human Development (MHEHD 2022)*, pp. 3–9. Atlantis Press, Dalian, China.

Yan, L., Martinez-Maldonado, R., and Gasevic, D. (2024). Generative artificial intelligence in learning analytics: Contextualising opportunities and challenges through the learning analytics cycle. In *Proceedings of the 14th Learning Analytics and Knowledge Conference*, pp. 101–111. ACM, Kyoto, Japan.

Yuan, Y., Li, H., and Sawaengdist, A. (2024). The impact of ChatGPT on learners in english academic writing: opportunities and challenges in education. *Language Learning in Higher Education*, *14*(1):41–56.

Zadorozhnyy, A. and Lai, W. Y. W. (2023). ChatGPT and L2 written communication: A game-changer or just another tool? *Languages*, *9*(1):5.

Zhang, W. (2024). The path of enhancement of traditional cultural heritage on moral education based on addie model. *Applied Mathematics and Nonlinear Sciences*, *9*(1):2.

CHAPTER 4

Learners' Emotion and Motivation while Learning with GenAI

Yuyue Zhang, Huaiya Liu, Xinyu Li, and Yizhou Fan

EMOTIONS AND MOTIVATIONS play an important role in the learning of the students. Human teachers can stimulate positive academic emotions and learning motivation, thus creating a positive academic environment, alleviating learning pressure and anxiety, promoting good teacher-student relationships, and providing a good learning environment. Many new technologies such as multimedia and intelligent teaching systems have also promoted positive academic emotions among students. Although GenAI (such as ChatGPT) has advantages in response speed and knowledge storage, it is not known whether it can enable students to achieve the same positive emotional state and learning motivation as human teachers when learning needs to be evaluated through empirical research. This chapter first reviews the current evaluation of the empathy ability of GenAI and compares the similarities and differences between GenAI and human teachers in teaching as well as their impact on students' emotions. Subsequently, we conducted an empirical study using facial emotion recognition technology based on deep neural networks. This study compared emotional changes and changes in essay scores between 16 learners who used GenAI to modify their essays and those who modified their essays under the guidance of the teacher. Research analyses the differences in emotional changes between two groups of

DOI: 10.4324/9781003632146-4

students and uses clustering analysis to group learners with different emotional changes into three groups. Finally, ENA technology was used to analyse the differences in teaching methods between GenAI and human teachers as well as their relationship with different emotional changes in students. In summary, this study evaluated the emotional differences between GenAI and human teacher tutoring for students, providing insight into how GenAI can provide more effective writing tutoring strategies to enhance students' positive emotional experiences.

4.1 INTRODUCTION

Non-cognitive factors in the learning process are increasingly considered to be as important as cognitive factors. Non-cognitive factors in learning refer to a series of attitudes, behaviors, and strategies, including learning motivation, emotional state, self-concept, goal orientation, perseverance, self-control, learning habits, learning environment, popularity, parental involvement, etc. They are important components of social-emotional development and contribute to overall learning success (Boylan et al., 2018)). They are usually a "soft factor" in contrast to the "hard factors" of cognitive factors, such as memory capacity, literacy, and arithmetic ability. Many studies have shown that there is an interaction between non-cognitive factors and cognitive factors, (Lee et al., 2017) and non-cognitive factors are also important indicators of students' academic success (Veas et al., 2015; Gray et al., 2016).

Among the many non-cognitive factors, learning motivation and academic emotions are considered to be two of the most critical components in a specific learning process. Learning motivation is an internal driving force that prompts people to take actions to meet needs. It is closely related to people's goal-oriented behavior and is an important force that drives individuals to complete specific tasks and maintain learning behavior (Atkinson, 1964). Academic emotions refer to students' emotional experiences related to academic tasks and learning situations. According to Pekrun's "Control-Value Theory," academic emotions are emotional reactions felt by students in learning and achievement situations (Pekrun, 2006). These emotions may be related to specific learning tasks, classroom activities, exams, or academic achievements. Positive emotions such as happiness, hope, and pride are usually associated with high self-efficacy and achievement expectations, whereas negative emotions such as anxiety, anger, and helplessness are usually accompanied by low efficacy and failure expectations.

Learning motivation is essential for achieving high-achieving academic performance. Since learning is essentially hard work and requires a lot of mental work, it can only be achieved with sufficient learning motivation. In addition, highly motivated students learn faster and make the class fun, while unmotivated learners learn less and make teaching painful and frustrating (Filgona et al., 2020). Learning motivation is divided into intrinsic motivation and extrinsic motivation. Intrinsic motivation refers to the individual's interest in the activity or satisfaction in the activity itself, rather than external rewards or pressure. Intrinsic motivation is often related to an individual's curiosity, spirit of challenge, and desire for personal growth, whereas extrinsic motivation refers to an individual's engagement in an activity because of external rewards (such as money, honor) or avoiding punishment (Deci and Ryan, 2013). Learning motivation is particularly important in online learning environments (Heryanti et al., 2022). Academic emotions also have an impact on student engagement and academic success. First, academic emotions can directly affect students' attention, memory, and reasoning ability. Studies have shown that moderate test anxiety can help improve students' attention and test performance, while excessive anxiety can lead to cognitive dysfunction and affect test scores (Gross, 1998). Secondly, different academic emotions can in turn affect learners' motivation (Artino et al., 2012). Positive emotions, such as enjoying a task, can lead to greater interest and greater intrinsic motivation, thereby engaging in the task for its own sake (Ryan and Deci, 2000; McConnell and Eva, 2012). Negative emotions (such as boredom, anxiety, and anger) can reduce interest in the task and intrinsic motivation, but can also increase extrinsic motivation (motivation to participate in the task as a means to achieve an end) (Schunk et al., 2014). For example, the fear of performing poorly in front of peers may lead to greater extrinsic motivation, thereby motivating learners to study hard. Individuals' cognitive evaluation of environmental events, personal past life experiences, personality traits, physiological states, and external social environments such as social support, family background, and teacher-student relationships can all affect students' academic emotions.

Past research has revealed some dilemmas, problems, and challenges in the field of emotional motivation. First, Deci's research showed that external rewards may cause students to focus more on external results and ignore the joy of learning itself (Deci, 1971). How to effectively balance intrinsic and extrinsic motivation in educational practice and avoid external rewards weakening students' autonomy and intrinsic learning interest is a challenge. Secondly, Bandura emphasised the role of self-efficacy in motivation formation, but many students tend to decline in self-efficacy after failure or setbacks, thus falling into a motivation trough (Bandura, 1990). Therefore, students' self-efficacy should be continuously improved in education to help them maintain motivation when facing failure or challenges. In addition, Eccles and Wigfield pointed out that the expectations and pressure of family, school, and society for academic achievement may lead to the complexity of motivation sources (Eccles and Wigfield, 2002). How to design individualised motivation incentive strategies to meet the needs of different students is also a difficulty. In the field of educational technology and psychology, many technologies have been designed and developed to solve the above emotional motivation problems and help students improve their motivation and improve their academic emotions. For example, learning platforms that combine emotional computing technology, such as DreamBox and MindSpark, can help students maintain positive emotions and motivation by analysing whether students feel confused, anxious or tired during the learning process, adjusting the difficulty of learning content or providing incentives in a timely manner. Another example is gamified learning, such as Classcraft and Duolingo, which introduces game elements (such as points, levels, leaderboards, rewards, etc.) into the learning environment to motivate students to continue to participate, which is particularly suitable for solving the problem of internal and external motivation conflicts. Online social learning platforms, such as Edmodo and Piazza, provide social support and alleviate isolation and learning pressure by enhancing peer interaction and cooperative learning.

The impact of technology on emotional motivation is a double-edged sword. Although technology has great potential in solving emotional and motivational problems in the learning process, it also brings some negative effects and new problems. First, incorrect or imperfect feedback may bring emotional frustration. For example, if the feedback of adaptive learning systems or intelligent tutor systems is not timely, accurate, or overly complex, it may cause confusion or frustration to students and may even amplify students' anxiety and helplessness (Baker and Yacef,

2009; Zhou and Winne, 2012; Bergdahl et al., 2020; Selwyn, 2021; Bulfin et al., 2015). Secondly, learning analytics technology uses big data to analyse students' learning behaviors and emotional states. Although it can help personalised teaching, it may also produce a "labeling effect". When students are identified by the system as "low motivation" or "high anxiety" groups, teachers or systems' expectations and feedback on them may change, and may even strengthen this label, thereby affecting students' self-cognition and forming a self-fulfilling negative prophecy (Clow, 2013). In addition, there is the problem of social isolation in digital learning. Some students who rely on technology may feel that their social connections with peers and teachers are weakened, leading to loneliness and a decline in learning motivation (Hrastinski, 2009; Carr, 2000). Finally, over-reliance on technological tools (such as the reward mechanism of gamified learning) may cause students to be more inclined to focus on external rewards (such as scores, badges, etc.) provided by technology rather than the fun and intrinsic meaning of the learning process, which has long led to a decrease in intrinsic motivation (Deci et al., 1999; Clark and Mayer, 2023; Plass et al., 2015).

Generative AI, through natural language generation and content creation, may not completely solve all of the above emotional motivation problems, but it may partially alleviate these challenges through personalisation, real-time feedback, emotion regulation, etc. First, generative AI has strong natural language understanding and generation capabilities to ensure the timeliness and accuracy of feedback. In addition, generative AI can help break the impact of labeling through dialogue and naturally generated content. Compared with relying on big data analysis to "classify" students, generative AI can interact with students and generate personalised, non-judgmental feedback, so that students can feel personalised support. At the same time, generative AI can reduce students' sense of social isolation in online learning through virtual peers and mentor-type dialogues. Finally, generative AI can enhance intrinsic motivation by generating dynamic personalised content, rather than relying solely on external incentives.

However, in the field of the impact of generative AI on students' motivation and emotional changes during learning, due to the relatively small number of existing literature and empirical studies, there is a lack of empirical research reviews to understand the current research status, opportunities and challenges of generative AI in the field of emotional motivation. It is also very necessary to carry out corresponding empirical case studies. Therefore, in this chapter, we first review the current literature and outline the current application status of generative AI in the field of education, especially in writing tutoring. Secondly, through the literature review, we further refine the opportunities and challenges of generative AI in educational applications. Finally, through an empirical case study, we preliminarily explore how GenAIs affect students' emotions in writing tutoring and observe how generative AI affects students' emotional changes during the writing tutoring process.

4.2 LITERATURE REVIEW ON EMOTIONAL AND MOTIVATIONAL DIMENSIONS

Using the keywords (((TS = (motivation)) OR TS = (emotions))) AND (TS = (GenAI) OR TS = (GenAIs) OR TS = (ChatGPT)) on WOS, 443 articles were screened out. At present, most of the literature focuses on evaluating the emotional response of AI, how GenAI can better identify human emotions, the motivational factors for using GenAI, and which emotions affect people's use of GenAI. After screening and removing these irrelevant literature one by one, 72 articles were obtained, of which there were 34 empirical studies in learning situations, including 7 qualitative empirical studies and 27 quantitative empirical studies.

4.2.1 GenAI May Improve Learners' Motivation

Students have intrinsic motivation to participate in GenAI to improve their reading and writing skills, summarise literature, and generate practice exams (Dai et al., 2023), and integrating GenAI in educational environments can also improve students' participation and emotional response. The positive impact of GenAI on learning motivation has been confirmed by large-scale empirical research. Gabriella et al. (2024) conducted a large-scale survey of more than 400 people and found that the use of GenAI was significantly associated with students' learning motivation. As students' motivation increased, their academic performance and self-efficacy also improved. Questionnaires from 481 students were collected and conducted through a questionnaire survey. The results showed that all nine hypotheses were accepted, that is, the use of GenAI had a positive impact on students' perceived autonomy, perceived ability, perceived relevance, intrinsic motivation, engagement, and satisfaction. It shows that the use of GenAI affects students' perceived autonomy, ability, and relevance, thereby enhancing intrinsic motivation.

The improvement of learning motivation is reflected in various disciplines. Due to the powerful text generation function, many scholars have conducted empirical research on using GenAI to help students write and learn languages. Some researchers compared the feedback generated by GPT-3.5 and the two groups of students who did not receive feedback to revise their writing papers. The results showed that GenAI had a positive impact on students' cognitive performance and motivation (Baker et al., 2024). Wang explored students' learning motivation and cognitive load when using the ChatPRCS system for English reading comprehension learning, and found that students who used the GenAI system to generate personalised questions significantly improved the enthusiasm of students in the experimental group compared with students who used the traditional method of learning and practicing with standardised questions (Wang et al., 2024). Cheng applied it to students' programming learning and found that it increased students' learning benefits, high participation and learning motivation (Cheng et al., 2024). Others have discussed the impact of the integration of GenAI and gamification on students' academic performance and motivation in physics courses and found that students developed more positive attitudes towards interest, usefulness, self-efficacy, active participation and personal satisfaction in physics courses (Beltozar-Clemente and Díaz-Vega, 2024).

Timely and personalised feedback plays a key role in improving motivation. Chen and Hou (2024) studied the difference in the impact of using chatbots as scaffolds on game-based learning motivation, developed a mobile contextualised educational game framework with GenAI interactive scaffolding, and divided 61 participants into a document scaffolding group ($n = 32$) and a GenAI group ($n = 29$). The flow, motivation, and anxiety of the two groups of learners were examined through scales. The results show that assisted learning through GenAI can help students maintain their interest in learning through instant feedback and personalised question design in a specific teaching environment, stimulate learners' potential, maintain a certain level of high motivation and participation, and relieve anxiety. Xu et al. (2024)

research shows that GenAI can effectively search across multiple sources and search engines in a personal learning environment, quickly provide students with relevant information, greatly speed up the work speed, and provide a complete perspective on relevant issues. Through real-time personalised feedback, learners' motivation and self-efficacy are improved. Similarly, Rezai et al. (2024) found that the timely evaluation and feedback of student performance by generative AI technology enhanced students' sense of success, and the increase in utility value would enhance students' enthusiasm for participating in tasks. Generative AI not only has a positive impact on short-term motivation and emotion but also promotes students' sustained motivation and self-regulation ability in long-term learning. Chiu (2024) research shows that GenAI can enhance students' self-regulated learning ability by supporting three stages: self-reflection, performance and self-regulation. In addition, Ng et al. (2024) found that the use of AI tools can effectively help students maintain regular learning habits and enhance their learning performance and enthusiasm.

4.2.2 The Impact of GenAI on Learners' Emotional Changes

Generative AI not only affects students' motivation in the learning process but also plays an important role in emotional regulation. Zou et al. (2024) showed that students showed higher happiness and lower sadness when using questionnaires generated by generative AI. Hmoud et al. (2024) interviewed 15 students and used inductive and deductive content analysis to investigate students' emotions when using GenAI for learning. It was found that students generated 3 positive emotions and 1 negative emotion when using it: (1) **Enjoyment**: Due to the high engagement and fun of the chat system, students did not feel the passage of time during the task execution. (2) **Satisfaction**: Completing tasks through GenAI instilled an intrinsic sense of satisfaction in students about task completion and increased their confidence in completing the task. (3) **Curiosity**: When students typed questions or inquiries into GenAI and waited for responses, students were curious about how the answer would turn out and how useful it would be. This curiosity prompted students to ask more and more about it, enriching and enhancing students' knowledge. (4) **Anxiety**: Despite satisfaction with tasks completed using GenAI, other students generally felt anxious. These concerns were attributed to several reasons, including a lack of complete trust in the program information and fear that the task would be labeled as "cheating."

However, in the context of self-learning, generative AI plays an important role in anxiety relief. In a survey by Hamid et al. (2023), students said that using GenAI helped alleviate their fear of expressing their findings or opinions because they viewed GenAI as a source of shared information. They no longer felt the pressure of being judged for potentially incorrect answers because they felt they could attribute any differences to GenAI. Gao's research also pointed out that AI applications can significantly reduce students' test anxiety and negative academic emotions (Hamid et al., 2023). Younis's research also reported that students' AI environment alleviated their writing anxiety and promoted the improvement of their writing ability, which may be attributed to the non-judgmental interactive environment provided by AI, which enables students to cope with learning tasks with a more relaxed attitude (Younis, 2024).

GenAI's role in emotion regulation is attributed to the following aspects. First, GenAI can provide timely feedback and suggestions based on students' situations, thereby enhancing their learning experience. Second, educators can also create personalised and adaptive learning experiences and provide interactive and personalised practices based on students' specific requirements and preferences to meet students' personalised needs, thereby improving students' emotional motivation and learning outcomes. GenAI can provide context-related answers to a wide range of questions, making it a valuable tool for personalised learning. They can adapt to the unique needs and rhythm of each student and provide customised feedback and guidance. By analysing students' responses and progress, GenAIs can identify areas where students may be struggling and provide targeted support to address these challenges.

In addition, GenAIs can bridge the gap between technology and human interaction. GenAIs may allow EFL (English as a foreign language) learners to express their thoughts, feelings, and concerns in an interactive environment, where they may become more self-aware and develop emotion regulation skills, which in turn may affect their well-being (Kasneci et al., 2023). While GenAIs may not possess true emotional cognition, their ability to simulate empathy can create more meaningful and engaging interactions. This ability is particularly useful in online and distance learning environments, where the lack of face-to-face interaction can make it challenging to meet students' emotional needs. By incorporating empathetic responses, GenAIs can help recreate the supportive and responsive atmosphere of traditional classrooms, enhancing students' overall learning experience (Sorin et al., 2023).

4.2.3 Mechanisms and Factors of GenAI's Influence on Students' Emotional Motivation

The mechanism of GenAI's influence on students' emotional motivation can be explained by self-determination theory (SDT), which proposes three innate needs: autonomy, relatedness, and competence (Ryan and Deci, 2000). When individuals' needs are supported and met, their motivation increases, shifting from unmotivated to intrinsic motivation. GenAI, as an artificial intelligence tool, has the ability to facilitate the SDT process (Ryan and Deci, 2000). For autonomy, GenAI provides flexibility and freedom to learn at one's own pace, ownership and control over learning activities, a safe practice space, and no fear of being judged; for competence, personalised feedback and correction, support and context-specific examples, increased self-efficacy and confidence in language tasks, but also concerns about the accuracy and relevance of answers and the inability to adjust language levels as students progress; for relevance, GenAI can be based on a sense of companionship and guidance (Du and Alm, 2024).

According to SDT theory, learning can be divided into the deliberative stage, the performance stage, and the self-reflective stage. In the deliberation stage, GenAI may provide more precise descriptions and examples of learning activities to clarify problems, as well as suggestions for learning strategies, and a clear understanding of the problem is more likely to keep students motivated; in the performance stage, students can use GenAI to gain new learning ideas and insights, prompting students to be more actively involved in learning activities (Wu et al., 2024); in the self-reflection stage, students can ask GenAI what they have learned and how to improve their learning, reflect and review their learning experience (Kasneci et al., 2023). Wang et al. (2024) believe that the reason why GenAI improves students' emotional motivation is attributed to the following reasons: First, GenAI can speed up learning by providing quick solutions to challenging tasks. Second, GenAI meets students' performance expectations, motivating them to use their time to deal with major academic challenges, and ultimately improving their motivation and research productivity. Third, GenAI enhances motivation and engagement by meeting students' autonomy needs. It fosters student autonomy by promoting personalised learning paths, autonomous learning goals, and problem solving through interaction and communication. Fourth, it promotes student thinking. Students delve deeper into their inquiries based on the feedback provided. In the process, they must reflect to think more effectively about how to correctly ask questions to get the answers they need, stimulating their inner curiosity and desire to explore, thereby promoting deeper reflection and understanding. In addition, learners' emotions when interacting with GenAIs are affected by a variety of factors, including the user's personal intrinsic factors and GenAIs' external factors. For learners' personal intrinsic factors, it is mainly reflected in the individual's conservatism towards technology. Castelo and Ward found that conservatism and resistance to innovation are predictors of negative emotions towards AI, such as whether they are from a lower income class and may care about their work, or whether the individual is less educated and may not understand technology (Castelo and Ward, 2021). At the demographic level, GenAI may cause dissatisfaction among the elderly, those with lower education levels and incomes, those who are predominantly female, or those who tend to be conservative. However, if the public's loneliness is higher, they are more likely to accept artificial intelligence. Zou et al. (2024) found that college students experienced higher happiness and lower sadness when answering questionnaires developed by GenAI compared with human-designed questionnaires, and that women showed higher happiness than men, and men tended to show stronger expressiveness, especially in specific emotions such as sadness, anger, and surprise.

4.2.4 Motivational and Emotional Issues and Challenges of Students When Using GenAI

Although generative AI has shown great potential in improving student motivation and regulating emotions, there are also some challenges. First, in some teaching scenarios, there are no significant differences between the GenAI and traditional groups in intrinsic motivation, cognitive load, and effectiveness of learning behavior (Chen and Hou, 2024).

Second, over-reliance on AI may weaken students' autonomous learning ability. Research by Li et al. (2024) showed that students may suffer from a decline in autonomy and learning motivation due to over-reliance on AI tools in their learning. Song also believed that in the long run, the convenience and speed of accessing information through chatbots may hinder students' motivation to learn in the long run, because they may over-rely on this quick access, and when they cannot use chatbots, they will feel less successful or autonomous (Song and Song, 2023). This may be solved by overcoming lazy thinking. Ye et al. (2024) conducted an online survey of 870 Taiwanese college students and found that lazy thinking was positively correlated with GenAI dependence, there was a significant association between lazy thinking and avoidance learning motivation, and avoidance learning motivation was positively correlated with GenAI dependence. Therefore, educators should help students overcome lazy thinking and avoid learning motivation to prevent dependence on emerging technologies.

Moreover, GenAI still faces some technical limitations in providing accurate feedback and adapting to students' personalisation. Creating your own robot may alleviate this. Woo et al. (2024) introduced GenAI to Hong Kong secondary school students and tried a 500-word English writing task with the support of GenAI. They found that the average motivation score of students before and after the workshop increased slightly, but there was no significant difference in motivation. However, Guo and Li (2024) organised undergraduates to use Poe to create chatbots and assist in their writing process. The results showed significant differences. By using GenAI, students can get customised support for their specific writing needs, have clearer writing goals, writing confidence, writing beliefs, and more positive writing attitudes, thereby improving motivation.

In addition, although generative AI has a sustained positive impact on students' self-efficacy, there are challenges in maintaining intrinsic motivation. As time goes by, students' interest in learning may weaken, so further exploration is needed on how AI can integrate features to maintain long-term motivation. In a long-term controlled experiment on 65 elementary school students, the GenAI group showed significant advantages in the first month after the intervention, but when the time frame was extended to a one-month follow-up, the advantage of the GenAI group in writing motivation seemed to weaken. However, after the scenario-based task enhanced by digital storytelling generated by GenAI, the situation improved significantly. According to the task value theory, task value represents the subjective assessment of students' interest, relevance, and importance of learning tasks. Integrating digital storytelling into learning activities increases task value, thereby improving students' motivation levels (Bai et al., 2024). Finally, facing reduced interpersonal interaction and emotional connection, lack of social belonging, and peer pressure. Interpersonal relationships are an important part of student motivation, such as peer assistance and group-based learning are beneficial. However, social learning can also present challenges, especially in terms of unequal participation levels, which can lead to negative emotions such as frustration. Therefore, although GenAI may improve students' learning motivation and emotions, this approach requires careful design, such as building courses around relevant and real situations, and further exploring how to continuously stimulate students' intrinsic motivation and learning interest through the optimised design of AI tools (such as gamification elements). For example, Torres-Peña et al. (2024) created a dynamic adaptive learning environment where students deepened their understanding of mathematical concepts such as derivatives through continuous interaction with virtual tutors, significantly improving their engagement and enthusiasm.

4.3 EMPIRICAL STUDY: COMPARING LEARNERS' EMOTIONS WHEN LEARNING WITH GENAI VS. A TEACHER

4.3.1 Introduction to the Empirical Study

Prior studies have mainly focused on GenAI, with little attention on how learners' emotions differ when receiving feedback from teachers. Comparing these learners' emotions is essential to determine whether GenAI can complement the engagement that teachers provide. Since teachers cannot always offer one-on-one support, AI can assist when continuous individual help is needed. This comparison will help educators understand the emotional impact of both approaches and guide the effective use of AI in educational settings.

Methods commonly used to measure learners' emotions during learning have limitations. Prior sections have reviewed empirical studies on learners' emotions when learning with GenAI, highlighting that existing studies have primarily relied on self-report questionnaires and interviews to measure emotions. Although these methods provide valuable insights, they also come with limitations due to their reliance on subjective recollection, which depends on learners' ability to accurately recall and assess their emotions, potentially introducing biases or inaccuracies (Montibeller and Von Winterfeldt, 2015). Both approaches are prone to distortion, as learners may not fully remember their emotions or may report what they believe researchers expect to hear (Sutton and Austin, 2015).

We conducted a case study to compare learners' emotions when studying with GenAI versus a teacher. The specific implementation example we focus on is English as a foreign language (EFL) writing tutoring. We used data-driven methods to measure emotions based on learning behaviour patterns, such as learners' real-time facial expressions and body movements. Data analytic techniques, including process mining, were then applied to identify emotional changes from these expressions and movements. This approach allows for more accurate and comprehensive measurement of emotional states, reducing bias and providing a holistic view of learners' emotions. As a result, it enables a detailed comparison of how learners emotionally engage with GenAI versus expert teachers, offering new insights into the emotional dynamics of different tutoring methods.

Our case study has two research questions:

> **RQ1**: How do learners' emotions differ when learning with GenAI versus a teacher?
>
> **RQ2**: What types of feedback from GenAI trigger negative emotions in learners?

4.3.2 Research Design, Data Collection and Analysis

We designed a two-stage task for non-native English speakers, where participants completed an English writing and revision assignment. They first read English texts on artificial intelligence and then wrote a 200–400 word essay discussing AI and education. To measure learners' emotions while working with GenAI and an expert teacher, we conducted a lab study. Twelve participants took part in a 2 hours writing session together, followed by a 1 hour revision session. During the revision phase, the participants were randomly divided into two groups: one group used GenAI 4.0 for revising their essays, while the other received personalised feedback from an expert teacher. We then compared the emotions and emotional changes of the learners between the two groups.

We used a computer's front-facing camera to record students' facial expressions and upper body while they revised their essays with GenAI or a teacher. To identify emotions from these learning videos, we applied a facial expression-based emotion recognition system developed by Jia and He (2021). This system is grounded in Paul Ekman's basic emotions theory, which posits that six innate emotions (anger, fear, disgust, happiness, surprise, and sadness) are universally expressed across cultures (Ekman, 1989).

Based on the analysis of six innate emotions and body language, we recoded them into four categories: focus, confusion, boredom, and happiness, as shown in Table 4.1. Learners were categorised as "focused" when their body language showed signs of attentiveness and engagement, such as leaning forward or nodding in agreement, indicating concentration on the content. "Confusion" was identified through facial expressions linked to emotions like anger and fear, as well as body language such as frowning or scratching the head, which reflect difficulty understanding or uncertainty. Facial expressions like sadness and disgust were recoded as "boredom," characterised by gestures such as leaning back, looking away from the screen, sighing, or resting the head on the hand, all suggesting a lack of interest."Happiness" was used for learners showing clear signs of happiness, with body language like gentle nodding.

To address the first question, we conducted process mining to analyse the emotional transitions learners experienced while learning with GenAI compared to a teacher. By mapping these transitions, we could observe how frequently learners shifted from one emotion to another during learning sessions with GenAI compared to sessions with a teacher. The process map illustrated these transitions with arrows, where the direction showed the flow of emotions and the numbers represented how often each transition occurred.

To address the second question, we analysed the learner emotions, as well as the dialogue texts during essay revisions between learners and teachers or GenAI. We then coded the data from two perspectives:

TABLE 4.1 Coding Framework for Learner Emotions Based on Facial Expressions and Body Language

Emotion	Facial Expression	Body Language Examples
Focus	N/A	Leaning forward, nodding in agreement
Confusion	Expressions associated with anger and fear	Frowning, scratching the head, reflecting difficulty understanding or uncertainty
Boredom	Expressions associated with sadness and disgust	Leaning back, looking away from the screen, sighing, or resting the head on the hand
Happiness	Expressions associated with happiness	Gentle nodding, arms open or at the sides, relaxed and open body language

learner emotions and teacher/GenAI feedback. Using Epistemic Network Analysis (ENA), we explored the relationship between feedback from teachers or GenAI and learner emotions.

The coding framework categorised data into various groups based on learners' emotions and the feedback from teachers or GenAI, as shown in Table 4.2. Feedback was categorised by analysing the dialogue texts from learners' online interactions with teachers and GenAI.Learners' emotions were coded from two perspectives. The first perspective, Code 1, distinguished between negative and positive emotions. Label 1 (Negative Emotion) referred to emotions such as boredom and confusion. In this study, these emotions were recoded based on the framework in Table 4.1, where, for example, "confusion" was defined by facial expressions associated with anger and fear, along with body language such as frowning and scratching the head, which reflected difficulty understanding or uncertainty. Conversely, Label 0 (Positive Emotion) included emotions like happiness and focus. The second perspective, Code 2, considered whether the emotion was intense or not. Label 1 (Intense Emotion) was characterised by emotions such as happiness and confusion, which were more expressive and outwardly visible. Meanwhile, Label 0 (Not Intense Emotion) included more subdued emotions like boredom and focus.

TABLE 4.2 Coding Framework for Learner Emotions and Teacher/GenAI Feedback

Code	Dimension	Label	Description
Code 1	Learner emotion type	1 (Negative emotion)	Learner emotions include boredom and confusion
		0 (Positive emotion)	Learner emotions include happiness and focus
Code 2	Learner emotion intensity	1 (Intense emotion)	Learner emotions include happiness and confusion
		0 (Not intense emotion)	Learner emotions include boredom and focus
Code 3	Teacher/GenAI feedback style	1 (Guided feedback)	Teacher or GenAI offers hints, prompts or suggestions
		0 (Answer)	Teacher or GenAI provides an answer
Code 4	Teacher/GenAI feedback completeness	1 (concise feedback)	Teacher or GenAI provides a clear, one-time feedback that addresses the question fully
		0 (Iterative feedback)	Teacher or GenAI encourages learners for further interaction, asking follow-up questions or providing clarifications as needed

In terms of feedback, Code 3 (Teacher/GenAI Feedback Style) was classified as either direct or guided. Label 1 (Guided Feedback), on the other hand, involved hints, prompts, or suggestions instead of a direct answer. It encouraged the learner to think critically and arrive at the solution independently, fostering problem-solving skills. For example, a learner asks, "Is my sentence correct?" The teacher replies, "Think about your verb tense here. What tense are you using? You might want to try a different one," guiding the student to reconsider and correct it. Label 0 (Answer) represented straightforward responses that directly provided the correct answer or correction, without further explanation or prompts. This feedback was clear and precise. Code 4 (Teacher/GenAI Feedback Completeness) was analysed as either concise or iterative. Label 1 (Concise Feedback) referred to clear, one-time feedback that directly addressed the learner's question or issue without the need for further interaction. For example, a learner asks, "Is my thesis statement clear?" The teacher replies, "Yes, it's clear but could be stronger by specifying your main argument," providing a brief and direct suggestion. This type of feedback delivered all necessary information efficiently, ensuring the immediate comprehension. Label 0 (Iterative Feedback) involved multiple exchanges, where the teacher or GenAI continued to guide the learner through a process. For example, the teacher says, "Your introduction needs more context. Can you explain why this topic is important?" After the learner adds information, teacher responds, "Good, now try linking it to your main argument," continuing to guide the revision in steps. This feedback style encouraged ongoing interaction, with follow-up questions and clarifications to support gradual improvement. This coding framework enabled a structured analysis of how learner emotions interacted with the different types and styles of feedback provided by teachers or GenAI.

Following the coding, we applied ENA to investigate how different types of feedback from the teacher and GenAI correlate with student emotions. ENA is a method that allows us to map and visualise the connections between coded elements, helping to identify patterns and relationships within the data. By creating network graphs, we were able to observe how specific feedback styles, such as direct or guided, and concise or iterative, influence different emotional states, including positive, negative, intense, or mild emotions.

4.3.3 Findings

4.3.3.1 Learners Feel more Bored but more Focused While Learning with GenAI than with a Teacher

Learners feel more bored but more focused with GenAI than with a teacher (RQ1). As shown in Figure 4.1, learners demonstrate varying patterns of emotions between teacher-led and GenAI-assisted learning environments. In the HE group, learners were focused a total of 38 times, with 4 transitions from "boredom" to "focus." Additionally, learners in the HE group experienced "boredom" 8 times. In contrast, learners in the AI group were recorded as "focused" 132 times, significantly more than in the HE group, with 19 transitions from "boredom" to "focus." Learners in the AI group also showed "boredom" 31 times, indicating that even when students felt bored, they were more likely to regain their focus in the GenAI-assisted environment than with a teacher.

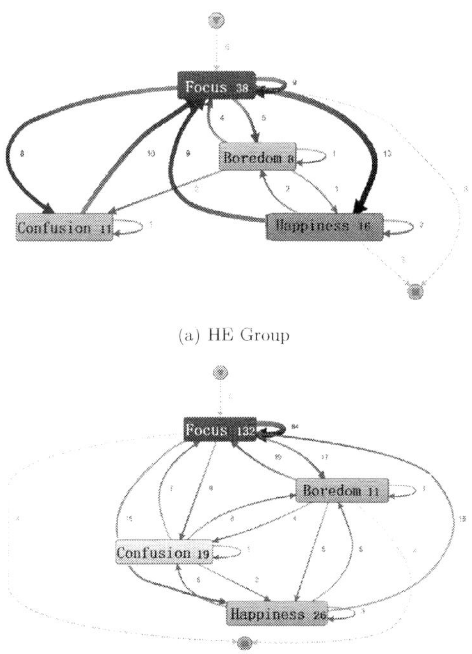

(a) HE Group

(b) AI Group

Figure 4.1 Process maps of HE (a) and AI group (b).

These findings suggest that while learners may experience moments of boredom more frequently with GenAI, they have a greater ability to refocus, possibly due to the consistent and immediate nature of GenAI feedback. This allows learners to navigate back to relevant content at their own pace, making it easier to re-engage with the writing after periods of disengagement. On the other hand, teacher-led sessions may provide a more dynamic and varied learning experience, which can reduce boredom but may also lead to occasional distractions where students find it harder to sustain focus.

The ability of GenAI to deliver immediate, on-demand feedback and explanations may help students quickly resolve confusion and return to a focused state without waiting for external assistance. This emotional dynamic highlights the potential of GenAI as an effective learning aid, particularly in scenarios that require sustained concentration.

4.3.3.2 Guided Feedback from GenAI Leads to Learners' Negative Emotions

Guided feedback from GenAI is associated with learners' negative emotions (RQ2). As shown in Figure 4.2, which presents the ENA subtraction between the AI group (solid line) and the HE group (dashed

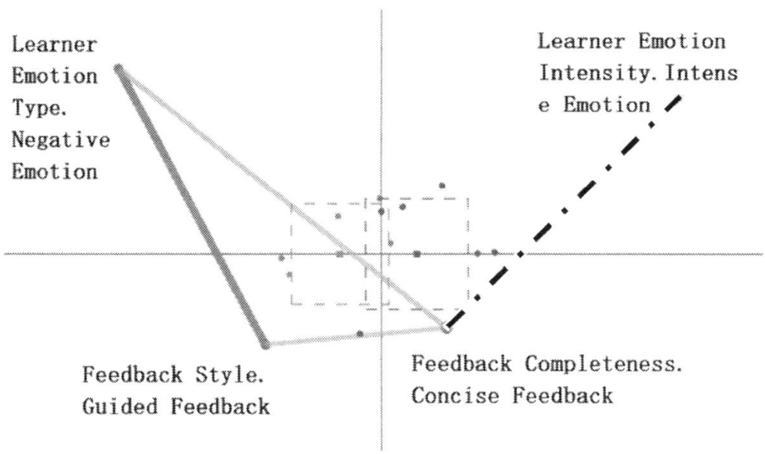

Figure 4.2 ENA subtraction between AI group(solid line) and HE group(dashed line).

line), based on the coding table in Table 4.2. "Negative Emotion" in the Learner Emotion Type (Code 1) refers to feelings such as boredom and confusion. "Intense Emotion" in the Learner Emotion Intensity (Code 2) is characterised by outwardly visible reactions like happiness and confusion."Guided Feedback" in the Teacher/GenAI Feedback Style (Code 3) refers to hints, prompts, or suggestions provided by the teacher or GenAI. "Concise Feedback" in Teacher/GenAI Feedback Completeness (Code 4) refers to clear, one-time feedback that fully addresses the question. The ENA network shows that in AI group (solid line), there is a strong connection between guided feedback and negative emotions. This pattern suggests that when GenAI provides guided feedback, learners are more likely to express confusion or boredom. This may be because guided feedback often requires students to think and reason actively, rather than providing direct answers, which they may expect from GenAI. This can lead to feelings of confusion or frustration, especially when students are unable to solve the problem independently. In contrast, HE group (dashed line) demonstrates a stronger link between concise feedback and intense emotions. This indicates that clear and precise feedback from teachers tends to elicit stronger emotions, such as happiness or confusion, depending on the clarity and comprehensibility of the feedback.

4.3.4 Discussion of the Case Study

Our case study has two main findings: learners feel more bored but more focused while learning with GenAI than with a teacher, and guided feedback from GenAI leads to learners' negative emotions. These findings suggest that while GenAI can help learners stay focused, but its feedback style may lead to boredom during the learning process. This effect is particularly evident when GenAI consistently provides guided feedback, as learners tend to experience negative emotions, including boredom. This also aligns with the earlier conclusion that some learners reported a lack of emotional connection when interacting with GenAI (Du and Alm, 2024), with feelings of boredom potentially contributing to this reduced sense of engagement. Additionally, our case study's findings differ from most of previous studies, which have suggested that GenAI, through personalised feedback, can enhance learner motivation and have a positive impact on their emotions (Almulla,

2024; Beltozar-Clemente and Díaz-Vega, 2024). These previous studies have primarily relied on questionnaires or semi-structured interviews to draw conclusions. While these methods capture learners' subjective experiences, they are limited by memory biases and the tendency to report what participants think researchers expect. In contrast, our case study adopts a data-driven approach, collecting multimodal data directly from learners' real interactions with GenAI during the learning process. This data includes videos featuring facial expressions and body movements, as well as dialogue texts between GenAI and the learners. Through the collection and analysis of such multimodal data, we can gain a more comprehensive and objective understanding of learners' emotions. Specifically, facial expressions and body movements captured in video data can help us identify learners' immediate, subconscious emotions during the learning process—responses that are often difficult to fully convey through questionnaires and interviews. Multimodal data allows for different types of data to complement each other, providing a multi-dimensional verification of the research findings' reliability (Saint et al., 2022). Through this data-driven method, our findings are more closely aligned with students' actual emotions in real learning scenarios.

The findings from our case study can be explained using Cognitive Load Theory (CLT). Research has shown that learners using GenAI experience significantly lower cognitive load compared to those using other tools, such as Google (Stadler et al., 2024). When cognitive load is too low, learners may not face enough challenges, which can lead to boredom. Additionally, guided feedback does not adapt to the learner's evolving needs and may fail to provide sufficient cognitive stimulation, resulting in boredom and negative emotions. CLT directly relates to focus, suggesting that when our cognitive load is too high, our ability to concentrate on a specific task decreases, as working memory becomes overloaded and struggles to effectively process new information (Atkinson, 1968). Conversely, GenAI presents a lower cognitive load, which can help learners maintain focus more effectively.

We explained the emotions exhibited by learners when learning with GenAI from a cognitive perspective. Although using GenAI may lead to negative emotions such as boredom, it can effectively reduce cognitive load, thereby enhancing learners' focus. However, whether this effect is ultimately beneficial or detrimental remains uncertain, and further empirical research is needed to validate this. In future learning models, especially in scenarios where teachers and AI collaborate, it will be important to explore how to balance learners' emotional and cognitive engagement. Emotional engagement can help stimulate learning motivation and interest, while cognitive engagement can improve learning outcomes and efficiency. Future research can focus on how to design AI-assisted teaching methods that allow learners to alternate between emotional and cognitive engagement at appropriate times, to achieve optimal learning outcomes. A key reflection on the case study is that the small sample size and the specific focus on student districts within certain fields may limit the generalisability of the findings to broader contexts.

4.4 IMPLICATION AND FUTURE WORK

In this chapter, we employed methods such as process mining and Epistemic Network Analysis (ENA) to analyse video and text data, conducting overall, temporal, and instructional strategy analyses. A notable contribution of this study lies in its examination of emotional sequences, not only assessing the static distribution of emotions but also analysing their temporal evolution. Another key contribution is the integration of emotional dynamics with instructional strategies, highlighting how specific teacher-student interactions can influence students' emotional trajectories. By addressing the research questions posed in the introduction, our study yields several significant insights.

Firstly, our findings reveal that students in the HE group predominantly exhibit emotion sequences such as "focused-happy-focused" and "focused-confused-focused," whereas students in the AI group demonstrate sustained "focused" states or "focused-bored-focused" sequences. Students in the AI group exhibited more boredom compared to those in the teacher group, likely due to the longer response times from GPT, which created a delay during their interactions.

Secondly, clustering based on student emotions identified three distinct learner types: highly focused, focused-confused, and focused-happy. Notably, the high-focus type is more common in the AI group, while the focused-happy type is predominantly observed in the teacher group. Human teachers, equipped with emotional intelligence, can perceive, interpret, and respond to students' emotional states effectively. This ability allows teachers to create a sense of warmth and security, fostering positive emotional experiences during learning (Saleh and Hibatullah, 2023). In contrast, while AI systems can recognise emotional cues, they lack the nuanced understanding and empathetic responses that human teachers provide, often resulting in a less emotionally supportive learning environment. For example, while AI chatbots can create relaxed environments for some students, they often fail to address the complex emotional needs that arise in educational settings (Wu and Yu, 2024). The emotional validation provided by human teachers is integral to students' learning experiences, fostering a sense of belonging and trust that AI systems are currently unable to replicate (Mafulah and Basthomi, 2023; Dong et al., 2021).

Thirdly, in the AI group, guided questioning was strongly correlated with negative student emotions, such as confusion and boredom. In contrast, in the teacher-led group, clear and comprehensive responses were strongly associated with positive emotional reactions, such as happiness and confusion. When students perceive that their teachers are invested in their understanding, they are more likely to experience positive emotions such as happiness. Although confusion is often considered a negative emotional state, it can also serve as a catalyst for deeper learning, as it may indicate that a student is grappling with complex concepts and is motivated to seek further clarification. On the other hand, while AI chatbots can enhance learning through personalis3ed and interactive experiences, they may lead to confusion when the guidance provided is perceived as inadequate or overly complex (Wu and Yu, 2024). Students may feel overwhelmed by AI responses, leading to frustration and disengagement (Almaiah et al., 2022). Though some studies suggest that AI can reduce negative emotions through immediate feedback and analytical assessments, emotional responses can vary widely depending on individual experiences and contextual factors (Nazari et al., 2021).

Based on these findings, we propose two scaffolding strategies for supporting learners emotion while learning with GenAI:

First, emotional Monitoring and Adjustment: Scaffolding should adapt in real-time to counteract negative emotions such as boredom and confusion. This could involve adjusting instructional methods to re-engage students and guide them toward a state of flow. Adaptive Virtual Learning Environments (AVLEs) are particularly effective in providing personalised learning experiences tailored to individual student characteristics. AVLEs can adjust learning paths and content delivery based on real-time assessments of student engagement and performance (Alshammari, 2020). This adaptability not only helps maintain student interest but also fosters deeper semantic processing of information, as noted by (Haynes et al., 2014). By setting GPT's prompts to dynamically adjust instructional methods, GenAI systems can re-engage students and guide them back to a productive learning state.

Second, differentiated Learning Paths: Students exhibiting high focus levels tend to achieve the highest performance, while those with greater emotional fluctuations show the most significant improvement. Therefore, it is crucial to select appropriate learning methods based on individual student characteristics. Students in the AI group, who demonstrate sustained focus, might benefit from deeper and more engaging content. Conversely, students in the teacher-led group, who exhibit both focus and emotional fluctuation, would benefit from more interactive and supportive guidance. Teaching strategies such as formative assessment, collaborative learning, and emotional coaching can help students navigate their emotional landscape while maintaining focus on academic tasks.

Regarding future research directions, several areas warrant further exploration. First, while current research suggests limitations in GenAI's ability to establish emotional resonance, improving models and algorithms to better recognise and respond to students' emotional needs represents an important avenue for future study. Research could explore how integrating additional human emotion recognition features—such as vocal tone, facial expressions, and body language—might enhance GenAI's emotional interaction capabilities.

Second, further investigation into hybrid teaching models that combine GenAI and human teachers in various educational contexts is needed. For example, in high-pressure or emotionally demanding learning environments, understanding how to optimally allocate roles between GenAI and human teachers could improve overall teaching effectiveness. Research into these hybrid models can help identify which educational stages benefit most from GenAI, and how to maximise its capabilities when human teachers take the lead.

Additionally, the emotional and cognitive responses of different learner groups to GenAI use merit further study. Future research could segment student populations to examine how students from diverse cultural backgrounds, and socioeconomic statuses respond to GenAI, providing a basis for more personalised educational solutions.

Finally, with the advancement of technology, future studies could explore the creation of more immersive teaching environments, such as those utilising Virtual Reality (VR) and Augmented Reality (AR), in combination with GenAI, to foster more interactive and emotionally resonant learning experiences. This multidimensional research will deepen our understanding of GenAI applications in education and help develop more intelligent, emotionally aware educational tools.

4.5 CHAPTER SUMMARY

This chapter reveals the multi-level mechanism of the impact of GenAI on students' learning motivation and emotion through a systematic review. GenAI, such as ChatGPT, has a significant impact on students' learning motivation and mood. Studies have shown that ChatGPT can significantly improve students' motivation by providing personalised feedback, solving problems quickly, improving learning autonomy, meeting students' performance expectations, and stimulating curiosity. Specifically, students showed higher motivation, engagement, and self-efficacy when using ChatGPT, especially in language learning, programming learning, and physics learning. In addition, timely, personalised feedback not only boosts student motivation but also alleviates anxiety and enhances the learning experience.

GenAI also play an important role in emotion regulation, helping students relieve anxiety and stress and increase their well-being and self-confidence by providing personalised, timely feedback. The study also found that students' emotional responses to GenAI were influenced by personal factors (e.g., technology acceptance, loneliness) and external factors (e.g., response quality, response speed). In addition, based on the Self-Determination Theory (SDT), ChatGPT supports students' autonomy, sense of competence, and connectedness, thereby enhancing their intrinsic motivation.

Although GenAI has shown great potential to improve students' motivation and emotional regulation, it also faces several challenges. First, over-reliance on AI tools may impair students' ability to learn on their own, especially when students rely too much on quick feedback, which may reduce long-term learning motivation. Future research needs to help students overcome lazy thinking and reduce their reliance on GenAI. Second, GenAI has technical limitations in providing personalised feedback and adapting to students' needs, and future research should develop more personalised models to better support students' writing. Third, although GenAI has a positive impact on students' self-efficacy, students' intrinsic motivation may weaken over time, so it is necessary to explore how to maintain long-term motivation. Some studies have shown that AI can promote students' long-term learning motivation by combining task value theory and self-regulated learning. Finally, students may face a lack of interpersonal interaction and social belonging when using GenAI, and proper instructional design can compensate for this shortcoming, and improve students' motivation and engagement by creating interactive and contextual learning environments.

Besides, this chapter compares the emotional changes experienced by students when using GenAI versus human teachers for essay revisions through an empirical study. The study examines the emotional and attitudinal impacts of interacting with either a human teacher or a GenAI during a writing exercise and involves pre-tests, online article reading, drafting, revision with either a human or AI and post-tests to analyse emotional attitudes and composition outcomes. Data was analysed from two perspectives: emotional data (captured through video analysis of facial expressions) and student attitude data (analysing pre- and post-test results). The emotional data was processed using deep neural networks and the K-means clustering algorithm to identify and analyse emotions during the experiment.

Through data analysis, we found that students interacting with human teachers experienced more positive emotions, particularly focus and happiness, compared to those interacting with GenAI, who experienced more boredom. The temporal sequence of emotions revealed that students in the teacher group frequently transitioned between focused and happy or confused states, while those in the AI group showed sustained focus or alternating between focus and boredom. The study examined how different instructional strategies influenced student emotions. It found that guiding responses from AI were often linked to negative emotions like confusion and boredom, while direct and complete answers from human teachers led to more intense emotional reactions, both positive and negative. The study suggests that clear, direct feedback is more effective in promoting emotional engagement among students, especially when provided by human teachers. Therefore, this chapter emphasises the need to better simulate and enhance emotional resonance in the application of GenAI in education to improve students' learning experiences and outcomes.

Although GenAI (GenAI) holds significant potential in the field of education, its success should not solely rely on technological innovation but must be intertwined with humanistic care. Effective education is not merely about the transmission of knowledge but also about the conveyance and resonance of emotions. This highlights the importance of remembering that the core of education is human-centered, where emotions and empathy are indispensable components. Consequently, future developments should aim to integrate emotional intelligence with technological advancements, ensuring that the emotional wisdom of human teachers is deeply embedded.

This chapter underscores the critical importance of emotional resonance in education, suggesting that future instructional design must place greater emphasis on the cultivation and application of emotional intelligence. The role of teachers has not been diminished in the digital and intelligent age; on the contrary, it has become even more crucial. Teachers should be regarded as indispensable emotional navigators in education, whose responsibilities extend beyond knowledge transmission to include the stimulation of students' motivation and creativity through rich emotional interactions. Therefore, teacher training should encompass strategies for collaborating with artificial intelligence, leveraging its strengths while maintaining and enhancing the unique emotional influence that human teachers bring to the educational process.

The collaborative teaching models that integrate AI with human educators aim to leverage the strengths of both, yet the emotional aspects of teaching remain predominantly human. While AI tutors can offer certain advantages, they cannot replace the emotional and social support provided by human educators (Pérez et al., 2020). The emotional regulation strategies employed by teachers not only mitigate their own stress but also positively influence students' emotional experiences in the classroom (Katz et al., 2018). This interplay underscores the irreplaceable role of human teachers in nurturing a supportive learning environment that promotes positive emotions and engagement.

In summary, it is critical to embrace the technological revolution without losing sight of the essence of education—namely, the development of well-rounded individuals who are empathetic, creative, and socially responsible. By striking a balance between technological innovation and humanistic care, we can pave the way for a future that is more emotionally resonant and educationally equitable.

Bibliography

Almaiah, M. A., Alfaisal, R., Salloum, S. A., Hajjej, F., Thabit, S., El-Qirem, F. A., et al. (2022). Examining the impact of artificial intelligence and social and computer anxiety in e-learning settings: Students' perceptions at the university level. *Electronics*, *11*(22):3662.

Almulla, M. A. (2024). Investigating influencing factors of learning satisfaction in AI ChatGPT for research: University students perspective. *Heliyon*, *11*(1):e41331.

Alshammari, M. T. (2020). Design and evaluation of an adaptive framework for virtual learning environments. *International Journal of Advanced and Applied Sciences*, *7*(5):39–51.

Artino Jr, A. R., Holmboe, E. S., and Durning, S. J. (2012). Can achievement emotions be used to better understand motivation, learning, and performance in medical education? *Medical Teacher*, *34*(3):240–244.

Atkinson, J. (1964). *An Introduction to Motivation.* Van Nostrand, Princeton, NJ.

Atkinson, R. C. (1968). A proposed system and its control processes. *The Psychology of Learning and Motivation*, *2*:89–195.

Bai, S., Gonda, D. E., and Hew, K. F. (2024). Write-curate-verify: A case study of leveraging generative AI for scenario writing in scenario-based learning. *IEEE Transactions on Learning Technologies 17*:1301–1312.

Baker, H. P., Dwyer, E., Kalidoss, S., Hynes, K., Wolf, J., and Strelzow, J. A. (2024). ChatGPT's ability to assist with clinical documentation: A randomized controlled trial. *JAAOS-Journal of the American Academy of Orthopaedic Surgeons*, *32*(3):123–129.

Baker, R. S. and Yacef, K.(2009). The state of educational data mining in 2009: A review and future visions. *Journal of Educational Data Mining*, *1*(1):3–17.

Bandura, A. (1990). Perceived self-efficacy in the exercise of control over aids infection. *Evaluation and Program Planning*, *13*(1):9–17.

Beltozar-Clemente, S. and Díaz-Vega, E. (2024). Physics XP: Integration of ChatGPT and gamification to improve academic performance and motivation in physics 1 course. *International Journal of Engineering Pedagogy*, *14*(6). https://doi.org/10.3991/ijep.v14i6.47127.

Bergdahl, N., Nouri, J., and Fors, U. (2020). Disengagement, engagement and digital skills in technology-enhanced learning. *Education and Information Technologies*, *25*(2):957–983.

Boylan, F., Barblett, L., and Knaus, M. (2018). Early childhood teachers' perspectives of growth mindset: Developing agency in children. *Australasian Journal of Early Childhood*, *43*:16–24. http://doi.org/10.23965/ajec.43.3.02.

Bulfin, S., Johnson, N. F., and Bigum, C. (2015). *Critical Perspectives on Technology and Education*. Springer, New York.

Carr, S. (2000). As distance education comes of age, the challenge is keeping the students. *Chronicle of Higher Education*, *46*(23):39–41.

Castelo, N. and Ward, A. F. (2021). Conservatism predicts aversion to consequential artificial intelligence. *PLoS One*, 16(12):e0261467.

Chen, Y.-C. and Hou, H.-T. (2024). A mobile contextualized educational game framework with ChatGPT interactive scaffolding for employee ethics training. *Journal of Educational Computing Research*, *62*(7):1737–1762.

Cheng, A. Y., Guo, M., Ran, M., Ranasaria, A., Sharma, A., Xie, A., et al. (2024). Scientific and fantastical: Creating immersive, culturally relevant learning experiences with augmented reality and large language models. In *Proceedings of the CHI Conference on Human Factors in Computing Systems*, Hawai'i, USA, pp. 1–23.

Chiu, T. K. (2024). A classification tool to foster self-regulated learning with generative artificial intelligence by applying self-determination theory: A case of ChatGPT. *Educational Technology Research and Development*, *72*:2401–2416.

Clark, R. C. and Mayer, R. E. (2023). *E-Learning and the Science of Instruction: Proven Guidelines for Consumers and Designers of Multimedia Learning*. John Wiley & Sons, Hoboken, NJ.

Clow, D. (2013). An overview of learning analytics. *Teaching in Higher Education, 18*(6):683–695.

Dai, W., Lin, J., Jin, H., Li, T., Tsai, Y.-S., Gašević, D., and Chen, G. (2023). Can large language models provide feedback to students? A case study on ChatGPT. In *2023 IEEE International Conference on Advanced Learning Technologies (ICALT)*, Orem, Utah, USA, pp. 323–325.

Deci, E. L. (1971). Effects of externally mediated rewards on intrinsic motivation. *Journal of Personality and Social Psychology, 18*(1):105.

Deci, E. L., Koestner, R., and Ryan, R. M. (1999). A meta-analytic review of experiments examining the effects of extrinsic rewards on intrinsic motivation. *Psychological Bulletin, 125*(6):627.

Deci, E. L., and Ryan, R. M. (2013). *Intrinsic motivation and self-determination in human behavior*. Springer Science & Business Media, New York.

Dong, Y., Wang, H., Luan, F., Li, Z., and Cheng, L. (2021). How children feel matters: Teacher–student relationship as an indirect role between interpersonal trust and social adjustment. *Frontiers in Psychology, 11*:581235.

Du, J. and Alm, A. (2024). The impact of ChatGPT on english for academic purposes (EAP) students' language learning experience: A self-determination theory perspective. *Education Sciences, 14*(7):726.

Eccles, J. S. and Wigfield, A. (2002). Motivational beliefs, values, and goals. *Annual Review of Psychology, 53*(1):109–132.

Ekman, P. (1989). The argument and evidence about universals in facial expressions. *Handbook of Social Psychophysiology, 143*:164.

Filgona, J., Sakiyo, J., Gwany, D., and Okoronka, A. (2020). Motivation in learning. *Asian Journal of Education and Social Studies, 10*(4): 16–37.

Gabriella, A., Gui, A., and Chanda, R. C. (2024). The use of Chatbot and its impact on academic achievement. In *2024 IEEE Symposium on Industrial Electronics & Applications (ISIEA)*, pp. 1–6. IEEE, Kristiansand, Norway.

Gray, G., Mcguinness, C., and Owende, P. (2016). In Swe Khine, M. and Areepattamannil, S., editors, *Non-Cognitive Skills and Factors in Educational Attainment*, pp. 199–237. Brill, The Netherlands.

Gross, J. J. (1998). The emerging field of emotion regulation: An integrative review. *Review of General Psychology*, *2*(3):271–299.

Guo, K. and Li, D. (2024). Understanding EFL students' use of self-made AI chatbots as personalized writing assistance tools: A mixed methods study. *System*, *124*:103362.

Hamid, H., Zulkifli, K., Naimat, F., Yaacob, N. L. C., and Ng, K. W. (2023). Exploratory study on student perception on the use of chat AI in process-driven problem-based learning. *Currents in Pharmacy Teaching and Learning*, *15*(12):1017–1025.

Haynes, J. A., Underwood, J. S., Pokorny, R., and Spinrad, A. (2014). What is adaptivity? Does it improve performance? In *Foundations of Augmented Cognition: Advancing Human Performance and Decision-Making through Adaptive Systems: 8th International Conference, AC 2014*, Held as Part of HCI International 2014, Heraklion, Crete, Greece, June 22–27, 2014. Proceedings 8, pp. 224–235. Springer.

Heryanti, E., Azrai, E. P., and Melvinasari, M. W. (2022). The relationship between motivation to learn biology and discipline with students' cognitive learning outcomes during online learning. *Bioedukasi: Jurnal Pendidikan Biologi*, *15*(2):126–140.

Hmoud, M., Swaity, H., Hamad, N., Karram, O., and Daher, W. (2024). Higher education students' task motivation in the generative artificial intelligence context: The case of ChatGPT. *Information*, *15*(1):33.

Hrastinski, S. (2009). A theory of online learning as online participation. *Computers & Education*, *52*(1):78–82.

Jia, J. and He, Y. (2021). The design, implementation and pilot application of an intelligent online proctoring system for online exams. *Interactive Technology and Smart Education*, *19*(1):112–120.

Kasneci, E., Seßler, K., Küchemann, S., Bannert, M., Dementieva, D., Fischer, F., et al. (2023). ChatGPT for good? On opportunities and challenges of large language models for education. *Learning and Individual Differences*, *103*:102274.

Katz, D. A., Harris, A., Abenavoli, R., Greenberg, M. T., and Jennings, P. A. (2018). Educators' emotion regulation strategies and their physiological indicators of chronic stress over 1 year. *Stress and Health*, *34*(2):278–285.

Lee, K., Ning, F., and Goh, H. C. (2017). Interaction between cognitive and non-cognitive factors: The influences of academic goal orientation and working memory on mathematical performance. In Lee, J. and Stankov, L., editors, *Noncognitive Psychological Processes and Academic Achievement*, pp. 83–101. Routledge, London, UK.

Li, Y., Sadiq, G., Qambar, G., and Zheng, P. (2024). The impact of students' use of ChatGPT on their research skills: The mediating effects of autonomous motivation, engagement, and self-directed learning. *Education and Information Technologies*, *2024*:1–32.

Mafulah, S. and Basthomi, Y. (2023). "I am scared of my teacher": Students' emotional responses towards teacher's feedback. In *20th AsiaTEFL-68th TEFLIN-5th iNELTAL Conference (ASIATEFL 2022)*, pp. 648–657. Atlantis Press, Chiang Rai, Thailand.

McConnell, M. M. and Eva, K. W. (2012). The role of emotion in the learning and transfer of clinical skills and knowledge. *Academic Medicine*, *87*(10):1316–1322.

Montibeller, G. and Von Winterfeldt, D. (2015). Cognitive and motivational biases in decision and risk analysis. *Risk Analysis*, *35*(7):1230–1251.

Nazari, N., Shabbir, M. S., and Setiawan, R. (2021). Application of artificial intelligence powered digital writing assistant in higher education: Randomized controlled trial. *Heliyon*, *7*(5):e07014.

Ng, D. T. K., Tan, C. W., and Leung, J. K. L. (2024). Empowering student self-regulated learning and science education through ChatGPT: A pioneering pilot study. *British Journal of Educational Technology, 55*(4):1328–1353.

Pekrun, R. (2006). The control-value theory of achievement emotions: Assumptions, corollaries, and implications for educational research and practice. *Educational Psychology Review, 18*:315–341.

Pérez, J. Q., Daradoumis, T., and Puig, J. M. M. (2020). Rediscovering the use of chatbots in education: A systematic literature review. *Computer Applications in Engineering Education, 28*(6):1549–1565.

Plass, J. L., Homer, B. D., and Kinzer, C. K. (2015). Foundations of game-based learning. *Educational Psychologist, 50*(4):258–283.

Rezai, A., Soyoof, A., and Reynolds, B. L. (2024). Disclosing the correlation between using ChatGPT and well-being in EFL learners: Considering the mediating role of emotion regulation. *European Journal of Education, 59*(4):e12752.

Ryan, R. M. and Deci, E. L. (2000). Intrinsic and extrinsic motivations: Classic definitions and new directions. *Contemporary Educational Psychology, 25*(1):54–67.

Saint, J., Fan, Y., Gašević, D., and Pardo, A. (2022). Temporally-focused analytics of self-regulated learning: A systematic review of literature. *Computers and Education: Artificial Intelligence, 3*:100060.

Saleh, A. Y. and Hibatullah, M. D. A. (2023). The role of emotional intelligence to teacher perception of student-teacher relationship. *Jurnal Pendidikan Progresif, 13*(2):803–816.

Schunk, D. H., Pintrich, P. R., and Meece, J. L. (2014). *Motivation in Education: Theory, Research, and Applications*. Pearson, Boston, MA.

Selwyn, N. (2021). *Education and Technology: Key Issues and Debates*. Bloomsbury Publishing, London.

Song, C. and Song, Y. (2023). Enhancing academic writing skills and motivation: Assessing the efficacy of ChatGPT in AI-assisted language learning for EFL students. *Frontiers in Psychology, 14*:1260843.

Sorin, V., Brin, D., Barash, Y., Konen, E., Charney, A., Nadkarni, G., and Klang, E. (2023). Large language models (LLMS) and empathy: A systematic review. *medRxiv*, pp. 2023–08.

Stadler, M., Bannert, M., and Sailer, M. (2024). Cognitive ease at a cost: LLMS reduce mental effort but compromise depth in student scientific inquiry. *Computers in Human Behavior*, *160*:108386.

Sutton, J. and Austin, Z. (2015). Qualitative research: Data collection, analysis, and management. *The Canadian Journal of Hospital Pharmacy*, *68*(3):226.

Torres-Peña, R. C., Peña-González, D., Chacuto-López, E., Ariza, E. A., and Vergara, D. (2024). Updating calculus teaching with AI: A classroom experience. *Education Sciences*, *14*(9):1019.

Veas, A., Castejón, J.-L., Gilar, R., and Miñano, P. (2015). Academic achievement in early adolescence: The influence of cognitive and non-cognitive variables. *The Journal of General Psychology*, *142*(4):273–294.

Wang, X., Zhong, Y., Huang, C., and Huang, X. (2024). Chatprcs: A personalized support system for English reading comprehension based on ChatGPT. *IEEE Transactions on Learning Technologies*, *17*:1762–1776.

Woo, D. J., Wang, D., Guo, K., and Susanto, H. (2024). Teaching EFL students to write with ChatGPT: Students' motivation to learn, cognitive load, and satisfaction with the learning process. *Education and Information Technologies*, *2024*(18):24963–24990.

Wu, R. and Yu, Z. (2024). Do AI chatbots improve students learning outcomes? Evidence from a meta-analysis. *British Journal of Educational Technology*, *55*(1):10–33.

Wu, T.-T., Lee, H.-Y., Li, P.-H., Huang, C.-N., and Huang, Y.-M. (2024). Promoting self-regulation progress and knowledge construction in blended learning via ChatGPT-based learning AID. *Journal of Educational Computing Research*, *61*(8):3–31.

Xu, X., Wang, X., Zhang, Y., and Zheng, R. (2024). Applying ChatGPT to tackle the side effects of personal learning environments from learner and learning perspective: An interview of experts in higher education. *PLoS One*, *19*(1):e0295646.

Ye, J.-H., Zhang, M., Nong, W., Wang, L., and Yang, X. (2024). The relationship between inert thinking and ChatGPT dependence: An i-pace model perspective. *Education and Information Technologies*, *30*:1–25.

Younis, B. K. (2024). Examining students' self-regulation skills, confidence to learn online, and perception of satisfaction and usefulness of online classes in three suggested online learning environments that integrates ChatGPT. *Online Learning*, *28*(2):n2.

Zhou, M. and Winne, P. H. (2012). Modeling academic achievement by self-reported versus traced goal orientation. *Learning and Instruction*, *22*(6):413–419.

Zou, Z., Mubin, O., Alnajjar, F., and Ali, L. (2024). A pilot study of measuring emotional response and perception of LLM-generated questionnaire and human-generated questionnaires. *Scientific Reports*, *14*(1):2781.

CHAPTER 5

The Impacts of GenAI on Learning: What Works and What Falls Short?

Zhanghan Wang, Yuan Shen, and Yizhou Fan

With the rapid development of education technology, its impact on learning is becoming increasingly significant. The birth of generative artificial intelligence (GenAI) has tremendously impacted education. GenAI is able to provide personalised feedback in a timely manner and assist learners in their learning through human-like interactions. However, the powerful capabilities of GenAI have also raised concerns among learners, educators, and researchers. They are concerned that using GenAI may lead to learners' over-reliance on AI, resulting in cheating and hindering learners' critical thinking. Although previous studies have reported GenAI's potential to promote learning, there is a lack of systematic sorting and critical discussion on its impact on learning. Therefore, this chapter seeks to provide a comprehensive and critical exploration of GenAI's impacts on learning, enabling researchers, educational application developers, and educators to harness its potential to enhance learners' learning more effectively. In this chapter, we form the taxonomy of the impact on learning based on existing studies and review the impact of applying traditional technology

DOI: 10.4324/9781003632146-5

to learning. Then, this chapter reviews GenAI's impacts on learning based on the taxonomy we form, which includes three dimensions, namely the impact on learning performance, the impact on higher-order thinking and the impact on learning experience. In order to provide a more critical understanding of GenAI's impact, this chapter provides an empirical study example that explores the impact of ChatGPT on learners' writing performance, knowledge gain, knowledge transfer, and algorithm aversion. Finally, this chapter summarises practical methods and challenges in applying GenAI to learning, providing further research directions.

5.1 THE IMPACT OF TECHNOLOGY ON LEARNING: TAXONOMY AND DEVELOPMENT

5.1.1 The Taxonomy of the Impact on Learning

Paying attention to the impact on learning is crucial to help learners learn better (Hattie, 2012). Researchers examine the impact of learning from various dimensions. Common variables to explore the impact on learning include learners' learning outcomes, learning performance, and academic retention. For example, when exploring the impact of technology on learning, Tamim et al. (2011) selected studies focusing on learners' achievement or performance as an outcome measure for second-order meta-analysis. McCrindle and Christensen (1995) measured learners' final exam scores to explore the learning journals' impact on learners' learning performance. Other studies explore the impact on specific skills or abilities related to the long-term development of learners, rather than only focusing on learners' performance in certain areas. Tiwari et al. (2006) measured learners' critical thinking disposition through the California Critical Thinking Disposition Inventory, comparing the impact of different learning methods on learners' critical thinking. Al-Zahrani (2015) examined the impact of the flipped classroom on learners' creativity through a qualitative creativity test. Besides these skills, several studies pay attention to learners' learning experiences. Rienties and Toetenel (2016) investigated learners' satisfaction with different learning designs through a questionnaire, focusing on how teaching design impacts learners' behaviour, satisfaction and performance. Barzilai and Blau (2014) used a questionnaire to measure learners' perceived flow and perceived enjoyment, discussing the impact of scaffolding game-based learning on learners' learning achievements, perceived learning, and game experiences. The above studies show that the impact on learning is not a specific variable but a general concept that is discussed from multiple dimensions, such as the impact on learning performance, critical thinking, and learners' satisfaction.

Based on this, this chapter mainly discusses the impact of GenAI on learning from three dimensions, namely **the impact on learning performance**, **the impact on higher-order thinking**, and **the impact on learning experience**. **Learning performance** refers to learners' performance in exams or tests about knowledge, as well as specific tasks such as writing or programming tasks. **Higher-order thinking** refers to the skills such as problem-solving, inferring, estimating, predicting, creative thinking and critical system thinking (Miri et al., 2007). These thinking skills are prominent for learners to translate their knowledge and skills into responsible action (Zoller, 2000, 2001). **Learning experience** refers to learners' perception of the learning experience, such as satisfaction and learning efficiency.

5.1.2 The Development of the Technology's Impact on Learning

Among all factors that impact learning, technology is an important one. Technology has profoundly transformed education by making it more accessible, interactive, and personalised. With the advent of digital tools and online platforms, learners are now able to access a wealth of information and learning resources from anywhere in the world, breaking down geographical and socioeconomic barriers (Lin et al., 2017; Kumari and Naaz, 2020). Interactive technologies, such as virtual and augmented reality, provide immersive learning experiences that enhance understanding and retention (Soliman et al., 2021; Saidin et al., 2015). Personalised learning algorithms and adaptive learning systems tailor educational content to individual learner needs, optimising the learning process (Kem, 2022). Furthermore, technology enables real-time collaboration and communication among learners and educators, fostering a more connected and dynamic learning environment (Wang and Liao, 2017; McDaniels et al., 2016). Overall, technology not only enhances the efficiency and effectiveness of education but also prepares learners for a future in an increasingly digital world. However, although various kinds of traditional technology positively impact learning from different aspects, they still have limitations. For example, designing and developing high-quality multimedia resources costs educators lots of time and energy. Learners may be affected by low-quality multimedia resources. In addition, although computer-assisted learning (CAL) offers learners more learning opportunities, developing and maintaining the CAL packages is expensive. If the contents of the CAL package become outdated, the resources will be wasted (Sharma, 2017). Therefore, although applying traditional technologies to learning has many advantages, there are also several shortcomings.

The emergence of GenAI has addressed several shortcomings mentioned above. GenAI is able to provide personalised learning experiences by adapting educational content to individual student needs, fostering better engagement and understanding (Hong, 2023). It is also capable of streamlining administrative tasks, giving educators more time to focus on instruction and student interaction (Lo, 2023). Additionally, GenAI offers real-time feedback and support, enhancing the overall learning experience and helping to identify and address learning gaps promptly (Songsiengchai et al., 2023). As the technology continues to evolve, its integration into education systems leads to more efficient, effective, and equitable learning environments, preparing learners for a technologically advanced future. Therefore, GenAI is widely applied to facilitate learners' learning. The impact of GenAI on learning has also become an important research topic. However, despite the various advantages of GenAI, there is still controversy over its impact on learning. In terms of the impact on learning performance, GenAI is able to answer learners' questions and help learners prepare for exams (Lo, 2023). However, how GenAI is applied to improve learners' learning performance remains to be explored. As for the impact on higher-order thinking, GenAI enables learners to explore their ideas through questioning and reflecting on the various answers provided by GenAI, which is able to promote learners' critical thinking (Risvold et al., 2024). However, learners may also directly use the content generated by GenAI to complete tasks and rely heavily on GenAI, which may hinder the development of their critical thinking. In addition, there is also no unified opinion on the impact of GenAI on learning experience. Although GenAI is able to generate human-like responses, it also provides incorrect, unrealistic, and biased responses that do not fully meet the needs of learners and may damage learners' learning experience (Liu et al., 2023a).

Although several studies have explored the impact of GenAI on learning, there is still controversy surrounding its impact on learning, particularly in the three dimensions that this chapter focuses on, namely the impact on learning performance, the impact on higher-order thinking, and the impact on learning experience. What kind of impact GenAI brings to the three dimensions, how it has such impact, and the reasons behind it have not been deeply analysed. Based on this, this chapter systematically reviews the literature from three dimensions, analysing the findings of existing studies. Then, we introduce the empirical study we conducted, providing more empirical evidence and practice insight for future research.

5.2 REVIEW OF GENAI'S IMPACT ON LEARNING

We conducted a comprehensive literature search in the Google Scholar database to identify empirical studies focusing on the impact of applying GenAI in learning. These studies explore the impact of GenAI from different dimensions, categorised into three main dimensions we have mentioned above: the impact on learning performance, the impact on higher-order thinking, and the impact on learning experience. The research directions and the types of impact are summarised in Table 5.1.

5.2.1 The Impact of GenAI on Learning Performance Is Not Always Positive

Lots of researchers integrate GenAI into learners' learning process and explore the impact of GenAI on learning performance. Patero (2023) integrated ChatGPT into the math curriculum as an auxiliary learning tool. He measured learners' performance metrics through math assessments and quizzes conducted before and after the ChatGPT invention (Patero, 2023). Results showed that learners' average score on math assessments improved by 12%, and the average score on math quizzes improved by 10%, suggesting the significant positive impact of integrating ChatGPT into math education on learning performance (Patero, 2023). Alneyadi and Wardat (2023) applied ChatGPT to learn electronic magnetism and compared the impact on learning through ChatGPT and traditional learning methods. The experimental group could use

TABLE 5.1 A Summary of Research Directions on the Impact of GenAI on Learning

Research Directions	Work	Not work
Impact on learning performance	Patero (2023), Alneyadi and Wardat (2023), Hakiki et al. (2023), Minh (2024), Song and Song (2023), Li et al. (2024), and Sun et al. (2024)	Kosar et al. (2024), Wecks et al. (2024), and Mahaini (2024)
Impact on higher-order thinking	Shanto et al. (2024), Minh (2024), Guo and Lee (2023), Li (2023), Liu et al. (2023b), Urban et al. (2024), and Lee et al. (2024)	Krupp et al. (2024)
Impact on learning experience	Altarawneh (2023), Sandu et al. (2024), Yusfi and Asmara (2023), Nguyen (2023), Castillo et al. (2023), and Tran (2023)	Sandu et al. (2024), Nguyen (2023), Tran (2023), and Thway et al. (2024)

ChatGPT whenever they required assistance with the course content. After four weeks of invention, the electronic magnetism unit test scores in the experimental group were significantly higher than those in the control group (Alneyadi and Wardat, 2023). Another research also found that learners who used ChatGPT during technology learning had higher scores in the exam than those who learned technology in conventional methods (Hakiki et al., 2023). In these studies, whenever learners need help, they are able to use GenAI for personalised assistance, interactive problem-solving, and conceptual explanations. The application of GenAI in learning helps learners better understand knowledge, improving their scores in several specific subjects such as math, electronic magnetism, and technology.

In addition, GenAI also has a positive impact on the performance of tasks related to specific skills, such as writing tasks and programming tasks. Several studies integrated ChatGPT into teaching English writing, finding that ChatGPT's assistance enabled learners to improve the organisation, coherence, grammar, vocabulary, and argumentation depth of their writings (Minh, 2024; Song and Song, 2023). Li et al. (2024) provided more detailed methods for using GenAI in English writing teaching and introduced a learning approach termed LLM-powered Chatbot-assisted argumentative writing (LCAW). This approach divided the writing process into four stages. In each stage, the LLM-powered chatbot provided support for learners based on the constructivist learning theory. Li et al. (2024) compared the impact of LCAW and the impact of the conventional approach on learners' writing performance. The results revealed significant differences in overall writing scores between the experimental and control groups. The experimental group learners performed better in writing content and language, but there was no significant difference in structure compared to the control group. These studies reveal the positive impact of GenAI on learners' writing skills. Based on LLM, GenAI is able to generate massive amounts of corpus and provide learners with personalised writing guidance quickly, which is difficult for teachers. This may be the reason why learners who use GenAI perform better than those who are taught by tutors in writing tasks. Besides writing skills, GenAI is also proved to be good at solving easy and medium programming problems written in C++ and Java (Bucaioni et al., 2024). GenAI is able to explain complex programming concepts by generating different examples, helping learners understand concepts better (Rahman and Watanobe, 2023). Sun et al. (2024) compared the impact of ChatGPT-facilitated programming (CFP) practice and the impact of self-directed programming (SDP) mode on learners' programming performance. Learners in the experimental group were able to ask ChatGPT questions and get feedback from ChatGPT after they completed programming tasks. The results showed that learners in the CFP mode had a higher average score than learners in the SDP mode, revealing the positive impact of integrating GenAI into programming learning.

However, the impact of GenAI on learning performance is not always positive. Most studies mentioned above allowed learners to interact with ChatGPT without restriction. Unlike these studies, Kosar et al. (2024) restricted learners' use of ChatGPT through experiment design. They adjusted the questions and assignments so that ChatGPT could not directly provide answers, thus avoiding learners unthinkingly relying on

ChatGPT. They also designed paper-based midterms to avoid the impact of ChatGPT on testing learners' learning performance. Consequently, the results showed no significant difference in grades between learners who used ChatGPT for task practice and those who did not use ChatGPT, suggesting that the learners' performance was not influenced by ChatGPT usage. Another study even found that GenAI had a negative impact on learning performance. Wecks et al. (2024) used GenAI detection systems to identify essays written using GenAI tools and compared the scores of essays written using GenAI tools with those written without GenAI tools. The results showed that the average essay score of learners who used GenAI tools to complete writing was lower than that of learners who did not, revealing the negative impact GenAI brought to their writing performance. Learners' passive participation is considered a vital reason underlying the negative impact. Wecks et al. (2024) attributed the negative impact on writing performance to a learning-hindering mechanism while using GenAI. This mechanism means if learners directly use GenAI to write an essay rather than writing essays by themselves based on their gains from using GenAI, they will lose opportunities to learn deeply and to experience the inherent rewards of figuring things out (Wecks et al., 2024). Learners with high potential will lose more if they rely on GenAI to complete tasks (Wecks et al., 2024). The results of Mahaini's research also demonstrate the importance of active participation. Mahaini (2024) investigated the impact of GenAI on the coding ability of computer science learners and found the correlation between engagement and grade improvements. Learners who felt more engaged in learning with GenAI tools believed GenAI improved their grades more firmly. Being actively involved in the learning process is possible to be the key to achieving deeper understanding and building knowledge when learners learn with GenAI.

5.2.2 GenAI Has the Potential to Improve Learners' Higher-Order Thinking

Higher-order thinking is considered a non-algorithmic, complex mode of thinking that often generates multiple solutions (Resnick, 1987). Compared to lower-order thinking, higher-order thinking extends essential memory and understanding (Hwang et al., 2018), involving uncertainty, application of multiple criteria, reflection, and self-regulation (Resnick,

1987). Researchers offer various definitions of higher-order thinking. Brookhart (2010) categorises the definitions of higher-order thinking into three distinct groups: (1) definitions that relate higher-order thinking to the concept of transfer, (2) those that equate it with critical thinking, and (3) those that associate it with problem-solving. Hwang et al. (2018) suggest that higher-order thinking encompasses advanced cognitive processes like critical thinking, problem-solving, and creativity. Miri et al. (2007) consider problem-solving, inferring, estimating, predicting, creative thinking, and critical thinking all as higher-order thinking. It is evident that higher-order thinking is not a specific term but a collective term for a specific type of thinking or cognitive skills. Existing studies mainly focused on the impact of GenAI on three kinds of higher-order thinking: critical thinking, creative thinking, and problem-solving.

Critical thinking refers to reasonable, reflective thinking that focuses on deciding what to believe or do (Norris and Ennis, 1989). Several empirical studies demonstrated the positive role of GenAI in enhancing critical thinking. Shanto et al. (2024) proposed a conceptual framework "AI-CRITIQUE" (AI-based Critical Reflection and Insightful Thought Unleashed for Education), which divided the process of using GenAI into seven stages to enhance learners' critical thinking and cognitive abilities. Participants needed to read an article first and answer an opinion-based question on the article's subjects two times. One time, they did not use any GenAI tools; another time, they used GenAI tools following the "AI-CRITIQUE" framework. The results of coding analysis on the two responses showed that learners' average thinking level significantly increased from recall to rationalisation under the "AI-CRITIQUE" framework (Shanto et al., 2024). GenAI prompted more in-depth mental engagement with the article, which helped learners enhance their critical thinking (Shanto et al., 2024). Other researchers used questionnaires or interviews to explore the impact on critical thinking. Minh (2024) integrated ChatGPT into the "English Writing 1" course over an academic year. The 66.7% learners reported in the semi-structured interviews that the suggestion provided by ChatGPT enabled them to evaluate their choices of words and the robustness of their arguments more critically. This not only improved their writing quality but also simulated their critical thinking. Guo and Lee (2023) applied ChatGPT into a chemistry curriculum. Participants needed to use ChatGPT to create an essay and then validate and revise the output produced by ChatGPT. The questionnaire results showed the significant improvement in participants' confidence in asking insightful and probing questions, analysing information, making logical conclusions, and understanding complex concepts. More participants would recommend using ChatGPT as a tool for others to enhance their critical thinking skills. The above studies reveal the feasibility of using GenAI to improve learners' thinking levels, stimulate critical thinking, and boost critical thinking confidence. The personalised suggestions and various perspectives generated by GenAI enable learners to evaluate their opinions more critically or think more deeply.

Besides critical thinking, creative thinking also receives lots of attention. Creative thinking refers to the cognitive process of original problem-solving using which original products are generated (Milgram, 1989). Creative thinking is necessary for the individual to be successful whenever he/she faces any problem (Ersoy and Baser, 2014). Several researchers explore the impact of GenAI integration on learners' creative thinking. Li (2023) developed a ChatGPT-based flipped learning guiding approach (ChatGPT-FLGA), integrating ChatGPT into a Modern Educational Technology course. Participants in the experimental group collaborated with learners and an AI "teacher" supported by ChatGPT in a QQ group, while the control group collaborated with other learners and a human teacher. This research used pre-questionnaire and post-questionnaire to measure participants' creative thinking tendencies. The results showed that the creative thinking tendencies of the experimental group were significantly higher than those of the control group. Reasonable solutions offered by the AI "teacher" expanded learners' thinking. Liu et al. (2023b) gave all participants educational content to cultivate their creative potential. The participants in the experimental group had opportunities to interact with ChatGPT during the learning process, while the participants in the control group were taught in traditional teaching methods, such as lectures and practical tasks. The questionnaire results showed that participants utilising ChatGPT had a higher level of creative potential than those in the control group. These studies prove GenAI's potential in promoting learners' creative thinking. Contrary to people's concerns, little empirical evidence proves that GenAI hinders learners' creative thinking. This may be related to the application scenarios of GenAI in experiments. Participants in the above two studies considered the feedback from GenAI as a resource for expanding their thinking rather than depending on GenAI to complete tasks. Learners retained the opportunity for creative thinking due to using GenAI, which may be the key to using GenAI to enhance learners' creative thinking.

The third type of high-order thinking that researchers pay attention to is problem-solving. It is defined as a cognitive process that focuses on accomplishing an objective for which the learners do not primarily know a solution technique (Mayer, 1992). Several studies explore the impact of applying GenAI to problem-solving. Urban et al. (2024) compared the problem solutions completed with ChatGPT assistance and those without ChatGPT assistance from three dimensions, namely quality, elaboration, and originality. The results showed that using ChatGPT had a strong impact on the quality of the solutions, a moderate impact on elaboration, and a moderate impact on originality, suggesting the positive role of GenAI on problem-solving. However, another research revealed different findings. Krupp et al. (2024) compared the differences in the impact of using ChatGPT and search engines to solve physics problems. The results showed that participants who used search engines had significantly better scores than those who used ChatGPT. Participants who used ChatGPT sometimes just copied the answer generated by ChatGPT as their answer to the problem without evaluations, while participants who used search engines tended to divide a question into multiple parts before using search engines, which indicated that over-reliance on GenAI might result in poor problem-solving. In response to this problem, researchers have proposed corresponding approaches. Lee et al. (2024) introduced the Guidance-based ChatGPT-assisted Learning Aid (GCLA). This design required learners to provide their answers to the questions first, and then the tool based on GCLA would determine whether learners had answered the questions correctly. If the answer was incorrect, the tool would provide guidance based on learners' answer and the specific question, helping learners correct the answer. This research compared the impacts of using the GCLA-based tool and ChatGPT on learners' higher-order thinking. The results showed that the experimental group notably outperformed the control group regarding problem-solving, critical thinking, and creativity, revealing the importance of using GenAI with independent consideration.

5.2.3 Impact of GenAI on Learning Experience Has Two Sides

In addition to GenAI's impact on learning performance and learners' higher-order thinking, scholars have also focused on learners' learning experiences, exploring the impacts of GenAI on personalised learning experiences, learning efficiency, and other aspects through surveys or interviews. In terms of personalised learning experience, GenAI is able to adjust feedback content based on student's ability level and learning pace, which helps learners carry out personalised learning (Altarawneh, 2023; Sandu et al., 2024). In a survey conducted in 2023, 73% of learners stated that ChatGPT was more effective in helping them learn than other applications (Altarawneh, 2023). In terms of learning efficiency, lots of learners pointed out that ChatGPT was able to quickly provide high-quality feedback, allowing them to access various relevant information in real time, which helped learners manage their time and complete learning tasks in a shorter amount of time, thereby improving their learning performance (Yusfi and Asmara, 2023; Nguyen, 2023; Castillo et al., 2023). Due to the functional advantages of GenAI, lots of learners widely applied it to various aspects of learning, believing that it helped them learn better (Altarawneh, 2023; Yusfi and Asmara, 2023; Nguyen, 2023; Castillo et al., 2023). For example, researchers investigated the impact of GenAI on IT learners' learning. IT and technology learners found ChatGPT helpful in clarifying complex concepts in the IT field, completing simple programming questions, summarising texts, generating ideas, and improving exam and homework performance (Nguyen, 2023; Tran, 2023). In addition, several learners pointed out that GenAI created a safe and inclusive learning environment for them, providing a more relaxed learning experience (Altarawneh, 2023).

While GenAI offers numerous advantages, it also introduces certain negative learning experiences. For instance, in Nguyen's survey, some participants reported that ChatGPT occasionally failed to provide accurate answers. As a result, learners had to spend additional time searching for the correct information due to the inaccuracies in ChatGPT's responses (Nguyen, 2023). In addition, several learners found that ChatGPT occasionally encountered difficulties in understanding complex queries, handling the latest topics, verifying facts, and citing sources, which might make it difficult for ChatGPT to provide high-quality feedback for specific needs of learners (Tran, 2023; Sandu et al., 2024). Another part of learners also found a lack of human interaction during conversations with ChatGPT, which might also affect their learning experience (Sandu et al., 2024). Faced with various problems with GenAI, several scholars further designed GenAI, developing a customised chatbot based on GenAI and applying it to learners' learning. Through exploring the learning experience of learners, researchers found that the customised chatbot not only provided personalised guidance and improved learners' learning performance, but also promoted learners' participation and positive perception of learning support by using colloquial language and establishing friendly character images, which to some extent alleviated the negative impact of ChatGPT's lack of human interaction on the learning experience (Thway et al., 2024).

5.3 EMPIRICAL STUDY: HOW GENAI IMPACTS LEARNING

Although several studies have explored the impact of GenAI on learning, several specific questions still need to be discussed. For example, the above literature review reveals the potential of GenAI to improve learners' writing. However, several studies also questioned the ability of GenAI. For instance, Yin et al. (2021) found no significant difference in overall learning performance by comparing the pre-post scores of learners utilising AI-powered chatbots with those interacting with human tutors. The impact of GenAI on learners' writing skills compared to humans or other tools still needs further discussion. In addition, although GenAI sometimes has a positive impact on learning performance, whether learners truly gain from the learning and are able to transfer what they learn remains to be discussed. Asare et al. (2023) found a negative influence on learners' mathematics performance after implementing ChatGPT. Their participants pointed out that ChatGPT only helped learners come up with solutions for the problems. Neither analysis for the problems nor explanations for the solutions were provided by ChatGPT (Asare et al., 2023). In other words, ChatGPT did not improve learners' understanding of what they studied. Whether GenAI is able to promote learners' knowledge gain and knowledge transfer is still controversial.

Based on the above analysis, the impact of GenAI on learning still has lots of specific questions to be explored. Therefore, this study proposed two research questions:

1. Are there, and if so, to what extent differences in task performance between learners supported by ChatGPT and human tutors?

2. Are there, and if so, to what extent differences in knowledge gain and knowledge transfer between learners supported by ChatGPT and human tutors?

Our experiment had 60 university learners as participants. They were all learning English as a foreign language and came from different majors. When the experiment began, they first took a pre-test, read the designated text, and completed the writing task within two hours. The reading materials were on three topics: AI, differentiated teaching, and scaffolding teaching. The participants needed to read these materials and write an essay that envisions the future of education in 2035 while integrating the three topics. After completing the writing task, they were divided into the AI and HE groups to revise the article. Learners in the AI group completed the revision with the help of ChatGPT 4.0. Learners in the HE group completed the revision under the guidance of human experts.

To answer the first research question, we considered differences in essay scores before and after revising as essay score improvement. To answer the second question, we also had participants complete a knowledge test on AI in education and AI in health care. We used the same knowledge test on AI in education to conduct pre-test and post-test on learners and considered differences between pre-test and post-test scores as knowledge gain. After completing the writing, we had the learners take a knowledge test on AI in health care and used the test scores as knowledge transfer.

5.3.1 ChatGPT Effectively Improves Learners' Writing Performance

We employed independent samples T-test based on the scores to analyse differences across the two groups. The T-test results indicated no significant differences in essay scores before revision, but significant differences in score improvements after revision. The AI group showed a higher score improvement than the HE group, suggesting that the AI group had a statistically significant higher task performance than the other group.

GenAI is able to provide learners with rich language materials and detailed writing suggestions (Hong, 2023). With the help of GenAI, learners' writing performance has been effectively improved, consistent with previous research findings (Song and Song, 2023; Minh, 2024). However, what surprised us was that the impact of GenAI on learners' writing performance even exceeded the impact of the very experienced human tutor on learners' writing performance, which gave us a new understanding of GenAI's ability to support learners' writing performance (Fan et al., 2024).

5.3.2 ChatGPT Doesn't Perform better than the Human Tutor in Improving Students' Knowledge Gain and Knowledge Transfer

However, although GenAI performed well in improving learners' writing performance, there was no difference compared to the human tutor in enhancing learners' knowledge gain and knowledge transfer. We compared learners' knowledge gain through T-test. The results indicated no significant differences between the two groups in terms of the pre-test score and post-test score, which means no significant differences in knowledge gain. We also compared the knowledge transfer test scores between the two groups, and T-test results showed no significant differences between the two groups.

By observing the process of learners' revisions, we found the possible cause of the problem. We found that several learners in the AI group continuously copied and pasted the contents generated by GenAI, and directly applied them to their essays to ensure that they met the rubric requirements (Fan et al., 2024). This meant that although learners had better writing performance, it might be because they directly used parts of the contents in the suggestions generated by GenAI, rather than because they had truly mastered the knowledge needed in writing. Therefore, when tested for knowledge gain and transfer, the AI group did not perform better than the HE group. For more details and findings from this study, see the paper led by Yizhou Fan "Beware of Metacognitive Laziness: Effects of Generative Artificial Intelligence on Learning Motivation, Processes, and Performance" (Fan et al., 2024).

5.4 IMPLICATION AND FUTURE WORK

Our literature review, together with the empirical case study, has yielded a more thorough and nuanced understanding of the effects of GenAI on learning performance, higher-order thinking, and the overall learning experience. Compared with the human tutor, GenAI is able to provide feedback that matches learners' ability level and learning pace more quickly, enabling learners to complete learning tasks in a shorter time. With the personalised assistance of GenAI, learners' learning performance in different subjects such as mathematics, English, science, and electromagnetics has been improved. In addition, GenAI is capable of enhancing several specific skills, such as writing and programming. Educators and educational application developers are able to apply GenAI to learning, reducing educators' workload and providing learners with personalised guidance (Guo and Wang, 2024; Hong, 2023).

However, it should be noted that GenAI only sometimes positively impacts learning performance. Over-reliance on GenAI, such as using GenAI to write, has a negative impact on learners' learning performance. The active participation of learners, such as evaluating the content generated by GenAI, is crucial for achieving the promoting impact of GenAI on learning performance. Educators, educational application developers, and researchers need to integrate GenAI properly, offering learners opportunities to participate actively in learning with GenAI. Methods like adjusting the question design and assignments design are helpful to avoid learners' over-reliance on GenAI.

GenAI also has the potential to promote learners' higher-order thinking, such as critical thinking, problem-solving, and creative thinking. GenAI is able to quickly provide learners with rich information and multiple perspectives, which helps learners better use critical thinking to solve problems. Rich information also inspires learners to solve problems and create new things. However, although GenAI is able to improve learners' learning performance, it has not performed well in improving learners' knowledge gain and knowledge transfer. This may be because learners only obtain more information through GenAI to achieve better grades, without truly participating in the process of understanding and internalising the knowledge (Wecks et al., 2024). In the future, educators and researchers should not only focus on the learning performance of learners supported by GenAI but also pay attention to their knowledge gains and knowledge transfer skills, ensuring that learners achieve deep learning with the support of GenAI.

In addition, learners, educators, educational application developers, and researchers need to understand GenAI's role rationally. Due to GenAI's inherent problems, it may provide incorrect or biased information, negatively impacting learners' learning (Maitland et al., 2024; Essel et al., 2024). Moreover, GenAI occasionally faces difficulties understanding complex queries, handling the latest topics, verifying facts, and citing sources (Tran, 2023; Sandu et al., 2024). The stakeholders need to recognise that they cannot fully trust the response provided by GenAI. In order to fully leverage the advantages of GenAI, educators, educational application developers, and researchers are able to design guidance frameworks based on their goals (Lee et al., 2024; Shanto et al., 2024; Li, 2023). They are also able to use prompt engineering to personalise the design of GenAI. Integrating teaching or learning strategies into GenAI promotes the development of learners' abilities more specifically (Li et al., 2024). Future educators, educational application developers, and educational researchers are able to start by integrating the framework design and instructional design of GenAI to further enhance its role in promoting learners' learning.

5.5 CHAPTER SUMMARY

In this chapter, we explore the impact of applying GenAI to learning. We first reviewed the positive and negative impacts of traditional technology on learning. Afterwards, we briefly outlined the improvements that GenAI brings to traditional problems and the new application opportunities it brings to learning. As more and more learners use GenAI, it is crucial to understand its impact on learning. Therefore, in the second part, we conducted a literature review and analysed the impact of GenAI on learning from three dimensions: the impact of GenAI on learning performance, the impact of GenAI on higher-order thinking, and the impact of GenAI on learning experience. To deepen our understanding of the impact of GenAI on learning, we propose one case study with two research questions in the third part. The first question finds that compared to human expert guidance, GenAI significantly improves learners' writing skills, which enhances their learning performance. The second question finds that GenAI fails to effectively improve learners' and knowledge transfer. The literature review and our case study provide a more comprehensive understanding of GenAI's impact on learning. GenAI has the potential to improve learners' learning performance, higher-order thinking such as critical thinking, and learning experience. However, whether GenAI is able to improve learning performance is related to whether learners actively participate in learning. In addition, although sometimes GenAI is able to improve learners' learning performance, it fails to improve learners' knowledge gain and knowledge transfer, which is conducive to learners' deep learning. The problems inherent in GenAI, such as model hallucination, may also affect learning experience. In short, although GenAI is able to bring positive impacts to learning, it also has weak or adverse impacts in certain aspects. Educators, educational application developers, and educational researchers need to have a rational view of the impact of GenAI on learning. They are responsible for guiding learners to use GenAI reasonably and actively by developing application frameworks and integrating teaching methods into GenAI, which helps maximise GenAI's advantages and avoid its problems.

Bibliography

Alneyadi, S. and Wardat, Y. (2023). ChatGPT: Revolutionizing student achievement in the electronic magnetism unit for eleventh-grade students in emirates schools. *Contemporary Educational Technology, 15*(4):ep448.

Altarawneh, H. (2023). ChatGPT impact on student educational performance: A conceptual analysis. *EAI Endorsed Transactions on e-Learning, 9*:1–5.

Al-Zahrani, A. M. (2015). From passive to active: The impact of the flipped classroom through social learning platforms on higher education students' creative thinking. *British Journal of Educational Technology, 46*(6):1133–1148.

Asare, B., Arthur, Y., and Boateng, F. (2023). Exploring the impact of ChatGPT on mathematics performance: The influential role of student interest. *Education Science and Management, 1*(3):158–168.

Barzilai, S. and Blau, I. (2014). Scaffolding game-based learning: Impact on learning achievements, perceived learning, and game experiences. *Computers & Education*, *70*:65–79.

Brookhart, S. M. (2010). *How to Assess Higher-Order Thinking Skills in Your Classroom.* ASCD, Alexandria, VA.

Bucaioni, A., Ekedahl, H., Helander, V., and Nguyen, P. T. (2024). Programming with ChatGPT: How far can we go? *Machine Learning with Applications*, *15*:100526.

Castillo, A. G. R., Rivera, H. V. H., Teves, R. M. V., Lopez, H. R. P., Reyes, G. Y., Rodriguez, M. A. M., Berrios, H. Q., Arocutipa, J. P. F., Silva, G. J. S., and Arias-Gonzáles, J. L. (2023). Effect of chat GPT on the digitized learning process of university students. *Journal of Namibian Studies: History Politics Culture*, *33*:1–15.

Ersoy, E. and Baser, N. (2014). The effects of problem-based learning method in higher education on creative thinking. *Procedia-Social and Behavioral Sciences*, *116*:3494–3498.

Essel, H. B., Vlachopoulos, D., Essuman, A. B., and Amankwa, J. O. (2024). ChatGPT effects on cognitive skills of undergraduate students: Receiving instant responses from AI-based conversational large language models (LLMS). *Computers and Education: Artificial Intelligence*, *6*:100198.

Fan, Y., Tang, L., Le, H., Shen, K., Tan, S., Zhao, Y., Shen, Y., Li, X., and Gasevic, D. (2024). Beaware of metacognitive laziness: Effects of generative artificial intelligence on learning motivation, processes, and performance. *British Journal of Educational Technology 56* (2):489–530.

Guo, K. and Wang, D. (2024). To resist it or to embrace it? Examining ChatGPT's potential to support teacher feedback in EFL writing. *Education and Information Technologies*, *29*(7):8435–8463.

Guo, Y. and Lee, D. (2023). Leveraging ChatGPT for enhancing critical thinking skills. *Journal of Chemical Education*, *100*(12): 4876–4883.

Hakiki, M., Fadli, R., Samala, A. D., Fricticarani, A., Dayurni, P., Rahmadani, K., Astiti, A. D., and Sabir, A. (2023). Exploring the impact of using Chat-GPT on student learning outcomes in technology learning: The comprehensive experiment. *Advances in Mobile Learning Educational Research, 3*(2):859–872.

Hattie, J. (2012). *Visible Learning for Teachers: Maximizing Impact on Learning*. Routledge, London, UK.

Hong, W. C. H. (2023). The impact of ChatGPT on foreign language teaching and learning: Opportunities in education and research. *Journal of Educational Technology and Innovation, 5*(1):37–45.

Hwang, G.-J., Lai, C.-L., Liang, J.-C., Chu, H.-C., and Tsai, C.-C. (2018). A long-term experiment to investigate the relationships between high school students' perceptions of mobile learning and peer interaction and higher-order thinking tendencies. *Educational Technology Research and Development, 66*:75–93.

Kem, D. (2022). Personalised and adaptive learning: Emerging learning platforms in the era of digital and smart learning. *International Journal of Social Science and Human Research, 5*(2):385–391.

Kosar, T., Ostojić, D., Liu, Y. D., and Mernik, M. (2024). Computer science education in ChatGPT era: Experiences from an experiment in a programming course for novice programmers. *Mathematics, 12*(5):629.

Krupp, L., Steinert, S., Kiefer-Emmanouilidis, M., Avila, K. E., Lukowicz, P., Kuhn, J., Küchemann, S., and Karolus, J. (2024). Unreflected acceptance–investigating the negative consequences of ChatGPT-assisted problem solving in physics education. In Fabian Lorig, Jason Tucker, Adam Dahlgren Lindström, Frank Dignum, Pradeep Murukannaiah, Andreas Theodorou, Pınar Yolum, editors, *HHAI 2024: Hybrid Human AI Systems for the Social Good*, pp. 199–212. IOS Press, Amsterdam, The Netherlands.

Kumari, P. and Naaz, I. (2020). Digital learning through MOOCs: Advantages, outcomes & challenges. *Sambodhi, UGC CARE Journal, 43*(4):18–22.

Lee, H.-Y., Chen, P.-H., Wang, W.-S., Huang, Y.-M., and Wu, T.-T. (2024). Empowering ChatGPT with guidance mechanism in blended learning: Effect of self-regulated learning, higher-order thinking skills, and knowledge construction. *International Journal of Educational Technology in Higher Education*, *21*(1):1–28.

Li, H. (2023). Effects of a ChatGPT-based flipped learning guiding approach on learners' courseware project performances and perceptions. *Australasian Journal of Educational Technology*, *39*(5):40–58.

Li, H., Wang, Y., Luo, S., and Huang, C. (2024). The influence of GenAI on the effectiveness of argumentative writing in higher education: Evidence from a quasi-experimental study in China. *Journal of Asian Public Policy*, 1–26.

Lin, M.-H., Chen, H.-C., and Liu, K.-S. (2017). A study of the effects of digital learning on learning motivation and learning outcome. *Eurasia Journal of Mathematics, Science and Technology Education*, *13*(7):3553–3564.

Liu, Y., Han, T., Ma, S., Zhang, J., Yang, Y., Tian, J., et al. (2023a). Summary of ChatGPT-related research and perspective towards the future of large language models. *Meta-Radiology*, *1*(2):100017.

Liu, Z., Vobolevich, A., and Oparin, A. (2023b). The influence of AI ChatGPT on improving teachers' creative thinking. *International Journal of Learning, Teaching and Educational Research*, *22*(12):124–139.

Lo, C. K. (2023). What is the impact of ChatGPT on education? A rapid review of the literature. *Education Sciences*, *13*(4):410.

Mahaini, D. (2024). Generative AI in computer science education: A study on academic performance. B.S. thesis, University of Twente.

Maitland, A., Fowkes, R., and Maitland, S. (2024). Can ChatGPT pass the MRCP (UK) written examinations? Analysis of performance and errors using a clinical decision-reasoning framework. *BMJ Open*, *14*(3):e080558.

Mayer, R. E. (1992). *Thinking, Problem Solving, Cognition.* WH Freeman/Times Books/Henry Holt & Co.,, New York.

McCrindle, A. R. and Christensen, C. A. (1995). The impact of learning journals on metacognitive and cognitive processes and learning performance. *Learning and Instruction*, *5*(2):167–185.

McDaniels, M., Pfund, C., and Barnicle, K. (2016). Creating dynamic learning communities in synchronous online courses: One approach from the center for the integration of research, teaching and learning (CIRTL). *Online Learning*, *20*(1):110–129.

Milgram, R. M. (1989). *Teaching Gifted and Talented Learners in Regular Classrooms*. Charles C. Thomas Publisher, Springfield, IL.

Minh, A. N. (2024). Leveraging ChatGPT for enhancing English writing skills and critical thinking in University Freshmen. *Journal of Knowledge Learning and Science Technology*, *3*(2):51–62. ISSN:2959-6386 (online).

Miri, B., David, B.-C., and Uri, Z. (2007). Purposely teaching for the promotion of higher-order thinking skills: A case of critical thinking. *Research in Science Education*, *37*:353–369.

Nguyen, K. (2023). The impact of ChatGPT on the learning process of technology students amongst higher education.

Norris, S. P. and Ennis, R. H. (1989). *Evaluating Critical Thinking: The Practitioners' Guide to Teaching Thinking Series*. ERIC, Pacific Grove, CA.

Patero, J. L. (2023). Revolutionizing math education: Harnessing ChatGPT for student success. *Mathematics Education*, *3*(1):807–813.

Rahman, M. M. and Watanobe, Y. (2023). ChatGPT for education and research: Opportunities, threats, and strategies. *Applied Sciences*, *13*(9):5783.

Resnick, L. B. (1987). *Education and Learning to Think*. National Academy Press, Washington, DC.

Rienties, B. and Toetenel, L. (2016). The impact of learning design on student behaviour, satisfaction and performance: A cross-institutional comparison across 151 modules. *Computers in Human Behavior*, *60*:333–341.

Risvold, W., Stratton, M., and Geddy, M. (2024). How to evaluate critical thinking in the age of AI. Accessed: 2024-08-17.

Saidin, N. F., Halim, N. D. A., and Yahaya, N. (2015). A review of research on augmented reality in education: Advantages and applications. *International Education Studies*, *8*(13):1–8.

Sandu, R., Gide, E., and Elkhodr, M. (2024). The role and impact of ChatGPT in educational practices: Insights from an Australian higher education case study. *Discover Education*, *3*(1):71.

Shanto, S. S., Ahmed, Z., and Jony, A. I. (2024). Enriching learning process with generative AI: A proposed framework to cultivate critical thinking in higher education using Chat GPT. *Tuijin Jishu/Journal of Propulsion Technology*, *45*(1):3019–3029.

Sharma, R. (2017). Computer assisted learning: A study. *Computer*, *4*(2):102–105.

Soliman, M., Pesyridis, A., Dalaymani-Zad, D., Gronfula, M., and Kourmpetis, M. (2021). The application of virtual reality in engineering education. *Applied Sciences*, *11*(6):2879.

Song, C. and Song, Y. (2023). Enhancing academic writing skills and motivation: Assessing the efficacy of ChatGPT in AI-assisted language learning for EFL students. *Frontiers in Psychology*, *14*:1260843.

Songsiengchai, S., Sereerat, B.-o., and Watananimitgul, W. (2023). Leveraging artificial intelligence (AI): Chat GPT for effective English language learning among Thai students. *English Language Teaching*, *16*(11):1–68.

Sun, D., Boudouaia, A., Zhu, C., and Li, Y. (2024). Would ChatGPT-facilitated programming mode impact college students' programming behaviors, performances, and perceptions? An empirical study. *International Journal of Educational Technology in Higher Education*, *21*(1):14.

Tamim, R. M., Bernard, R. M., Borokhovski, E., Abrami, P. C., and Schmid, R. F. (2011). What forty years of research says about the impact of technology on learning: A second-order meta-analysis and validation study. *Review of Educational Research*, *81*(1):4–28.

Thway, M., Recatala-Gomez, J., Lim, F. S., Hippalgaonkar, K., and Ng, L. W. (2024). Harnessing GenAI for higher education: A study of a retrieval augmented generation chatbot's impact on human learning. *arXiv preprint arXiv:2406.07796*.

Tiwari, A., Lai, P., So, M., and Yuen, K. (2006). A comparison of the effects of problem-based learning and lecturing on the development of students' critical thinking. *Medical Education*, *40*(6):547–554.

Tran, T. (2023). Exploring the impact of ChatGPT on learning experience of it students. *Frontiers in Education 9*:1379796.

Urban, M., Děchtěrenko, F., Lukavskỳ, J., Hrabalová, V., Svacha, F., Brom, C., and Urban, K. (2024). ChatGPT improves creative problem-solving performance in university students: An experimental study. *Computers & Education*, *215*:105031.

Wang, Y.-H. and Liao, H.-C. (2017). Learning performance enhancement using computer-assisted language learning by collaborative learning groups. *Symmetry*, *9*(8):141.

Wecks, J. O., Voshaar, J., Plate, B. J., and Zimmermann, J. (2024). Generative AI usage and academic performance. *arXiv preprint arXiv:2404.19699*.

Yin, J., Goh, T.-T., Yang, B., and Xiaobin, Y. (2021). Conversation technology with micro-learning: The impact of chatbot-based learning on students' learning motivation and performance. *Journal of Educational Computing Research*, *59*(1):154–177.

Yusfi, M. and Asmara, C. H. (2023). Exploring the impact of ChatGPT on english education department student's motivation and performance. *Journal of Teaching of English*, *8*(4):383–392.

Zoller, U. (2000). Teaching tomorrow's college science courses–are we getting it right? *Journal of College Science Teaching*, *29*(6):409.

Zoller, U. (2001). Alternative assessment as (critical) means of facilitating HOCS-promoting teaching and learning in chemistry education. *Chemistry Education Research and Practice*, *2*(1):9–17.

CHAPTER 6

How GenAI Affects Metacognition in Self-Regulated Learning: Between Enhancement and Inhibition

Zijian Li and Yizhou Fan

LEARNING HOW TO LEARN is a crucial skill, especially in the rapidly evolving landscape of artificial intelligence technology. In this context, a key component of "learning how to learn" is metacognition. Metacognition along with self-regulated learning plays a pivotal role in education by empowering learners to understand and manage their learning processes, leading to more effective and autonomous learners. With the recent emergence of generative artificial intelligence (GenAI) represented by ChatGPT, the application of GenAI in education inevitably impacts learners' learning processes, attainments, and strategies. As a consequence, as the application of GenAI continues to advance, its influence on the development of learners' metacognition and the cultivation of self-regulated learning skills becomes an important

DOI: 10.4324/9781003632146-6

topic. Therefore, we reviewed the application of GenAI in recent empirical studies related to metacognition and self-regulated learning, elucidating its effects on metacognition in SRL. We found that, from a positive perspective, the application of GenAI in the learning process and activities is able to promote learners' metacognition in three phases of self-regulated learning. Using the GenAI tool, indicators such as self-efficacy, self-reflection, goal setting, and planning motivation are shown to be improved. However, GenAI is also viewed as a double-edged sword. Subsequently, metacognitive laziness in learners' behavioural patterns when using GenAI tools was identified in the recent published paper and introduced here in this chapter as an example. Building on the above research findings, we assert that the application of GenAI tools holds substantial potential for enhancing learners' metacognition in self-regulated learning. Nevertheless, the issue of metacognitive laziness arising from using these tools demands greater academic scrutiny and resolution. Future research should enhance the understanding and in-depth analysis of the phenomenon of metacognitive laziness induced by GenAI tools.

6.1 METACOGNITION AND SELF-REGULATED LEARNING IN THE AGE OF GENAI: DEFINITIONS AND EVOLUTION

Metacognition and self-regulated learning (SRL) have long been pivotal areas of academic research and discourse. The term "metacognition", introduced by John Flavell in the 1970s, refers to "cognition about cognition" or "thinking about thinking" (Flavell, 1979). Metacognition encompasses knowledge about cognition and cognitive processes as well as the ability to monitor and regulate cognition processes consciously (Schraw and Moshman, 1995). As illustrated above, the monitoring of the cognitive process links metacognition to self-regulated learning (Griffith and Ruan, 2006). The concept of self-regulated learning has also evolved, with various scholars proposing different models. For example, the SRL model of Zimmerman (2000) views SRL as self-generated thoughts, feelings, and behaviours aimed at achieving personal goals. Pintrich's model defines SRL as the use of cognitive, metacognitive, and resource management strategies to control one's learning process (Pintrich and De Groot, 1990). Winne, from a metacognitive perspective, considers SRL a process driven by metacognition, where learners apply cognitive strategies and tactics to learning tasks (Winne, 1996, 2011). Generally, self-regulated learning is a complex process involving cognitive, metacognitive, behavioural, motivational, and emotional components (Zimmerman, 2002, 2008). It integrates metacognitive practices into a more holistic framework that includes cognitive, behavioural, and emotional components (Winne and Azevedo, 2022). A core component of self-regulated learning is the metacognitive process (Veenman et al., 2006; Zimmerman and Moylan, 2009). Learners apply metacognitive strategies such as goal setting, self-monitoring, and self-evaluation, which are essential for effective learning (Zimmerman, 2008). In previous chapters, we discussed the impact of GenAI on learners' cognitive processes, such as cognitive dialogues, interventions, and emotional states. However, the discussion on the metacognitive level has been relatively limited. Therefore, in this chapter, we focus on the influence of GenAI on metacognition, specifically on the metacognitive processes within learners' self-regulated learning.

Metacognition comprises two fundamental elements: metacognitive knowledge and cognitive regulation (Flavell, 1979). Metacognitive knowledge encompasses declarative knowledge, procedural knowledge, and conditional knowledge (Schraw and Moshman, 1995). Declarative knowledge refers to the "know-what" aspect, while procedural knowledge pertains to the "know-how" which involves utilising learning strategies and actions to achieve goals based on declarative knowledge. Conditional knowledge, on the other hand, relates to the "know-why-when-where" aspect, which includes understanding when, in what context, and why to apply various procedures, skills, and cognitive actions or strategies. These three types of knowledge are closely intertwined, collectively forming metacognitive knowledge. Cognitive regulation, also as known as metacognitive control, involves learners' actions to manage their thinking or learning processes. This includes three fundamental components or skills: planning, monitoring, and evaluating (Flavell, 1979; Schraw and Moshman, 1995). Planning involves selecting appropriate strategies and providing effective resources to achieve goals, including goal setting, activating prior knowledge, and managing time. Monitoring refers to the self-regulation skills necessary for learning, involving a critical analysis of the effectiveness of the implemented strategies or plans. Evaluation entails checking the progress toward goals, which can lead to further planning, monitoring, and evaluation.

Among the SRL models widely used in academia, Zimmerman's SRL model delineates three phases: forethought, performance, and self-reflection. Each phase encompasses specific subprocesses, such as goal setting and strategic planning in the forethought phase, time management and help-seeking in the performance phase, and self-evaluation in the self-reflection phase (Zimmerman, 2000, 2002). Pintrich's model, on the other hand, outlines four phases: forethought, planning and activation, monitoring, control and reaction and reflection. Each phase includes different areas or components of regulation such as cognition, motivational/effect, and behaviour, providing a comprehensive view of SRL processes (Pintrich and De Groot, 1990). As researchers continue to explore self-regulated learning, from the view of metacognition, Winne (2011) introduced four interrelated phases: task definition, goal setting and planning, enacting study tactics and strategies and metacognitive adaptation. This model also emphasises five facets of tasks (conditions, operations, products, evaluations, standards, abbreviated as COPES) that interact throughout the SRL process (Winne and Hadwin, 1998). Additionally, the concept of socially shared regulation of learning (SSRL) has emerged, addressing collaborative learning contexts where self-regulation, co-regulation, and shared regulation occur (Hadwin et al., 2011). With the development of AI technology, humans and AI gradually merge to form a hybrid system, and AI as a machine is able to provide learners with the necessary regulatory support according to SRL theory, which leads to the emergence of hybrid human-AI regulation theory (HHAIR) (Molenaar, 2022).

These theories have guided subsequent educational applications and practices, including instructional design, teaching methods, and the design of educational interventions. A key aspect of these research practices is the influence of technology and its development on learners' metacognition and self-regulated learning. Advances in technology have led to significant innovations in fostering learners' metacognitive and SRL skills. Research shows that metacognition is teachable, and the development of cognitive knowledge and cognitive regulation can be enhanced through various technological tools, leading to improvements in both metacognitive abilities and academic achievement (Saenz et al., 2019). For example, learning analytics provide visual dashboards that display learning data and offer metacognitive feedback to learners, enabling them to better monitor and regulate their learning processes

(Alonso-Mencía et al., 2020). Interactive feedback systems, powered by visual dashboards, allow teachers to track learners' learning activities by collecting data from online learning platforms. This data is presented using visualisations that help educators intervene effectively, facilitating the self-regulated learning process. Learners can also receive direct feedback from these analytics to guide their own learning regulation (Heikkinen et al., 2023).

Furthermore, data mining techniques are increasingly being used to measure and support SRL. These techniques analyse students' learning behaviours, create learner models, and provide personalised suggestions that enhance self-regulated learning. The insights gained from data mining are often used to deliver targeted metacognitive feedback to students, supporting their SRL development through actionable data-driven insights (Alonso-Mencía et al., 2020). AI agents, chatbots, and embedded systems are also emerging as valuable tools in this field. These technologies can provide real-time suggestions and guidelines for students as they engage in learning tasks, helping them to self-regulate more effectively. Through AI-driven feedback, students can adjust their strategies and behaviours to optimise their learning outcomes (Ng et al., 2024).

With the rise of the GenAI era, a new generation of generative AI tools, represented by ChatGPT, is gradually being applied in the education sector. The powerful capabilities of GenAI are expected to bring significant convenience to both students and teachers by enhancing the learning experience, supporting personalised and interactive learning, and increasing motivation while deepening engagement in the learning process (Bai et al., 2023; Baidoo-Anu and Ansah, 2023; Kasneci et al., 2023). As the latest cutting-edge technology, GenAI is progressively gaining traction as an instrumental tool in a growing body of research in the intricate realms of students' metacognition and self-regulated learning processes. It has been suggested that ChatGPT has great potential to improve metacognitive self-regulation learning (Dahri et al., 2024). Chang et al. (2023) argued that using ChatGPT as a representative chatbot, configured with relevant SRL prompts, can guide students' self-regulated learning and monitoring, helping them to reflect on and specify SRL strategies. Despite the notable advantages conferred by the advent of GenAI technologies, their application continues to grapple with a suite of challenges. These include the proliferation of inaccuracies within responses, the emergence of hallucinations, an inherent lack of transparency, and the propensity to provide answers that can perpetuate discrimination or exhibit bias (Montenegro-Rueda et al., 2023; Kasneci et al., 2023). Students may experience over-reliance on GenAI tools to the detriment of critical thinking, leading to a diminished depth of learning engagement and fostering an educational experience characterised by superficiality rather than profundity (Bai et al., 2023; Memarian and Doleck, 2023).

Although GenAI has been increasingly integrated into educational landscapes, there are currently no reviews of its application in the studies of metacognition and self-regulated learning. Therefore, this chapter provides a review in the following section that illustrates the questions including: **(1) What is the impact of GenAI technology on learners' metacognition? (2) What challenges are posed by GenAI technology in the realm of metacognition**. In the course of our review, a critical issue has emerged, which we refer to as "metacognitive laziness." We will explore this concept in more detail, alongside an empirical study, in the third section. Our goal is to uncover how learners exhibit metacognitive laziness when using GenAI as a learning aid and to examine its impact on the overall learning process (Fan et al., 2024).

6.2 REVIEW OF GENAI'S IMPACT ON METACOGNITION

A comprehensive literature search was performed using the Google Scholar database to identify empirical studies on the influence of GenAI on metacognition. The search included keywords such as metacognition, metacognitive skills, self-regulated learning, learning strategy, ChatGPT, and generative artificial intelligence. This search yielded 13 relevant empirical studies that align with the theme of this chapter. These studies provide a diverse and comprehensive perspective on how GenAI tools, particularly ChatGPT, are shaping learning practices and affecting learners' metacognitive processes. They cover various aspects of metacognition within self-regulated learning, offering insights into how students interact with GenAI to enhance their learning experience. Zimmerman's model outlines three phases of self-regulation: forethought, performance, and reflection(Zimmerman, 2002). Each of these phases corresponds to specific metacognitive processes, such as planning, monitoring, and evaluation (Schraw and Moshman, 1995; Zimmerman, 2002). In the following subsections, we will review the existing literature to summarise the impact of GenAI on these metacognitive processes within self-regulated learning phases. By examining these empirical studies in detail, we aim to highlight the key findings and discuss their implications for understanding how GenAI supports metacognitive skills and strategies. This review will also address the potential benefits and challenges of integrating GenAI into education, particularly in fostering metacognition and promoting effective self-regulation among students (Table 6.1).

6.2.1 Impact of GenAI in the Forethought Phase

In the forethought phase, learners engage in goal setting and strategic planning, which corresponds to the planning process of metacognition. During this phase, learners use their metacognitive knowledge to evaluate task requirements, anticipate potential challenges, and select suitable strategies to address them.

TABLE 6.1 A Summary of Research Contents within SRL Phases

SRL Phase	Research Content	Research List
Forethought	Goal setting and planning Motivation	Levine et al. (2024), Lin et al. (2024) and Ng et al. (2024)
Performance	Monitoring	Minh (2024), Šedlbauer et al. (2024), and Yan et al. (2024)
	Time management	Majumdar et al. (2024) and Ng et al. (2024)
	Help-seeking	Ng et al. (2024)
Reflection	Adaptation of learning strategies	Yan et al. (2024)
	Reflection and evaluation	Lin et al. (2024), Minh (2024), Levine et al. (2024), Li et al. (2024), Urban et al. (2024), and Majumdar et al. (2024)

Levine et al. (2024) conducted a naturalistic case study to understand how learners use ChatGPT for planning. Coding of learners' prompts to ChatGPT revealed that most of the prompts fell into the planning category, which includes goal-setting, idea generation, and organising. Then they conducted a more in-depth analysis of a specific case, focusing on the detailed interactions with ChatGPT. The researchers found that in the planning stage, learners did not delegate the planning process to ChatGPT. Instead, the prompts they proposed were not directly related to planning. The researchers' analysis indicated that creating these prompts required prior planning. It suggested that learners had already engaged in planning before interacting with ChatGPT. Thus, ChatGPT did not disengage learners from the planning process; instead, it may have provided an opportunity for learners to practice goal-setting (Levine et al., 2024)

Similarly, Lin et al. (2024) found that some learners use ChatGPT to help initiate discussions around challenging topics. It indicates that ChatGPT assists learners in planning, establishing relationships between concepts and building links between them. Ng et al. (2024) conducted a comparative study on the impact of a GenAI-based SRLbot and a rule-based AI chatbot (Nemobot) on learners' self-regulated learning. They found that GenAI can effectively enhance the planning process. In the semi-structured interviews, learners reported that using SRLbot helped them with goal setting, including setting clear learning objectives and constructing study schedules.

Furthermore, the study of Wu et al. (2024) uses standardised scales to measure various aspects of SRL before and after using GenAI tools. They found that compared to traditional Google search, GenAI improved the planning phase by fostering the motivation of learners. Yıldız (2023) examined the impact of ChatGPT assistance on student motivation by analysing their use of motivational strategies. The study employed a motivational strategies questionnaire that encompassed self-regulation strategies, including planning, monitoring, and evaluation. The findings revealed that ChatGPT's assistance enhanced learners' motivation during post-class activities, encouraging learners to be more proactive in planning, monitoring, and evaluating their learning efforts.

In summary, the integration of GenAI tools into the planning process of metacognition appears to have a multifaceted impact. GenAI offers a supportive role by facilitating goal-setting, idea generation, and conceptual linking. These tools not only assist in the initial stages of planning but also enhance learners' motivation to engage in strategic planning. Rather than diminishing the role of planning in metacognition, GenAI potentially amplifies it, providing learners with additional resources and scaffolding to refine and execute their planning processes.

6.2.2 Impact of GenAI in the Performance Phase

In the performance phase, learners engage in self-monitoring and control while completing tasks, which corresponds to the monitoring component of metacognition. During this phase, learners employ metacognitive monitoring strategies to evaluate their progress and adjust their strategy as needed.

Minh (2024) found that suggestions provided by AI prompt students to critically evaluate their word choices and the rigour of their arguments. Similarly, Šedlbauer et al. (2024) found that some learners reported that ChatGPT's responses were superficial and lacked reliability, thus prompting learners to think critically and seek additional resources to verify these responses. It revealed that the response of GenAI impacts students' monitoring process and critically adjusts their strategies. The study of Yan et al. (2024) revealed that learners adopted a more sceptical and self-evaluative approach during help-seeking interactions with ChatGPT. Before posing questions, learners engaged in a reflective process, analysing their comprehension of the issue and selecting different strategies for asking questions based on their self-assessment. This behaviour illustrates learners' monitoring of their learning processes. Another notable strategy involved analysing and paraphrasing ChatGPT's responses, integrating them into their own words. This paraphrasing represents a form of self-monitoring, helping learners to identify which aspects they had mastered and which areas remained unclear.

Ng et al. (2024) 's study also found that GenAI can effectively enhance the monitoring process by recommending learning strategies and methods. GenAI improved their time management by encouraging them to create study plans and helped them allocate dedicated time slots for different activities. In terms of help-seeking, SRLbot provided effective support by offering numerous examples and learning materials, aiding learners in problem-solving. The study of Majumdar et al. (2024) put insights into the time performance of students in the learning process.

It is found that with the introduction of ChatGPT, more time may be spent on interaction and review, which may indicate the shift of time management strategies of learners.

GenAI tools have a significant influence on the monitoring component of metacognition during the performance phase of learning. It prompts learners to critically evaluate their work, refine their strategies, and engage in deeper reflection on their learning processes. The interaction with GenAI enhances learners' monitoring of their progress and fosters a more reflective and self-evaluative approach, particularly in help-seeking and time management. By encouraging learners to reassess their understanding and adapt their strategies accordingly, GenAI supports a more dynamic and responsive monitoring process.

6.2.3 Impact of GenAI in the Reflection Phase

The reflection phase involves the evaluation and reflection on the learning process and outcomes, aligning with the evaluation component of metacognition. At this stage, learners reflect on their performance, assess the effectiveness of their strategies, and set improvement plans for future learning.

Yan et al. (2024) studied how learners collaborate with ChatGPT in programming, observing the evolution in communication strategies. Learners initially used simple Q&A interactions but gradually progressed to deeper dialogues, rethinking their approaches and clarifying their thoughts based on ChatGPT's responses. This shift indicates learners' growing ability to critically assess and reflect on their learning characteristics, aligning ChatGPT with their needs. In the study of Lin et al. (2024), learners integrated ChatGPT's responses with their viewpoints, which promotes further reflection, highlighting the enhancement of the metacognitive reflection process through the use of ChatGPT. Analysis of semi-structured interview content in the study of Minh (2024) revealed that AI suggestions prompted learners to critically evaluate their word choices and the coherence of their arguments, often leading to revisions that made their writing more persuasive and coherent. This suggests that ChatGPT not only served as a Q&A assistant but also promoted metacognitive reflection and evaluation.

However, Levine et al. (2024) found that learners were most likely to treat ChatGPT as a "cheating tool." After asking ChatGPT to "correct" or "revise" their work, learners often accepted its suggestions without question, sometimes adopting entire paragraph revisions. This behaviour suggests that learners may overlook the metacognitive processes of evaluation and reflection.

The above findings indicate that learners could become overly reliant on ChatGPT, potentially neglecting the critical metacognitive processes of evaluating and reflecting on its responses. However, in a more detailed case analysis, Levine et al. (2024) found that learners maintained a level of metacognitive awareness. They recognised differences between their own writing style and ChatGPT's responses, and did not fully accept the revisions; instead, they engaged in evaluation and reflection. This suggests that ChatGPT can offer opportunities for learners to practice metacognitive evaluation and reflection on their learning process and content. Li et al. (2024) investigated the impact of ChatGPT's hints on psychological factors in learners' programming education. The study found that learners in the ChatGPT-assisted groups, compared to the control group, did not attribute their success to their own critical thinking. This could be because they believed their success was largely due to ChatGPT's assistance. These findings suggest that ChatGPT may influence learners' metacognitive self-assessment and judgements about their learning, leading them to attribute their achievements more to ChatGPT's help.

Additionally, Urban et al. (2024) conducted a study comparing the effects of using ChatGPT on learners engaged in complex creative tasks. They found that ChatGPT usage could impact learners' self-assessment, with the perceived usefulness of ChatGPT contributing to greater inaccuracies in their self-evaluation judgements. Majumdar et al. (2024) observed that learners who arrived at incorrect answers tended to focus on repeatedly using tools like ChatGPT to find solutions. Even though their final solutions were incorrect, the interaction with ChatGPT still encouraged them to reflect on their problem-solving process and evaluate the solutions it provided.

GenAI tools have a complex and nuanced impact on the evaluation component of metacognition during the reflection phase. On the one hand, ChatGPT can enhance metacognitive reflection by prompting learners to critically evaluate their choices and integrate new perspectives. This reflective engagement fosters deeper self-awareness and supports the development of more effective learning approaches. On the other hand, there is a potential risk that learners may overly rely on ChatGPT, accepting its suggestions without sufficient critical evaluation, which could undermine their metacognitive self-assessment and lead to inaccuracies in self-evaluation. Despite this risk, when used thoughtfully, ChatGPT can provide valuable opportunities for learners to engage in metacognitive evaluation and prompt a more reflective and iterative learning process. Ultimately, the impact of GenAI on the evaluation phase is determined by how learners balance its use with their own reflective practices. This highlights the importance of maintaining metacognitive awareness and active engagement in the evaluation process.

6.2.4 Concerns and Risks of Over-Reliance on GenAI

GenAI, exemplified by tools like ChatGPT, is often viewed as a double-edged sword. Its integration into learning may enhance metacognition and self-regulated learning while its improper use in educational contexts can raise numerous concerns and ethical risks (Lo, 2023). As a seemingly omnipotent tool, there is a significant truth that students may develop or have already developed reliance when using it (Stojanov et al., 2024).

However, when the reliance becomes over-reliance on GenAI, it turns into a critical issue that cannot be overlooked. Several studies have also identified the potential negative impacts of GenAI applications on students in experimental settings. For instance, over-reliance on GenAI can lead to a struggle with accurate self-assessment(Urban et al., 2024), a lack of reflection (Lin et al., 2024) and a neglect of metacognitive monitoring (Li et al., 2024). Urban et al. (2024) conducted a study comparing the effects of using ChatGPT on learners engaged in complex creative tasks and found that ChatGPT usage can impact learners' self-assessment. Specifically, the perceived usefulness of ChatGPT seemed to affect their self-evaluation judgements, leading to greater inaccuracies in self-assessment. This finding suggests that ChatGPT may contribute to learners misjudging their learning status, potentially leading to a neglect of learning process management, reflection, and the adjustment of learning strategies. Consequently, this could hinder the effectiveness of self-regulated learning.

In the study of Yan et al. (2024), some students reported complete dependence on GenAI when errors occurred and were unable to independently identify the causes of recurring mistakes. Students struggled to reach a mutual understanding with GenAI, making it difficult for them to propose improvements. Similarly, Lin et al. (2024) observed that some learners exhibited over-reliance on ChatGPT, often accepting its suggestions with little to no critical judgements or consideration. This behaviour highlights a deficiency in metacognitive processes, particularly in reflection and monitoring. This finding aligns with Li et al. (2024) that, while ChatGPT's assistance seems to help alleviate the negative impact of task anxiety on cognitive engagement, it also reduces learners' pursuit of the feeling of knowledge, leading to dependency on ChatGPT. As a result, even when faced with complex tasks and high task anxiety, learners might not develop strong intrinsic motivation or judgements of learning, potentially neglecting the monitoring and reflection of their cognitive processes. In Chapter 8, we will delve into the ethical issues brought about by GenAI, with a particular focus on the concerns related to over-reliance.

6.3 EMPIRICAL STUDY: SEEKING EVIDENCE OF OVER-RELIANCE IN GENAI UTILISATION: A METACOGNITIVE PERSPECTIVE

The issue of learners' over-reliance on ChatGPT has recently become a focal point in research. While many studies and scholars have discussed the effects of this dependency, very few have empirically examined what this over-reliance means in concrete terms, particularly concerning its implications for learners' metacognitive processes. Although several previous studies have identified that students tend to develop over-reliance when using ChatGPT for learning (Yan et al., 2024; Lin et al., 2024; Li et al., 2024), the more critical task is intervening and addressing this issue. This requires an operational understanding of the relatively abstract and broad concept of over-reliance from a metacognitive perspective.

However, constructing this understanding cannot be achieved solely through students' self-reports or questionnaires. We need to dive deep into the micro-level aspects of students' learning behaviours. Therefore, in this section, we aim to address this gap by conducting an empirical study that analyses learners' specific learning behaviours to uncover the concrete metacognitive implications of over-reliance on GenAI. By understanding these implications, we can devise targeted interventions to guide learners' learning behaviours, helping them break free from the trap of over-reliance and return to more active and effective learning.

6.3.1 Background: From Cognitive Offloading to Over-Reliance

In the previous section, we found that learners sometimes depend heavily on GenAI during learning tasks, frequently seeking additional support and assistance. This behaviour, where individuals shift part or all of their cognitive load to external tools or resources during the execution of cognitive tasks, is referred to as cognitive offloading (Risko and Gilbert, 2016). The core of cognitive offloading lies in the use of external resources (such as paper, technological devices, or the environment) to alleviate the pressure on working memory and other cognitive systems. This strategy involves various aspects, including the use of external tools and metacognitive factors, such as the perception of task difficulty and beliefs about one's cognitive abilities. From a metacognitive perspective, Dunn and Risko (2016) consider cognitive offloading as a form of metacognitive control, also known as cognitive regulation (Flavell, 1979).

While cognitive offloading can help learners reduce cognitive load and investment, potentially improving their performance in the short term (Risko and Gilbert, 2016), it can also lead to negative cognitive consequences (Dergaa et al., 2024; Shum, 2024). Here, we focus on discussing these consequences from a metacognitive perspective. Reliance on GenAI for immediate feedback and answers may undermine learners' confidence in their cognitive abilities, leading to a decline in metacognitive confidence. As previous research has shown, frequent dependence on external resources like the internet or AI tools to retrieve information can inflate individuals' estimations of their knowledge reserves and reduce their reliance on internal memory and problem-solving abilities (Dunn and Risko, 2016). Moreover, within the framework of metacognitive development, the frequency and extent of cognitive offloading are closely related to individuals' metacognitive evaluations, such as their judgements about task difficulty and their own abilities (Risko and Gilbert, 2016). And the bias toward offloading can be predicted by erroneous metacognitive under-confidence in their memory abilities (Gilbert et al., 2020).

When learners excessively rely on GenAI, the metacognitive evaluation process may be supplanted by external tools, thereby weakening their perception and adjustment of task difficulty and cognitive strategies. This reliance not only limits learners' opportunities for independent problem-solving but also may lead to erroneous assessments of task complexity and their abilities. This viewpoint aligns with previous research findings (Urban et al., 2024). Furthermore, this process is self-reinforcing, as individuals in environments with effective cognitive technologies gradually shift away from relying on their internal capabilities (Risko and Gilbert, 2016). This phenomenon of excessive reliance on GenAI for cognitive offloading has also been observed in the empirical study. A representative study is the paper "Beware of Metacognitive Laziness: Effects of Generative Artificial Intelligence on Learning Motivation, Processes, and Performance" (Fan et al., 2024), and in this chapter, we use this study as a case study to demonstrate relevant empirical study.

6.3.2 Experiment Introduction: Design, Questions and Findings

This study designed a two-stage English reading and writing task that asked participants (non-native English speakers) to complete, which includes stage 1 reading and writing and stage 2 revising. The participants were required to complete an English writing and revising task. In this task, researchers provided participants with reading materials on three topics: AI, differentiated teaching, and scaffolding teaching. The participants were expected to read these materials and write an essay that envisions the future of education in 2035 while integrating the three topics. Alongside these materials, a rubric was provided to introduce the grading criteria of the essay. The participants could refer to this rubric while writing their essays, and researchers would score essays based on this rubric after the experiment. The participants came from a diverse array of disciplines. They were randomly assigned to four experimental groups: one group did not have any support and finished the task by themselves (CN group, 30 participants); one group of learners were supported by ChatGPT 4.0 (AI group, 35 participants); one group of participants were supported by a human expert (HE group, 25 participants). Additionally, researchers conducted the experiment in the lab, requiring participants to use a computer to complete the whole learning task on the platform. In the empirical research, through detailed analysis of learners' learning behaviour data, researchers have similarly encountered the phenomenon of excessive dependence on ChatGPT among learners, which we refer to as metacognitive laziness (Fan et al., 2024). Hence, in the following section of the empirical study, researchers aim to thoroughly investigate the learner metacognitive laziness induced by ChatGPT. This research focuses on the following research questions:

> **RQ1**: Whether learners' interaction behaviours demonstrate noticeable patterns of cognitive offloading or even dependency under ChatGPT?
>
> **RQ2**: What are the characteristics of interactions between students and human teachers?
>
> **RQ3**: How do the effects of ChatGPT support on student behaviour differ from the effects of teacher support?

To address the research questions, researchers gathered learning trace data to capture learners' behaviours throughout the study, covering both the initial stages of reading and writing as well as the later revision phase. This data included navigational logs (e.g., page views), click streams, mouse movements, and keystrokes. Using the trace parser approach, researchers transformed the raw trace data into identifiable learning actions and processes (Saint et al., 2020; Fan et al., 2022a,b). For instance, if a learner opened a task instruction or rubric page and scrolled through it, this was categorised as an "instruction action" according to the action library, and subsequently labelled as part of the "orientation process" in the process library, as such actions suggest the learner was trying to grasp task requirements. It also represents the node of "Orientation" in the process map. Similarly, the "Monitoring" node in the map suggests that the learner was trying to monitor the learning process, and the "Evaluation" node suggests the learner was trying to evaluate his essay. The "Elaboration/Organization" node suggests that the learner was refining the essay. The "Reading" node suggests that the learner was reading the provided material. The "Other" node, which occurs in the HE group and AI group, refers that the learner was communicating with human expert or ChatGPT.

Moreover, the objective was to explore how learners engaged with various learning processes sequentially and over time. To analyse the temporal patterns and process models of learners' interactions with different agents, researchers applied the process mining method (pMineR)

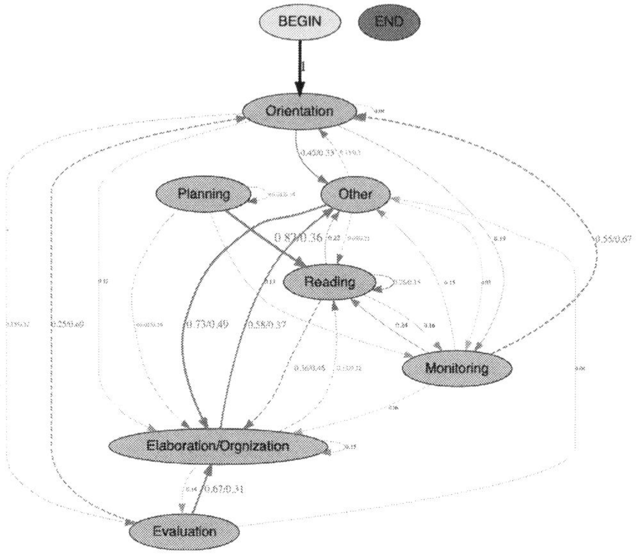

Figure 6.1 Process map of learning process between AI group and CN group.

utilising the First-Order Markov Model (FOMM). By overlaying group-specific process maps provided by pMineR, researchers highlighted key distinctions between groups, marking significant transitions (with probabilities differing by more than 10%) with red and green edges to emphasise important variations in the learning process models.

To answer RQ1, researchers compared the process map of AI group and CN group produced by pMineR. As illustrated in Figure 6.1, the prevalence of red transitions pointing to the "Other" node was reflected in the process map, indicating that the AI group learners frequently returned to interact with ChatGPT after engaging in processes such as orientation, elaboration/organisation, monitoring. Moreover, the probability of transitions from the "Other" node to the "Elaboration/Organisation" node is much higher. It indicates that, after interacting with ChatGPT, participants usually continue editing their essays. However in the CN group, without the support of ChatGPT, participants go back to reading materials to refine their essays. This suggests that participants in the experimental group offloaded part of the burden of revising their essays onto ChatGPT. Learners in the

AI group show an off-loading behaviour and reliance on ChatGPT to finish the learning tasks compared to the CN group. For example, in the post-interview a participant said that he used ChatGPT to polish grammar and language in his essay, and believed that ChatGPT makes the text more natural, improving the clarity and organisation of sentences, and enhancing overall readability. Another participant, under the pressure of time constraints, used ChatGPT to enrich the content of his essay and directly incorporated its suggestions into the final text. In summary, it reveals that learners engage in offloading activities during the revising stage. More specifically, this offloading occurs within a series of metacognitive processes, suggesting that learners may need to offload in these stages to reduce metacognitive load. For instance, they seek revision suggestions and assistance from ChatGPT rather than reading the material. This implies that students tend to opt for a more effortless approach, directly asking ChatGPT for assistance rather than continuing to refine their essays through their own reading and critical thinking. As the process progressed, these offloading behaviours gradually evolved into reliance, driven by the increasing frequency of interactions with ChatGPT.

To answer RQ2, researchers compared the process map of HE group and CN group shown in Figure 6.2. From the process map, researchers can see the same transitions from nodes like the comparison in the AI and the CN group. In the figure, there is also a clear mutual transition between the "Other" nodes and the "Elaboration/Organization" nodes. It seemed that learners in the HE group also have off-loading behaviour. Seeking help from the expert can be also viewed as a way of off-loading but the expert usually would not directly give the answer to learners which makes the obvious differences from ChatGPT. Therefore, in the process map, transitions from the "Other" node to the "Reading" node as well as that from "Evaluation" to "Orientation" are also significant. This suggests that learners were guided by the instructor to engage with the reading material and actively evaluate and reflect on their essays according to the task instructions and rubrics. In contrast, the participants in the control group experienced less guidance. They shifted more frequently between evaluating and orienting themselves, and between reading and editing their essays. Without sufficient direction, students were more inclined to focus on the task instructions rather than deeply engaging with the content. It reveals that after seeking help from

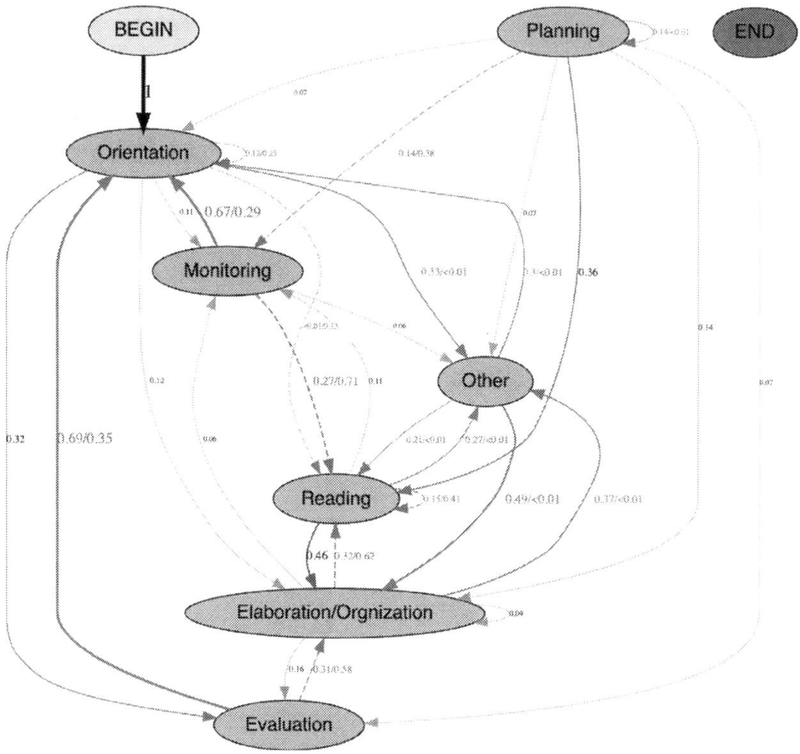

Figure 6.2 Process map of learning process between HE group and CN group.

the teacher, students' metacognitive processes were activated, including planning, monitoring, and evaluation. For example, a participant in the post-interview said that, through the teacher's feedback, he not only resolved the structural issues in his essay but also reflected on the rationale behind the chosen arrangement of the essay's structure. Some learners felt that their ideas conflicted with the teacher's feedback during the revision process. They attempted to reflect on and evaluate the suggestions provided. While some accepted the feedback, others chose to disregard it. From this, researchers can already observe that the AI and HE groups produced different results and impacts compared to the CN group.

Regarding RQ3, researchers will dive deeper into the comparison of learner behaviours between the AI group and the HE group. From the

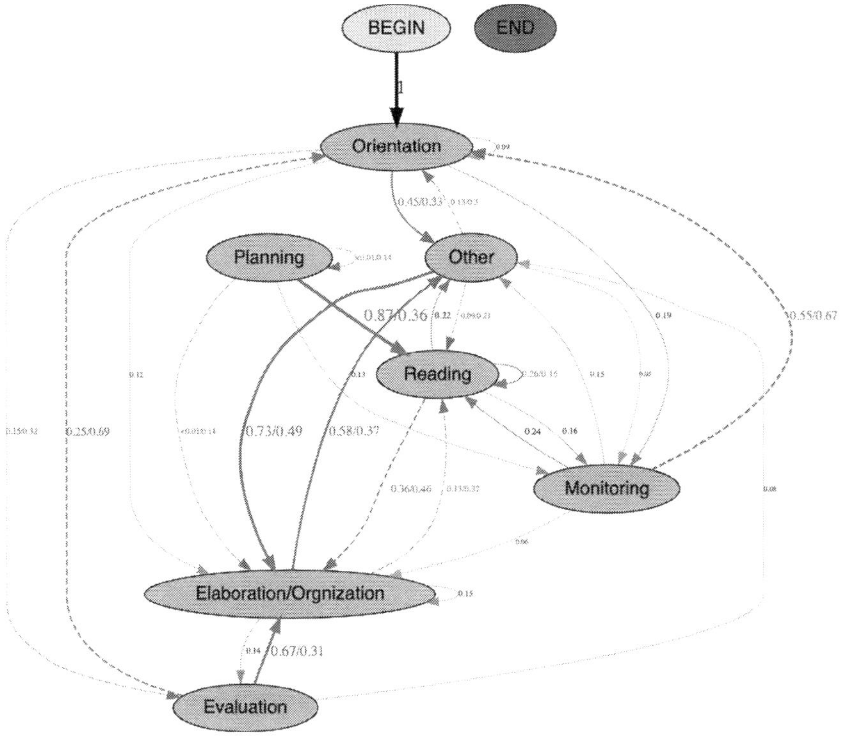

Figure 6.3 Process map of learning process between AI group and HE group.

process map shown in Figure 6.3, notably, there is a significant and continuous loop including nodes of "Orientation", "Other" and "Elaboration/Organization" compared with the HE group. The significant green transitions from nodes such as "Evaluation", "Orientation" and "Reading" demonstrate a more enriched process, particularly emphasising metacognitive processes. From the loop, researchers conclude that ChatGPT became the central component of learners' writing revision tasks during the revising stage in the AI group. In other words, ChatGPT seemed to dominate the revising stage so that learners "voluntarily" became caught in the loop. However, when learners interact with human experts, it enhances the revising with various learning processes such as reading, orientation, monitoring, and evaluation. From the perspective of metacognition, when comparing the AI group to other groups, the process map revealed that the learning processes in the AI group were heavily influenced by interactions with ChatGPT. Unlike the HE group, the AI group demonstrated relatively fewer metacognitive processes, such as evaluation, monitoring, and orientation.

Another difference researchers found lay in the learning strategy. Learners in the AI group adopted more singular and linear learning strategies and learning processes than other groups. The loop in the process map indicated that learners' common process was to consult ChatGPT, evaluate and revise their essays based on the suggestions, and then continue asking for further feedback on their revisions. This cyclical interaction suggested that AI group learners made ChatGPT their primary strategy for refining and assessing their work. Under the influence of ChatGPT, learners' strategies appeared to shift towards an interaction-dominated approach centred on ChatGPT. In contrast, learners in the other groups demonstrated relatively more diverse learning strategies. For example, in the CN group learners demonstrated a more balanced approach by connecting their revising activities to other resources like reading materials (reading) and task instructions (orientation), indicating a more independent and resource-diverse learning process. Similarly, in the HE group, learners demonstrated greater flexibility by incorporating feedback from human experts into their revisions. It facilitated more dynamic connections between revising, reading, and other processes such as task orientation and evaluation.

6.3.3 Discussion: Metacognitive Laziness

In a learning environment where ChatGPT or similar AI tools are easily available, learners may frequently turn to AI for suggestions, feedback, or even the evaluation of their work. Instead of critically reviewing their essays, identifying weaknesses, and thinking through revisions themselves, they rely on GenAI to provide corrections or suggestions (Yan et al., 2024; Lin et al., 2024; Li et al., 2024). The excessive reliance on ChatGPT for offloading tasks and the reduction in metacognitive processes point to a critical issue: potential **metacognitive laziness** (Fan et al., 2024). In the context of human-AI interaction, metacognitive laziness is defined as learners' dependence on AI assistance, offloading metacognitive load, and less effectively associating responsible metacognitive processes with learning tasks. Metacognitive laziness occurs when learners become overly dependent on external tools like GenAI, to manage cognitive tasks that would traditionally require self-regulation, reflection, and critical thinking. This dependency results in the learners avoiding the effortful mental processes needed to plan, monitor, and evaluate their learning, thereby diminishing their engagement in these crucial metacognitive processes (Fan et al., 2024).

The findings align with previous empirical studies and position papers suggesting that GenAI tools like ChatGPT can induce metacognitive laziness (Yan et al., 2024; Lin et al., 2024; Li et al., 2024). The observation that learners become stuck in a loop of interacting with ChatGPT supports the position that over-reliance on GenAI tools may lead to an educational experience characterised by superficiality (Bai et al., 2023; Memarian and Doleck, 2023). As Urban et al. (2024) pointed out learners using AI tools should focus on effective metacognitive cues rather than relying on the perceived ease of AI-assisted problem solving, therefore learners should be trained to recognise and utilise metacognitive strategies that enhance their critical thinking and self-regulation. Moreover, the findings also show that GenAI may take over (offload) regulation from learners like adaptive learning technologies, which might be problematic as GenAI may hinder learners' ability to effectively control and monitor their own learning (Bannert et al., 2017; Molenaar, 2022). There is a strong consensus that learners should develop self-regulated learning skills and maintain metacognition activity (Järvelä et al., 2021). However, the collaboration between learners and AI in future learning and hybrid intelligence is inevitable, so offloading and onloading cognitive and metacognitive load should be a dynamic and developmental process (e.g., see Molenaar (2022)'s HHAIR model), and learners do need scaffolding to learn how to ethically and effectively divide labour with AI and actively develop their metacognitive skills. For more details and findings about this study, see the paper led by Yizhou Fan and Dragan Gasevic "Beware of Metacognitive Laziness: Effects of Generative Artificial Intelligence on Learning Motivation, Processes, and Performance" (Fan et al., 2024).

6.4 IMPLICATION AND FUTURE WORK

A comprehensive review of GenAI in the realm of metacognition in self-regulated learning, along with the empirical study, reveals both the potential of GenAI tools in promoting learners' metacognition and the phenomenon of metacognitive laziness among learners during GenAI usage. GenAI tools like ChatGPT have a multifaceted impact on metacognition and self-regulated learning, influencing learners' planning, monitoring, and reflection processes. In the forethought phase, GenAI supports goal-setting and planning by aiding idea generation and conceptual linking, enhancing motivation without fully replacing the planning process. During the performance phase, learners use GenAI to monitor their progress, critically assess strategies, and refine their learning approaches, especially in time management and help-seeking. In the reflection phase, while GenAI promotes evaluation and self-assessment, there is a risk of over-reliance, where learners may accept AI responses without critical reflection, undermining metacognitive awareness. Therefore, teachers and researchers are required to be cautious and attentive when applying GenAI technology. The empirical case study also found that learners might exhibit "metacognitive laziness" when using ChatGPT tools. In their learning process, learners often centre around ChatGPT, frequently interacting with it to complete learning tasks, but this interaction lacks crucial metacognitive processes. The engagement with ChatGPT does not trigger learners' reflection and self-monitoring, leading their learning strategies into a cycle of "ask ChatGPT - modify based on answers - continue asking", devoid of essential metacognitive processes.

Furthermore, the preceding review reveals that only a limited number of studies have explored the influence of GenAI on learners' metacognition, with even fewer investigations addressing its impact from a behavioural perspective. The long-term impact of GenAI tools on learners' learning remains to be explored. Future research should integrate metacognitive and SRL theories to explore how to design prompts and utilise learning analytics to develop agents that support learners' metacognitive and SRL abilities. The interaction between learners and GenAI tools can also serve as a focal point for research, investigating the unique features and behavioural patterns of the learning process supported by GenAI. Longitudinal studies should be conducted to assess the long-term impact of GenAI on learners' metacognitive and self-regulatory skills. More importantly, future research urgently needs to address this new concept of metacognitive laziness in the age of generative AI. Researchers need to delve into the mechanisms underlying this phenomenon, explore more targeted measurement methods, and uncover the complex mechanisms of cognitive and metacognitive load management in learners. Additionally, future studies should focus on the design of scaffolding and human-machine interaction mechanisms within the learning process to help learners overcome potential metacognitive laziness, thereby promoting better collaboration between learners and AI, and advancing human-machine hybrid intelligence.

6.5 CHAPTER SUMMARY

In this chapter, we explore the influence of GenAI on learners' metacognition within the context of self-regulated learning.

Firstly, we review classical metacognitive theories and widely adopted metacognitive models in the academic field. We briefly outline the positive impacts of GenAI on metacognition and SRL in the age of generative artificial intelligence, along with the ethical issues and challenges it presents. The second section gathers recent empirical studies on GenAI related to metacognition and SRL and synthesises findings from empirical studies on GenAI's impact on metacognitive processes within the self-regulated learning framework. The review reveals how GenAI tools facilitate learners' goal-setting, idea-generation, and strategic planning in the forethought phase. During the performance phase, GenAI fosters self-monitoring, prompting learners to critically assess their progress and adapt their strategies. In the reflection phase, while GenAI can enhance learners' evaluative capacities, promoting deeper self-reflection, there are also concerns regarding learners' tendency to over-rely on GenAI, which may undermine their ability to self-assess and reflect on their learning outcomes accurately. To deepen our understanding of the impact of GenAI technology on learners' learning processes and behaviours, we present a case study in the third section, focusing on learners' learning behaviours and processes supported by ChatGPT. The case study identified a significant phenomenon termed "metacognitive laziness." We define this concept and observe that metacognitive laziness is characterised by a central reliance on ChatGPT and a reduction in metacognitive processes during task completion. The rise of metacognitive laziness poses challenges to effective self-regulated learning in the GenAI age. Our research urges educators to be vigilant in how GenAI tools like ChatGPT are integrated into learning environments. Specifically, they should focus on creating scaffolds that encourage active reflection and critical thinking to mitigate over-reliance on AI. Additionally, future research is essential to investigate how metacognitive laziness can be measured and addressed, including exploring mechanisms for human-AI hybrid regulation. This chapter highlights the need for longitudinal studies to understand better how AI shapes learners' learning behaviours over time, and how AI can evolve from being a tool for automation into a facilitator for deeper learning processes.

Bibliography

Alonso-Mencía, M. E., Alario-Hoyos, C., Maldonado-Mahauad, J., Estévez-Ayres, I., Pérez-Sanagustín, M., and Delgado Kloos, C. (2020). Self-regulated learning in MOOCs: Lessons learned from a literature review. *Educational Review*, *72*(3):319–345.

Bai, L., Liu, X., and Su, J. (2023). ChatGPT: The cognitive effects on learning and memory. *Brain-X*, *1*(3):e30.

Baidoo-Anu, D. and Ansah, L. O. (2023). Education in the era of generative artificial intelligence (AI): Understanding the potential benefits of ChatGPT in promoting teaching and learning. *Journal of AI*, *7*(1):52–62.

Bannert, M., Molenaar, I., Azevedo, R., Järvelä, S., and Gašević, D. (2017). Relevance of learning analytics to measure and support students' learning in adaptive educational technologies. In *Proceedings of the Seventh International Learning Analytics & Knowledge Conference*, Vancouver British Columbia Canada, pp. 568–569.

Chang, D. H., Lin, M. P.-C., Hajian, S., and Wang, Q. Q. (2023). Educational design principles of using AI chatbot that supports self-regulated learning in education: Goal setting, feedback, and personalization. *Sustainability*, *15*(17):12921.

Dahri, N. A., Yahaya, N., Al-Rahmi, W. M., Aldraiweesh, A., Alturki, U., Almutairy, S., Shutaleva, A., and Soomro, R. B. (2024). Extended TAM based acceptance of AI-powered ChatGPT for supporting metacognitive self-regulated learning in education: A mixed-methods study. *Heliyon*, *10*(8):e29317.

Dergaa, I., Ben Saad, H., Glenn, J. M., Amamou, B., Ben Aissa, M., Guelmami, N., Fekih-Romdhane, F., and Chamari, K. (2024). From tools to threats: A reflection on the impact of artificial-intelligence chatbots on cognitive health. *Frontiers in Psychology, 15*: 1259845.

Dunn, T. L. and Risko, E. F. (2016). Toward a metacognitive account of cognitive offloading. *Cognitive Science*, *40*(5):1080–1127.

Fan, Y., Lim, L., Van der Graaf, J., Kilgour, J., Raković, M., Moore, J., Molenaar, I., Bannert, M., and Gašević, D. (2022a). Improving the measurement of self-regulated learning using multi-channel data. *Metacognition and Learning*, *17*(3):1025–1055.

Fan, Y., Tang, L., Le, H., Shen, K., Tan, S., Zhao, Y., Shen, Y., Li, X., and Gašević, D. (2024). Beware of metacognitive laziness: Effects of generative artificial intelligence on learning motivation, processes, and performance. *British Journal of Educational Technology*, 1–42. http://doi.org/10.1111/bjet.13544.

Fan, Y., van der Graaf, J., Lim, L., Raković, M., Singh, S., Kilgour, J., Moore, J., Molenaar, I., Bannert, M., and Gašević, D. (2022b). Towards investigating the validity of measurement of self-regulated learning based on trace data. *Metacognition and Learning*, *17*(3):949–987.

Flavell, J. H. (1979). Metacognition and cognitive monitoring: A new area of cognitive–developmental inquiry. *American Psychologist*, *34*(10):906.

Gilbert, S. J., Bird, A., Carpenter, J. M., Fleming, S. M., Sachdeva, C., and Tsai, P.-C. (2020). Optimal use of reminders: Metacognition, effort, and cognitive offloading. *Journal of Experimental Psychology: General*, *149*(3):501.

Griffith, P. L. and Ruan, J. (2006). What is metacognition and what should be its role in literacy instruction? In Susan E. Israel, Cathy Collins Block, Kathryn L. Bauserman, Kathryn Kinnucan-Welsch, editors, *Metacognition in Literacy Learning*, pp. 25–40. Routledge, New York.

Hadwin, A. F., Järvelä, S., and Miller, M. (2011). Self-regulated, co-regulated, and socially shared regulation of learning. *Handbook of Self-Regulation of Learning and Performance*, *30*:65–84.

Heikkinen, S., Saqr, M., Malmberg, J., and Tedre, M. (2023). Supporting self-regulated learning with learning analytics interventions: A systematic literature review. *Education and Information Technologies*, *28*(3):3059–3088.

Järvelä, S., Malmberg, J., Haataja, E., Sobocinski, M., and Kirschner, P. A. (2021). What multimodal data can tell us about the students' regulation of their learning process? *Learning and Instruction*, *72*:101203.

Kasneci, E., Seßler, K., Küchemann, S., Bannert, M., Dementieva, D., Fischer, F., et al. (2023). ChatGPT for good? On opportunities and challenges of large language models for education. *Learning and Individual Differences*, *103*:102274.

Levine, S., Beck, S. W., Mah, C., Phalen, L., and PIttman, J. (2024). How do students use ChatGPT as a writing support? *Journal of Adolescent & Adult Literacy*. https://doi.org/10.1002/jaal.1373.

Li, S., Ding, G., and Zheng, J. (2024). Examining college students' psychological dynamics in ChatGPT assisted programming. In *Proceedings of the 18th International Conference of the Learning Sciences-ICLS 2024*, pp. 963-966. International Society of the Learning Sciences, Buffalo, New York.

Lin, X., Luterbach, K., Gregory, K. H., and Sconyers, S. E. (2024). A case study investigating the utilization of ChatGPT in online discussions. *Online Learning*, *28*(2):n2.

Lo, C. K. (2023). What is the impact of ChatGPT on education? A rapid review of the literature. *Education Sciences*, *13*(4):410.

Majumdar, R., Prasad, P., and Sane, A. (2024). Mining epistemic actions of programming problem solving with Chat-GPT. In *Proceedings of the 17th International Conference on Educational Data Mining*, Atlanta, Georgia, USA, pp. 628–633.

Memarian, B. and Doleck, T. (2023). ChatGPT in education: Methods, potentials and limitations. *Computers in Human Behavior: Artificial Humans*, *1*(2):100022.

Minh, A. N. (2024). Leveraging ChatGPT for enhancing English writing skills and critical thinking in University Freshmen. *Journal of Knowledge Learning and Science Technology*, *3*(2):51–62. ISSN:2959-6386 (online).

Molenaar, I. (2022). The concept of hybrid human-AI regulation: Exemplifying how to support young learners' self-regulated learning. *Computers and Education: Artificial Intelligence*, *3*:100070.

Montenegro-Rueda, M., Fernández-Cerero, J., Fernández-Batanero, J. M., and López-Meneses, E. (2023). Impact of the implementation of ChatGPT in education: A systematic review. *Computers*, *12*(8):153.

Ng, D. T. K., Tan, C. W., and Leung, J. K. L. (2024). Empowering student self-regulated learning and science education through ChatGPT: A pioneering pilot study. *British Journal of Educational Technology*, *55*(4):1328–1353.

Pintrich, P. R. and De Groot, E. V. (1990). Motivational and self-regulated learning components of classroom academic performance. *Journal of Educational Psychology*, *82*(1):33.

Risko, E. F. and Gilbert, S. J. (2016). Cognitive offloading. *Trends in Cognitive Sciences*, *20*(9):676–688.

Saenz, G. D., Geraci, L., and Tirso, R. (2019). Improving metacognition: A comparison of interventions. *Applied Cognitive Psychology*, *33*(5):918–929.

Saint, J., Whitelock-Wainwright, A., Gašević, D., and Pardo, A. (2020). Trace-SRL: A framework for analysis of microlevel processes of self-regulated learning from trace data. *IEEE Transactions on Learning Technologies*, *13*(4):861–877.

Schraw, G. and Moshman, D. (1995). Metacognitive theories. *Educational Psychology Review*, *7*:351–371.

Šedlbauer, J., Činčera, J., Slavík, M., and Hartlová, A. (2024). Students' reflections on their experience with ChatGPT. *Journal of Computer Assisted Learning*, *40*:1526–1534.

Shum, S. B. (2024). Generative AI for critical analysis: Practical tools, cognitive offloading and human agency. In *LAK Workshops*, Kyoto, Japan, pp. 205–213.

Stojanov, A., Liu, Q., and Koh, J. H. L. (2024). University students' self-reported reliance on ChatGPT for learning: A latent profile analysis. *Computers and Education: Artificial Intelligence*, *6*:100243.

Urban, M., Děchtěrenko, F., Lukavskỳ, J., Hrabalová, V., Svacha, F., Brom, C., and Urban, K. (2024). ChatGPT improves creative problem-solving performance in university students: An experimental study. *Computers & Education*, *215*:105031.

Veenman, M. V., Van Hout-Wolters, B. H., and Afflerbach, P. (2006). Metacognition and learning: Conceptual and methodological considerations. *Metacognition and Learning*, *1*:3–14.

Winne, P. H. (1996). A metacognitive view of individual differences in self-regulated learning. *Learning and Individual Differences*, *8*(4):327–353.

Winne, P. H. (2011). A cognitive and metacognitive analysis of self-regulated learning: Faculty of education, Simon Fraser University, Burnaby, Canada. In Dale H. Schunk, Barry Zimmerman, editors, *Handbook of Self-Regulation of Learning and Performance*, pp. 29–46. Routledge, New York.

Winne, P. H. and Azevedo, R. (2022). Metacognition and self-regulated learning. In Morris, A. S. and Smith, J. M., editors, *Cambridge Handbooks in Psychology*, pp. 93–113. Cambridge University Press, Cambridge.

Winne, P. H. and Hadwin, A. F. (1998). Studying as self-regulated engagement in learning. In Hacker, D. J., Dunlosky, J., and Graesser, A. C. L., editors, *Metacognition in Educational Theory and Practice*, pp. 277–304. Routledge, London, UK.

Wu, T.-T., Lee, H.-Y., Li, P.-H., Huang, C.-N., and Huang, Y.-M. (2024). Promoting self-regulation progress and knowledge construction in blended learning via ChatGPT-based learning AID. *Journal of Educational Computing Research*, *61*(8):3–31.

Yan, W., Nakajima, T., and Sawada, R. (2024). Benefits and challenges of collaboration between students and conversational generative artificial intelligence in programming learning: An empirical case study. *Education Sciences*, *14*(4):433.

Yıldız, T. A. (2023). The impact of ChatGPT on language learners' motivation. *Journal of Teacher Education and Lifelong Learning*, *5*(2):582–597.

Zimmerman, B. J. (2000). Attaining self-regulation: A social cognitive perspective. In Monique Boekaerts, Paul R. Pintrich and Moshe Zeidner, editors, *Handbook of Self-Regulation*, pp. 13–39. Academic Press, Cambridge, MA.

Zimmerman, B. J. (2002). Becoming a self-regulated learner: An overview. *Theory into Practice*, *41*(2):64–70.

Zimmerman, B. J. (2008). Investigating self-regulation and motivation: Historical background, methodological developments, and future prospects. *American Educational Research Journal*, *45*(1):166–183.

Zimmerman, B. J. and Moylan, A. R. (2009). Self-regulation: Where metacognition and motivation intersect. In Hacker, D. J., Dunlosky, J., and Graesser, A. C., editors, *Handbook of Metacognition in Education*, pp. 299–315. Routledge, London, UK.

CHAPTER 7

Enhance Assessing Students' Learning with GenAI: Challenges, Opportunities and Future Directions

Luzhen Tang, Kejie Shen, and Yizhou Fan

ASSESSMENT, AS A CRUCIAL component of the educational process, guiding teachers in adjusting their teaching methods to meet students' learning needs, as well as aiding students in understanding their progress, thereby fostering self-reflection and the adjustment of learning strategies. Computer Assisted/Aided Assessment (CAA) enhances the efficiency and quality of learning assessment. The emergence of generative artificial intelligence (GenAI), a forefront technology, has further propelled advancements in CAA. ChatGPT, as an exemplar of GenAI, is able to perform several traditional assessments through dialogue, such as grading students' work and providing feedback based on rubrics. Furthermore, ChatGPT is also used to assess complex skills that are difficult to quantify in standard rubrics, such as divergent thinking, programming abilities, and experimental operations. However, GenAI introduces significant challenges to assessment, such as academic

 DOI: 10.4324/9781003632146-7

integrity, ethical hazards, complex problem understanding, higher-order skills assessment, and algorithm stability. Therefore, this chapter will review 39 recent empirical studies on GenAI in learning assessment and introduce our two empirical studies on how GenAI can be utilised in the learning product and process. We found that most studies focus on formative and summative assessment, research contents including analysing the quality of GenAI's assessments, validating the consistency of GenAI's scoring and feedback, generating innovative assessment methods and questions, leveraging existing assessment frameworks, and modifying models to enhance assessment quality. Our studies also provide evidence for the efficacy of GenAI in assessing students' learning, particularly highlighting ChatGPT's capabilities in grading essay and providing feedback, as well as in enhancing learners' self-assessment competencies. Building on these findings, we posit that GenAI has significant potential to promote the development of stealth and generative assessments, though the cultivation of robust human-computer relationships remains indispensable.

7.1 LEARNING ASSESSING: DEFINITION, CLASSIFICATION AND DEVELOPMENT

A concise yet comprehensive definition of learning assessment states: "To assess is to make judgements about students' work, inferring from this what they have the capacity to do in the assessed domain, and thus what they know, value, or are capable of doing" (Joughin, 2008, p.16). Assessment plays a crucial role in learning, enabling teachers to gauge the extent of students' understanding of subject matter and to make teaching decisions accordingly (Brookhart, 2011; Yorke, 2003). Moreover, through assessment, students can enhance their self-awareness, develop personal learning paths by identifying their strengths and weaknesses, and engage in effective collaboration with peers (Broadfoot and Black, 2004; Black and Wiliam, 1998).

Assessment can be categorised into three distinct types based on its stages and objectives: Diagnostic Assessment, Formative Assessment, and Summative Assessment (Bloom et al., 1971; Spolsky et al., 2008; Chufama and Sithole, 2021; Scaife and Wellington, 2010). **Diagnostic Assessment** assists students in determining their initial proficiency or knowledge in a particular subject, aiming to rectify any misunderstandings before learning is given (Boud, 2012). **Formative assessment** offers continuous feedback and insights during the educational process, while learning is taking place (Brown and Knight, 2012). **Summative assessment** provides information and feedback to summarise the entire educational process, it is usually conducted after learning has been completed or must be carried out at the end of the course (Shepard, 2000). Diagnostic assessments are typically conducted through pre-tests and brief interviews; while formative Assessment are commonly based on classroom observations, homework exercises, and reflective journals; summative assessment, on the other hand, often rely on final examinations, term papers, projects (Chufama and Sithole, 2021).

Both formative and summative assessment occur after formal learning has begun, and Cizek (2010) delineated specific criteria in order to further differentiate them. Summative assessment is recognised by two main features: (1) It is conducted after a certain teaching stage, for example, at the end of a unit, semester, or school year; (2) Its main purpose is to collect the performance of students. Therefore, the main goal of summative assessment is to grasp current achievements in order to use them for decision-making, grading, rewards and punishments, issuing certificates, and categorising the student into grades such as good, better, best (Cizek, 2010). Conversely, Formative Assessment focus more on individual diagnosis, providing valuable feedback, specifically meeting two criteria: (1) It is conducted during teaching or a certain teaching stage; (2) Its main purpose is to identify students' strengths and weaknesses, to provide teachers with insights for subsequent teaching, to assist students in refining their learning strategies and fostering self-assessment and self-learning ability (Cizek, 2010). Among these three types of assessment, formative assessment has been notably emphasised and debated (Bennett, 2011). For example, formative assessment assessors are more diverse than the other two types, formative assessment not only requires teachers to serve as assessors but also emphasises students to actively engage in generating and utilising feedback (e.g. self-assessment and peer-assessment) (Wanner and Palmer, 2018). Through the act of giving and receiving feedback, students are able to generate deeper insights into the expectations of assessments and improve the quality of their work (Nicol and Macfarlane-Dick, 2006; Orsmond et al., 2004; Wanner and Palmer, 2018).

Applying the above three assessments presents significant challenges. One of the main challenges is that the quality of any specific assessment is usually determined by standards of reliability and validity (Broadfoot and Black, 2004). Reliable and valid assessments require continuous information collection and feedback quality improvement during the teaching process, which imposes a heavy workload on teachers (Yorke, 2003; Black and Wiliam, 2018). The rapid advancement of information technology and the internet have led to the emergence of practical applications for **Computer Assisted/Aided Assessment (CAA)**. CAA is capable of automatically assessing both objective multiple-choice questions (Blayney and Freeman, 2004) and subjective questions (e.g. long essays and short free texts) (Roy et al., 2015; Pérez-Marín et al., 2009) in the test. Furthermore, CAA is able to record and analyse students' interactions to provide a richer understanding of learning (Conole and Warburton, 2005), which helps capture more learning process's details that surpass the limitations of paper-based assessments, ultimately enhancing assessment. CAA is also used in programming education, and various automated assessment techniques including dynamic, static, and hybrid approaches are being consistently developed and explored (Ullah et al., 2018; Bey et al., 2018). These automated assessment techniques or systems enhance grading consistency and provide timely feedback, enabling teachers to redirect their attention from grading towards other instructional activities (Hahn et al., 2021). Furthermore, automated assessment fosters students' self-regulated learning (Ouyang et al., 2022). For instance, automated peer feedback within a learning platform is able to provide learners with a benchmark for comparison, engender learners' self-reflection and self-explanation of their actions, and ultimately foster the development of self-assessment and adjust the learning strategies (Persico et al., 2020; Gross and Pinkwart, 2015).

The utilisation of artificial intelligence (AI) in education has led to significant advancements in the technical efficiency, speed, and sophistication of automated assessment. AI-based assessments are predominantly established in summative assessment, such as Automated Essay Scoring (AES) and Computerised Adaptive Testing (CAT), while formative assessment is expected to be enhanced by the application of machine learning based on big data and learning analytics (Gardner et al., 2021). However, the ethical issues of artificial intelligence in educational applications are still being discussed, especially problems related to assessment, such as discrimination, bias, and lack of transparency (Pedró et al., 2019). For example, biased training datasets may result in prejudiced algorithmic outputs, consequently, algorithms used in automated assessments could propagate injustice, adversely affecting students' final grades and future professional opportunities (Akgun and Greenhow, 2022; Nguyen et al., 2023a). Moreover, automated assessment systems, such as AES, face several significant challenges: although these systems eliminate the subjective biases inherent in human assessments, they lack the cognitive awareness and contextual understanding of a human assessor; students may try to 'trick' the computer to obtain high scores; these systems struggle to assess higher-order human capabilities, such as creativity and practical application (Hussein et al., 2019).

Recently, the emergence of Generative Artificial Intelligence (GenAI) has provided both new opportunities and challenges for learning assessment (Mao et al., 2024). GenAI utilises sophisticated algorithms and expansive datasets to generate novel content, significantly extending beyond the capabilities of conventional software in data processing and analysis. Research has examined the reliability and accuracy of ChatGPT as an automated essay scoring tool, and the results suggest that ChatGPT reduces the time required for scoring, ensures consistency in grading, and can provide timely feedback on student performance and writing skills (Mizumoto and Eguchi, 2023). However, the use of GenAI in assessment also faces ethical and moral issues. Moreover, GenAI may involve issues related to content plagiarism and academic integrity (Chan and Hu, 2023). The application of technologies like ChatGPT might compromise the validity of traditional assessment methods, particularly those concerning written tasks, therefore, teachers need to consider innovative forms of assessment, especially those that encourage creativity and require critical thinking (Zhai, 2022). The National Education Technology Plan (NETP) discussed how technology can lead to improved assessments along seven dimensions, including enabling enhanced question types, measuring complex competencies, providing real-time feedback, increasing accessibility, adapting to learner ability and knowledge, embedded in the learning process, and assessing for ongoing learning (Cardona et al., 2023). The emergence of GenAI as a new technology is worth considering how it should be applied in assessments.

Though GenAI has been in use for a while, there is currently no review of empirical studies discussing the application of generative artificial intelligence in assessment. Exploring the application of GenAI in learning assessment allows us to comprehensively analyse the current landscape of assessments, identify existing research gaps, and address the potential challenges and issues that future assessments may encounter. Therefore, the second section of this chapter aims to collect empirical research and practical examples to address the following questions: (1) How can GenAI contribute to existing assessments? (2) What novel assessment opportunities can be generated by GenAI? (3) What are the assessment challenges posed by GenAI? Furthermore, in the third section, we intend to illustrate the application of ChatGPT in conducting assessments through two empirical studies. The first study involves directly employing ChatGPT to grade students' essays, while the second investigates ChatGPT's impact on facilitating students' self-assessment practices.

7.2 REVIEW OF APPLYING GENAI IN LEARNING ASSESSMENT

We conducted a literature search in the Google Scholar database, employing search terms such as 'learning assessment, ChatGPT, content, quality, evaluation, accuracy, consistency, teacher, and Generative artificial intelligence' to swiftly identify empirical studies relevant to the theme of learning assessment. This process was complemented by argumentative research introducing the capabilities of generative artificial intelligence (GenAI). We can divide the past research into two parts from the perspective of summative assessment and formative assessment. The specific research directions of these studies are shown in Table 7.1.

Summative assessment evaluates student learning outcomes over a period through exams or projects, with GenAI focusing on automated grading and question generation. Formative assessment emphasises persistent, multidimensional evaluations, primarily providing explanatory feedback to adjust learning strategies. GenAI explores its potential in assessing open-ended textual responses and logic-based coding, aiming to deliver high-quality formative feedback that enhances understanding of learning tasks. Our literature review included 24 studies on formative assessment and 15 on summative assessment.

TABLE 7.1 Research about GenAI in Learning Assessment

Assessment Type	Specific Research Content	Research List
Summative assessment	Automatic scoring quality	Latif and Zhai (2024), Lu et al. (2024), Mansour et al. (2024), Yancey et al. (2023), Liu et al. (2023), and Hou and Ji (2023)
	Assessment and feedback consistency	Kung et al. (2023) and Yaneva et al. (2023)
	Generate assessment methods and problems	Cheung et al. (2023)
	Ability to pass existing assessment systems	Keiper et al. (2023), (Clark, 2023), (Zhu et al., 2023), and (Ali et al., 2023)
	Modify the GenAI model to improve the assessment quality	Organisciak et al. (2023) and Liu et al. (2023)
Formative assessment	Analysis and evaluation quality (e.g., with human teachers' assessment)	Jukiewicz (2024), Hutt et al. (2024), Wang et al. (2024), Pinto et al. (2023), Nguyen et al. (2023b), Nimpattanavong et al. (2023), Téllez et al. (2024), Revell et al. (2023), and Busch and Hausvik (2023)
	Assessment and feedback consistency	Luo et al. (2023), Hackl et al. (2023), Jang and Lukasiewicz (2023), Ahmad et al. (2023), and Zuccon et al. (2023)
	Generate assessments methods and problems	Kwan (2023), Salinas-Navarro et al. (2024), and Cingillioglu (2023)
	Ability to pass existing assessment systems	Friederichs et al. (2023), Dunder et al. (2023), Nikolic et al. (2023), Popovici (2023), and Revell et al. (2023)
	Modify the GenAI model to improve the assessment quality	Sovrano et al. (2023)

We extracted specific content from each study to identify common themes in research. The research directions are categorised into five aspects: analysing the quality of GenAI's assessments, validating the consistency of GenAI scoring and feedback, generating assessment methods and questions, leveraging existing assessment frameworks, and modifying models to improve assessment quality. In both formative and summative assessment, the majority of studies focused on the quality of GenAI assessments, examining their ability to understand assessment tasks, criteria, and the correctness of student responses. Specifically, six studies on summative assessment investigated GenAI's accuracy in automated grading, and ten studies on formative assessment examined the quality of GenAI-generated formative feedback texts, particularly comparing them to human-provided feedback in terms of textual and substantive alignment.

In learning assessment, the consistency of scoring and feedback is a fundamental precondition for ensuring quality, fairness, and objectivity. Despite GenAI's powerful generative capabilities, the vast and diverse training data lead to inconsistent responses to the same question, influenced by different contexts and knowledge learned from the data. Consequently, seven studies have specifically focused on this issue of consistency in GenAI's performance across multiple assessments of the same task, exploring whether GenAI maintains consistency in automated grading and feedback provision. Additionally, the assessment method and related questions form another critical foundation for the effectiveness of learning assessments, with 4 researchers conducting empirical studies on using GenAI to generate assessment questions and innovate assessment methods.

Finally, our review includes nine studies investigating whether GenAI operates within existing assessment systems. The inclusion of these studies is because of the sub-research questions in these studies related to assisted learning assessment. More importantly, these studies reflect to some extent whether GenAI understands existing assessment frameworks, revealing potential issues that arise in learning assessment which highlights the risks and challenges associated with applying GenAI in this context. Notably, three studies have responded to some of these challenges, attempting to modify the models and improve the assessment quality of GenAI. Through all these 39 studies, we can make an overview of the attempts of GenAI in learning assessment and what are the opportunities, shortcomings, and challenges for applications.

7.2.1 Automating Traditional Summative Assessment with GenAI

The main purpose of summative assessment is to assess the student's learning outcomes at the end of the learning period. This form of assessment aims to quantify a student's mastery of the course objectives, whether through an exam, essay or project. A score or rating from a summative assessment is often used to determine a student's grade and is sometimes used to meet standardised test requirements. The application of GenAI in automated scoring has been proven. GenAI is able to automate the summative assessment methods of scoring in traditional learning, reduce the teacher's workload while generating learner insights and promote classroom innovation (Latif and Zhai, 2024). Several studies have shown that GenAI technology performs well through various professional knowledge tests, indicating its ability to comprehend professional expertise. For example, GenAI correctly answered two-thirds of all multiple choice questions (MCQs) at the German state licensing exam level in Progress Test Medicine (Friederichs et al., 2023). In physical education, GenAI provides high-quality, complete, and accurate short-answer responses (Keiper et al., 2023). In the context of software testing, GenAI is capable of answering 77.5% of the questions in a popular software testing curriculum, and it provides correct or partially correct answers in 55.6% of cases out of these questions (Jalil et al., 2023). Similarly, GenAI excellently identifies concepts containing multiple chemical symbols in high school chemistry's closed questions (Clark, 2023). Since these tests or questionnaires mentioned above are commonly used in summative assessment across different disciplines, GenAI's proficiency in accurately responding to their contents underscores its foundational capability to perform automated scoring tasks effectively.

In addition to measuring GenAI's ability to pass tests in different disciplines, some studies have applied GenAI to the actual scoring of learner responses. Comparing the consistency of automatic scoring by GenAI with teacher scoring, showing the effectiveness of this technology in automatically scoring and highlighting its prospects as an educational tool (Organisciak et al., 2023; Zhou et al., 2023; Lu et al., 2024). Organisciak et al. (2023)'s study based on a large dataset constructed from nine previous studies shows that automatic scoring by GenAI is highly correlated with human scorers. Jukiewicz (2024) compared the differences between teachers and the ChatGPT system in assessing

Python course assignments, and the results showed that although the scores given by teachers were higher than those by ChatGPT, there was a strong positive correlation between the two scores, proving consistency in scoring. Additionally, Mansour et al. (2024)'s study compared the capabilities of different GenAI models (ChatGPT and Llama) in comprehensively assessing written essays, finding that their performance in predicting student essay scores greatly depended on the given prompts and task type. The automated scoring research above assesses learners' performance in open-ended responses such as writing and coding based on grading rubrics. The research above consistently indicates that GenAI's scoring is similar to that of human teachers, demonstrating the ability to perform basic automated grading tasks competently. However, Some studies have reported shortcomings of GenAI in automating scoring tasks. For example, GenAI sometimes identifies errors in a student's solution where there is no reality. GenAI does not always return identical grades (Jukiewicz, 2024). Some research suggests we still need to prompt engineering and fine-tune AI to improve auto-scoring performance (Yancey et al., 2023). Combining GenAI with domain-specific corpora and fine-tuning based on context makes it possible to achieve more precise, fair, and domain-adapted automated scoring, the model's reliability and credibility can be further improved (Liu et al., 2023). Overall, GenAI complement traditional teacher scoring methods and benefits from time efficiency and elimination of human subjectivity bias in grading, but teachers still need to carefully verify potential risks in actual applications.

Case Study of GenAI in Automatic Scoring Application in Mathematical Thinking in Science

In order to address the challenges in learning assessment, improve scoring efficiency and reduce the burden of manual grading, Latif and Zhai (2024)'s research focuses on the ability of GenAI to score learners' answers automatically. The study involved a variety of assessment tasks, including multi-label and multi-class tasks, which required students to use scientific knowledge and mathematical reasoning to solve scientific problems. PASTA provides two multi-label assessment tasks aimed at evaluating middle school students' abilities to explain scientific phenomena using multi-label knowledge. The Mathematical Thinking in Science(MTS) project offers four multi-category assessment tasks requiring students to solve scientific problems using scientific knowledge and mathematical reasoning. Latif and Zhai (2024) underscores that Large language models such as BERT show remarkable performance in automatic scoring due to their bi-directional context understanding, especially in the field of written response scoring in science education, but directly using pre-trained models is insufficient. This is because the language used by students differs from that of trained in GenAI, which is found in journals or Wikipedia, necessitating specific contextual information for accurate grading. GenAI such as GPT-3.5, while excellent at language understanding, often lacks a deep understanding of a specific domain. Fine-tuning helps models better understand and adapt to domain-specific terms, concepts, and contexts. Therefore, the article proposes fine-tuning domain-specific models to improve the automatic scoring accuracy of models. ChatGPT's fine-tuning and validation work utilised a diverse middle school student responses dataset and expert grading from the PASTA and MTS projects. Results showed that GPT-3.5 significantly improved automatic scoring accuracy by 9.1% across six tasks compared to a model without fine-tuning, with GPT-3.5's scoring accuracy significantly surpassing BERT's for multi-label and multi-category tasks. The study also discussed the applications of automatic scoring in education, including using machine learning algorithms to provide timely information for teachers to make instructional decisions and offering personalised feedback to guide students' self-regulated learning. Lastly, the article suggests future research directions, including implementing automatic scoring in real classroom environments and examining experimental designs to check student learning outcomes. It also addresses ethical dilemmas and related issues of integrating generative AI into learning assessment. In summary, the assessment problem mainly relates to multi-label and multi-class assessment tasks in science education in this study. In situations where students are required to demonstrate an understanding of complex concepts, multi-label and multi-class tasks provide rich information to help assess students' cognition and understanding of multiple dimensions. Whereas this type of summative assessment is common in learning assessment, The results of this study lead us to believe that GenAI will be able to automate the analysis of learners' responses and make scorings consistent with those of human teachers. In addition, educators have to fine-tune the model to improve the large model and the accuracy of automatic scoring. The fine-tuning in this study is completed based on the official API, which means that while some programming may be required to prepare data and set fine-tuning parameters, the fine-tuning method given by this research is instructive for educators.

7.2.2 New Assessment Opportunities with GenAI

Automatic scoring is one of the core manifestations of summative assessment, based on a series of established standards to assess learners' learning outcomes, measuring students' progress. In contrast, formative assessment is defined as the process of continuous exchange of information and feedback between learners and teachers. It aims to improve learners' learning efficiency by adjusting teaching methods and learning activities through continuous communication (Dixson and Worrell, 2016). GenAI usually requires a deep understanding of the internal patterns and structure of data, making them better at understanding and reasoning. The improvement of technology has made GenAI provide opportunities for the application of formative assessment at different cognitive levels, such as know-what, know-how and show-how. Most importantly, the key goal of formative assessment is to make students more aware of the gap between the existing learning outcomes and learning objectives so they can learn from their mistakes and continuously improve their abilities. GenAI has the ability to generate explanatory feedback, which helps teachers and learners better understand why their feedback is effective or not effective enough, thus providing them with directions for learning improvement (Hutt et al., 2024). For example, in Hutt et al. (2024)'s study, GenAI was used to provide learners with real-time scaffolding when they write feedback comments. Students receiving peer feedback categorised as "1 - least robust" may be encouraged to increase the length of annotations or include more adjectives.

In fields such as programming and engineering, concepts are often highly abstract and technical, which creates quite a few challenges for learners. Formative assessment enables learners to immediately know what aspects they need to improve, how to adjust their learning strategies, promote an in-depth understanding of complex concepts and achieve learning goals in these subjects. It has been found that GenAI has demonstrated capabilities in fixing programming errors and composing complex texts (Dunder et al., 2023). GenAI effectively demonstrates its application potential in critical thinking and problem-solving skills through online quizzes and programming tasks (Nikolic et al., 2023; Popovici, 2023). On the other hand, formative assessment usually focuses more on open-ended questions. GenAI shows strong language processing capabilities in open-ended questions, performing better when generating multiple answers to the same question (Zhu et al., 2023). Especially in the field of writing, GenAI not only understands and evaluates the complexity of academic articles but has also been proven to support teachers in assessing and providing feedback on student writing, improving the efficiency and quality of assessments (Lu et al., 2024). Research shows that the feedback provided by ChatGPT is often more comprehensive and balanced than teachers, especially in terms of content, organisation, and language (Dai et al., 2023). In this way, ChatGPT provides effective support and feedback for learning tasks involving advanced cognitive skills, such as writing and engineering design, thereby promoting learners' deep learning and capability development.

In continuation of its multifaceted contributions to learning assessment, GenAI is seen as an important tool for providing real-time feedback, solving problems, and assisting learners (Wang et al., 2024). By adopting the adaptive feedback system of GenAI, learners are able to receive formative, instantaneous, and personalised support, significantly improving their engagement and learning outcomes (Yang et al., 2022). Research shows that GenAI can align closely with teachers' assessments and sometimes provide more detailed, fluent, and coherent feedback than human teachers. For example, Pinto et al. (2023)'s study found that chatGPT is capable of identifying semantic details in students' responses and detected that while the student had used the correct term, the understanding of the term in the answer was incorrect. GenAI not only gives a score but also provides an explanation for the score. This interpretive feedback helps learners understand why GenAI assessment is effective or ineffective enough (Hutt et al., 2024). Especially in providing real-time feedback on learners' learning performance, helping learners adjust their learning strategies on time, and promoting their understanding and growth (Pearce and Chiavaroli, 2023). This precise feedback mechanism helps learners better understand and grasp the learning content and improves their trust in the underlying algorithms and their control over their learning progress. Therefore, GenAI exhibits its value in the context of formative assessment.

In addition to assessing learners based on established rubrics, GenAI designs preliminary assessment schemes according to teaching objectives and content. Kwan (2023)'s study shows that ChatGPT is competent for the generation of a learning assessment scheme task. The assessment script generated by ChatGPT has many application-oriented questions but few analysis-based questions and no evaluation-based questions at all, as per Bloom's Taxonomy. Teachers and learners use GenAI to generate multiple-choice questions, short-answer questions, and case study drafts that can be edited and improved later (Gonsalves, 2023). For example, Cheung et al. (2023) study allowed ChatGPT to generate 50 multiple-choice questions from undergraduate medical textbooks. Results showed that ChatGPT takes far less time to create questions than human teachers, minimal use of negative stem other factors, and there was no significant difference in question quality or other areas between drafted questions. Research has proven ChatGPT's effectiveness in identifying common issues with question creation by analysing 200 student-generated questions across different subjects (Moore et al., 2023). This research suggests that we need to embed some rule-based methods in GenAI to accurately and efficiently evaluate the quality of multiple-choice questions from multiple domains. Through the above cases, we believe that GenAI aids teachers in designing tests and promotes in-depth reflection on the assessment design itself. Technological advances in generative artificial intelligence prompt teachers to shift the focus from mere knowledge testing to cultivating higher-order capabilities such as learners' creativity and critical thinking (Organisciak et al., 2023).

By integrating GenAI technology, the nature of assessments can become more collaborative, personalised, scalable, and interactive, thus effectively encouraging knowledge creation (Salinas-Navarro et al., 2024). Innovative formative assessment activities, such as educational games, require students to simulate real-world tests of ability, promote student engagement and critical thinking, and provide significant learning experiences (Nguyen et al., 2023b). Nimpattanavong et al. (2023)'s study proposed a new method for integrating ChatGPT in fighting game commentary generation tasks. The results show that different prompts significantly affect the generated comments, which suggests that GenAI shows versatility in generating fighting game commentary. GenAI allows educators to create personalised and interactive formative assessment through assisted writing code or other ways (Yang et al., 2024). For example, Salinas-Navarro et al. (2024) summarised the use of GenAI tools to facilitate authentic assessment considering constructive alignment in different learning stages, like the use of ChatGPT to create self-assessment tools that help students track their progress and identify areas where they need to improve. Embedding AI in various assessment activities that provide learners with simulated real-life learning and assessment scenarios (Pearce and Chiavaroli, 2023). This approach provides real-time feedback to learners, dynamically assessing their performance. AI-assisted scenario creation optimises the assessment process, providing insights into learner performance and learning outcomes (Rajendran and Santhanam, 2024).

In summary, advancements in GenAI enable educators to continue adopting and optimising traditional learning assessment schemes, simplify the assessment process, increase student engagement, and ultimately improve learning outcomes in the educational environment.

Case Study of GenAI in Formative Assessment Application in History Essays Written

In recent years, advancements in artificial intelligence technology have made automated writing evaluation (AWE) feasible, which helps alleviate the burden on teachers to provide frequent feedback to a large number of students. Steiss et al. (2024)'s study evaluated the quality of formative feedback on history classroom essays written by middle school students, generated by both human teachers and ChatGPT, across five dimensions: whether the feedback was standards-based, whether it provided clear directions for improvement, accuracy, whether it prioritised important features of writing, and whether it adopted a supportive tone. To assess these aspects, Steiss et al. (2024) developed an inductive coding framework and trained researchers to code feedback generated by humans and ChatGPT. After coding, the study specifically compared the feedback quality of ChatGPT and human teachers across the entire sample and within essays of different quality levels, as well as between feedback for native English speakers and non-native English speakers. The results showed that teachers provided higher-quality feedback in all categories except standards-based feedback. The quality of feedback for both teachers and AI did not vary with the language status of the student (Steiss et al., 2024). While well-trained human evaluators provided higher quality feedback than ChatGPT, the convenience and overall quality of ChatGPT-generated feedback make generative AI suitable in contexts such as formative drafts or where well-trained evaluators are lacking (Steiss et al., 2024). Additionally, the article explored how tools like ChatGPT could be utilised to enhance writing instruction, including the need for educators and learners to use these tools critically and reflectively, improving output quality through iterative questioning and requests to ChatGPT. In summary, this study compared the quality of formative feedback from GenAI and human teachers on writing based on certain assessment rubrics. The Researchers used a deductive framework to assess the quality of feedback and conducted joint coding practices, which let the score for each feedback ensure consistency. And then, descriptive statistics and analysis of variance were used to answer the research questions. The paradigm of this research method is similar to our study. While this study focuses on the quality of formative feedback generated on text features, ours focuses more on the quality of feedback related to writing content. In addition, the study also draws some important conclusions, like GenAI feedback, which especially lacks clarity in the case of low-quality essays and may not be sufficient in a supportive tone. GenAI may fail to identify a student's mistakes or give suggestions that are inconsistent with the student's actual level of writing, or it may not identify the next steps for improving a high-quality paper. These conclusions also inspire us to dig deeper into the textual features of GenAI's feedback in the formative assessment of writing, such as emotional state and syntactic structure.

7.2.3 Assessment Challenges Posed by GenAI

GenAI is presenting noteworthy challenges to academic integrity, plagiarism, and loyalty in learning assessment. Tools such as ChatGPT are causing educators to feel concerned about the authenticity and originality of student assignments (Bin-Nashwan et al., 2023). Assessment tasks, like essays or short responses, are at risk of plagiarism from AI-generated content. This is especially true for open-ended writing tasks where educators worry students may use AI tools to generate answers. Revell et al. (2023) have raised concerns regarding using AI-generated content in tasks requiring complex scenarios and critical thinking. For example, Busch and Hausvik (2023)'s study found that ChatGPT can generate generally good-quality answers that may pass as human-written text by examiners in an actual Information System exam. The prevalence of AI-generated texts highlights the importance of detecting these contents to ensure academic honesty (Revell et al., 2023). Educators are currently facing the challenge of differentiating between AI-generated content and genuine student assignments in order to effectively combat plagiarism. This highlights the urgent need to develop new tools and robust strategies to identify AI-generated content and address academic integrity issues (Cingillioglu, 2023). Some tools and techniques have already emerged that can help identify AI-generated content, such as copyleaks, Turnitin, metadata analysis, and stylometric analysis. However, the limitations of these methods should also be acknowledged, including the possibility of manipulated metadata and the reliance on machine learning algorithms, and efforts should be made to improve and develop more reliable detection methods (Uzun, 2023).

GenAI has emphasised its feedback generation capability, which can summarise student performance smoothly and provide more comprehensive feedback than human teachers (Pinto et al., 2023; Dai et al., 2023). However, research has revealed its limitations, such as favouring lexically similar answers, reasoning errors, and a lack of understanding of instructions (Luo et al., 2023). In specific professional fields, GenAI may not have sufficient capability to understand complex issues' deep logic and requirements (Kwan, 2023). The performance of ChatGPT fails in reasoning, proofs, and model construction in mathematical problems (Téllez et al., 2024). ChatGPT independently solved 19 out of 127 programming tasks generated and assessed by Kattis and was found to encounter difficulties with more complex programming tasks because of lacking effective debugging and error correction mechanisms compared to humans (Dunder et al., 2023). Additionally, GenAI accuracy in specific professional fields is limited since the inability to access relevant databases hinders GenAI's ability to provide accurate and reliable information. For example, ChatGPT showed that only half the answers were correct based on contextual context clues alone in neurosurgery (Ali et al., 2023). Therefore, it is important to carefully assess the accuracy and applicability of GenAI in specific complex disciplines. Fine-tuning is a specific strategy in AI training, which refers to further training on an already trained model to adapt to a new task or data set to improve the understanding of AI in the professional field. Appropriate fine-tuning is still required when applying GenAI to specialised areas that require complex logical thinking or where generative AI lacks understanding (Yancey et al., 2023).

Assessment consistency and stability are other major challenges when using GenAI in learning assessment (Jang and Lukasiewicz, 2023; Hackl et al., 2023). Some studies have tested the stability of GenAI in terms of assessment, some of which have concluded that GenAI has better consistency, and others have highlighted the problem of GenAI illusion. According to Kung et al. (2023), ChatGPT had high repeatability, which consistently approached or maintained the passing line in multiple tests in the Medical Licensing Examination without any specific training. Hackl et al. (2023) study showing that ChatGPT exhibited extremely high accuracy and repeatability when assessing the responses to higher education macroeconomics tasks. However, ChatGPT and similar GenAIs may face the issue of 'AI hallucinations' when answering questions, producing answers that seem reasonable but are actually incorrect (Fui-Hoon Nah et al., 2023). For example, (Ahmad et al., 2023) research indicates that ChatGPT tends to provide inconsistent information when a series of contextual questions are asked for language and literature learning. Because of this hallucination. This phenomenon is mainly caused by a lack of data and information, leading the model to generate inaccurate answers randomly (Hou and Ji, 2023). Research still found that GenAI yields different responses to repeated questions, raising concerns about potential inconsistencies (Yaneva et al., 2023). Therefore, it is necessary to ensure GenAI's effectiveness through expert verification and demand that GenAI generate the corresponding evidence sources through prompt engineering to avoid inconsistencies (Zuccon et al., 2023). By combining question generation and answer retrieval algorithms with GenAI while mitigating hallucination shortcomings (Sovrano et al., 2023).

7.3 EMPIRICAL STUDY: HOW CAN GENAI BE USED IN ASSESSING LEARNING PRODUCT AND PROCESS

7.3.1 Using ChatGPT to Assess Learner's Performance

A straightforward approach to using ChatGPT for assessment is to ask ChatGPT to act as a teacher and grade student work. ChatGPT's capability in automated essay scoring has been examined, showing a high correlation between its automated scores and those given by human teachers. Additionally, ChatGPT provides feedback to learners on their writing. Research comparing the feedback from ChatGPT 3.5 and that of human teachers indicates that the feedback quality from ChatGPT closely mirrors that from humans (Steiss et al., 2024; Dai et al., 2023). Given the balance between the feedback quality and the training time required, ChatGPT demonstrates potential as an assessment tool (Steiss et al., 2024). Furthermore, ChatGPT can generate feedback on student performance that is more detailed, fluid, and coherent than that of human teachers, showing high consistency with teachers in assessing the topics of student assignments (Dai et al., 2023). Thus, in the empirical study, we aim to explore ChatGPT's capabilities in terms of scoring and offering feedback. Our study is guided by the following question:

> **RQ1**: How consistent are ChatGPT scoring of learners' essay performance with human scoring?
>
> **RQ2**: What are the characteristics of ChatGPT feedback compared to human feedback?

We designed an essay writing task that required participants (non-native English speakers) to complete an English writing and revising task, where they were asked to read and study English material on three different topics: artificial intelligence, differentiation in the classroom, and scaffolding of learning. Based on the reading material, participants were required to integrate these three topics into a 200–400 word essay, envisioning school education in 2035. Alongside these materials, participants received detailed instructions and a rubric. This rubric was designed to serve a dual purpose: guiding the participants in structuring their essays, and providing a criterion for the researcher and ChatGPT to assess learners' essays and give feedback upon the conclusion of the experiment. Specifically, we sent the essays along with the rubric to the GPT, requesting it to score the essays according to the rubric while also assuming the role of a teacher to provide a commentary approximately 200 words in length. A total of 118 learners (average age 22.56, SD = 2.79, with 64% female and 51% undergraduates) from a university participated in the experiment. To ensure the accuracy of learners' essay scores, two researchers independently utilised the same rubric to evaluate essays. A total of 12 written essays were assessed by both researchers. The inter-rater reliability was determined using the intraclass correlation coefficient and absolute agreement measure, indicating a very good agreement level (all ICCs > 0.85). Considering this high inter-rater reliability, the remaining essays were assessed by only one researcher.

To answer RQ1, we computed Spearman correlations between the Researcher Assessment Scores (RA-Scores) and ChatGPT Assessment Scores (GPT-Scores), where a stronger positive correlation indicated higher consistency. Table 7.2 shows the correlation between RA-Scores and GPT-Scores based on the same rubric. The results show that there is a strong correlation in basic writing skills, academic writing skills, and

TABLE 7.2 Correlations between RA-Scores and GPT-Scores

	Spearman Correlation
Word count	0.080
Basic writing skills	0.374^{a}
Academic writing skills	0.369^{a}
Originality	0.069
Scaffolding to optimise learning	0.282^{a}
The role of AI in education	0.214^{b}
Differentiation practices in the classroom	0.262^{b}
Integration of three topics	0.205^{b}
Future vision on education	0.290^{a}
Total score	0.484^{a}

$^{a}p < 0.01$.
$^{b}p < 0.05$.

total scores (0.374, 0.369, and 0.484, $p < 0.01$). However, the correlation in originality and word count was low. Furthermore, significant but moderate correlation was observed between RA-Scores and GPT-Scores in specific writing content (i.e. Scaffolding to Optimise Learning, The Role of AI in Education, Differentiation Practices in the Classroom, Integration of Three Topics, and Future Vision on Education). These results indicate a high consistency between ChatGPT and human assessments in areas such as spelling, grammar, and writing style. In contrast, the assessment of essay depth and originality shows lower consistency, highlighting ChatGPT's limitations in assessing advanced writing abilities like creativity and critical thinking. Unexpectedly, the consistency in basic aspects such as Word Count was low. In the experiment, the researchers used a character calculator to ensure the accuracy of the word count. ChatGPT's low consistency in word count indicates potential errors and performance instability. Nonetheless, the effectiveness of ChatGPT in assessing specific writing content cannot be dismissed, aligning with the findings of Dai et al. (2023).

We also plotted the distribution of RA-Scores and GPT-Scores. As shown in Figure 7.1, RA-Scores primarily cluster between 14 and 18 points, peaking at 16 points, which indicates a relatively tight and symmetrical distribution, closely approximating a normal distribution. In contrast, GPT-Scores cover a wider range from 6 to 24 points and are more uniformly spread, lacking a clear concentration and exhibiting a slight skewness in the distribution. Generally, scores from human demonstrate greater concentration, while those from GPT are more dispersed. These results suggest that human grading tends to rely on experience and perceptions of student performance, often conforming to a normal distribution. Conversely, the GPT shows the difficulty in distinguishing between varying student performances, possibly due to looser scoring criteria, resulting in a failure to identify distinctively higher or lower performing student groups.

To answer RQ2, we used natural language processing methods to conduct word frequency analysis, sentiment analysis and syntactic structure analysis of ChatGPT's Assessment Feedback (GPT-Feedback) and Researcher Assessment Feedback (RA-Feedback) (Table 7.3). The result of word frequency analysis presents that GPT-Feedback mainly relates to the topics of the essay content (e.g., "vision future education", "artificial intelligence differentiation scaffolding", and "compelling vision

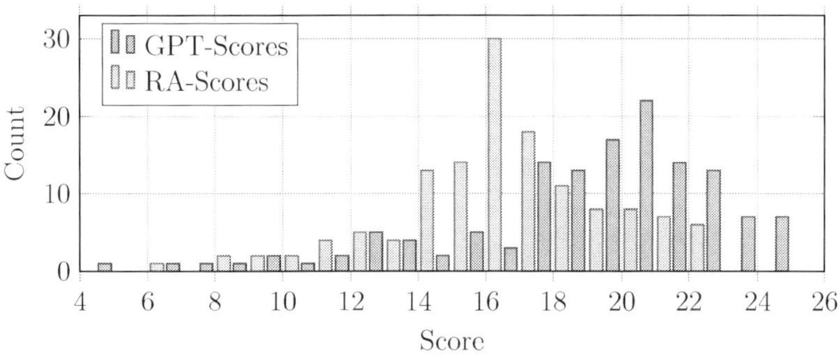

Figure 7.1 Distribution of GPT-essay and TA-essay sum score.

future education"), and it also generates topics not found in the reading materials (e.g., "potential challenges ethical considerations"). On the other hand, RA-Feedback is more varied, covering aspects such as the essay's topic (e.g., "differentiated instruction scaffolding"), word count (e.g., "article meets word count"), and grammar (e.g., "spelling grammatical errors").

The result of sentiment analysis shows that 79% of GPT-feedback and 86% of RA-feedback are neutral, and the positive proportion of GPT-feedback (18%) was higher than that of RA-feedback (10%). The result of syntactic structure analysis shows that RA-Feedback, on average, has longer sentence lengths than GPT-Feedback, suggesting that they are more detailed or have a more complex structure. Researchers also use nouns and verb phrases more frequently than ChatGPT, which suggests their feedback is likely more specific and direct. While both use independent clauses at a similar rate, researchers more frequently utilise dependent clauses, indicating their feedback might be logically more intricate, or they tend to employ conditional, comparative, and causal structures more often.

7.3.2 Facilitating Learner's Self-Assessment by Providing Feedback through ChatGPT

Self-assessment means that learners assess their own performance in work and study and judge whether they have reached the established goals or standards so as to make corresponding adjustments. In writing tasks, accurate self-assessment can help learners develop important skills

TABLE 7.3 Example of GPT-Feedback and RA-Feedback

GPT-Feedback	RA-Feedback
As your teacher, I commend you for tackling complex issues like AI, differentiation, and scaffolding in education. Your essay shows promise and a good understanding of the basic concepts. However, there are areas for improvement. Firstly, the essay would benefit from better organization. It's not always clear how the different sections relate to one another, making it hard to follow your line of argument. Second, while the essay touches on all the required topics, it does so superficially. Each topic could be elaborated upon to present a more nuanced argument. Third, the essay contains numerous grammatical errors and awkward phrasings that detract from its readability and effectiveness. Your future vision for education in 2035 brings in some interesting ideas, but they could be developed further to paint a more vivid picture. AI's role, for example, could be more specifically tied to your discussions of differentiation and scaffolding. The ultimate purpose of AI, differentiation, and scaffolding in education could be explored in greater depth to provide a more insightful view.	This is an article with significant room for improvement, and I will comment on it from two aspects: (1) **Language and expression**: The article meets the word count requirements but contains several spelling or grammatical errors, such as "aeroplane" and "applys." In terms of originality, the author presents their own ideas and perspectives rather than merely summarizing the reading material. Academically, it's commendable that the author has divided the article into sections using subheadings, which helps to clarify the structure. However, further improvement is needed in the logical flow and coherence between sentences and sections. Additionally, it's important to spell out abbreviations when they are first introduced in the text to avoid confusing readers who are not experts in the field (for example, "RLHF"). (2) **Content**: The author has a basic understanding of the concepts of artificial intelligence and differentiated instruction but appears to be somewhat unclear about the theme of scaffolding. The article also fails to delve into specific applications of these three

(*Continued*)

TABLE 7.3 (*Continued*) Example of GPT-Feedback and RA-Feedback

GPT-Feedback	RA-Feedback
Overall, your essay shows effort and understanding but needs refinement in structure, depth, and language to meet academic standards. Keep up the hard work! Total Score: 13/25	themes in education. Many specific examples could be further elaborated on, such as how teachers or AI can group students based on performance, and activity data to achieve differentiated instruction; or how scaffolding could be systematically applied in real-world classrooms. Moreover, the article neglects the interconnectedness among these three themes. The author could explore, based on specific examples, how AI could facilitate differentiated instruction and scaffolding, and also discuss the potential for integrating these approaches. Lastly, in terms of education in 2035, I hope to see the author offer more innovative insights or critical thinking, such as considering the potential ethical impacts of AI in education or the disparities in technology access, rather than merely focusing on the reading material or existing applications.

to analyse their own work and improve future writing performance. As an important part of self-regulated learning (SRL), self-assessment is essential for promoting learners' agency and autonomy during the learning process (Nicol and Macfarlane-Dick, 2006; Wilby, 2022). Writing analysis tools appear to help students implement self-assessment in writing. The strength of writing analysis tools provide personalised feedback that pinpoints strengths and areas for improvement, it also allows learners to develop writing strategies (Yang and Ogata, 2023; Kovanović et al., 2018; Pantiwati and Husamah, 2017). Such writing analysis tools utilise technical approaches such as dictionary-based approaches, expert-defined rules, and natural language processing to focus on assessing various aspects of writing such as grammar, style, and sentence diversity (Conijn et al., 2022). The emergence of ChatGPT is expected to be a powerful writing analysis tool to support learners in writing. Thus, in this empirical study, we aim to explore the impact of ChatGPT on the accuracy of self-assessment and the implementation of the self-assessment process in writing tasks. Our study is guided by the following question:

> **RQ1**: Do ChatGPT influence how accurately learners self-assess their writing products during revision?
>
> **RQ2**: How does ChatGPT influence the process of learners' self-assessment?

We designed a two-stage task that required participants (non-native English speakers) to complete an English writing and revising task, a detailed information was mentioned in Section 2.2. A total of 61 learners (average age 22.56, SD = 2.79, with 64% female and 51% undergraduates) from a university participated in the experiment. These learners come from a diverse array of disciplines, they were randomly divided into two groups, with both sets completing the English writing task within the same learning environment in stage one. However, during stage two, one group had the support of ChatGPT (AI group, 30 participants) to revise their essays, while the other group did not (CN group, 31 participants). During the task, we collected the Researchers' Assessment scores of essay (RA-Scores) and Learners' Self-Assessment scores of essay (SA-Scores) to evaluate the accuracy of self-assessment, and we also collected mouse and keyboard data during the task.

TABLE 7.4 Correlations between SA-Scores and RA-Scores

CN Group	**Before Revision**	**After Revision**
Basic writing skills	0.384[a]	0.162
Academic writing skills	0.155	0.403
Originality	0.179	−0.202
Integration of three topics	0.087	−0.158
Future vision on education	0.206	−0.136
Total score	0.071	−0.453[b]
AI Group	**Before Revision**	**After Revision**
Basic writing skills	0.097	−0.148
Academic writing skills	0.215	0.060
Originality	0.655[b]	0.007
Integration of three topics	0.446[a]	0.106
Future vision on education	0.557[b]	0.023
Total score	0.596[b]	0.047

[a] $p < 0.05$.
[b] $p < 0.01$.

To answer RQ1, we examined the Spearman correlations between the SA-Scores and RA-Scores before and after the revision task. Table 7.4 shows that there is a weak positive correlation between SA-Scores and RA-Scores in the CN group before revision, while there is a strong negative correlation between SA-Scores and RA-Scores after the completion of stage two (after revision), and this correlation coefficient has statistical significance. In the AI group, there is a strong positive correlation between SA-Scores and RA-Scores before the revision, and this correlation coefficient is statistically significant, but there is a weak positive correlation between SA-Scores and RA-Scores after the revision.

Together, our findings clearly show that the accuracy of SA-Scores decreased in both groups throughout the task in both groups. To assess whether ChatGPT improves the accuracy of learners' self-assessment, we compared the absolute accuracy of self-assessment between two groups. As shown in Table 7.5, the two groups in self-assessment accuracy during stage one did not differ significantly ($t(58.91) = 1.035, p = 0.305$, $d = 0.264$). However, during stage Two, the t-test showed a statistically significant difference in the accuracy of self-assessment between two groups, ($t(58.57) = 2.280, p = 0.026$, $d = 0.583$). The results from the t-test demonstrated that the AI group exhibited superior absolute

TABLE 7.5 Changes in Learners' Self-Assessment Accuracy

		Before Revision		After Revision		Difference	
Group	**N**	**Mean**	**SD**	**Mean**	**SD**	**Mean**	**SD**
AI group	30	2.133	1.502	2.833	2.086	−0.700	1.968
CN group	31	2.581	1.858	4.129	2.349	−1.548	2.173

Note: The learners in each group are the same in the pre-measurement (writing) and the post-measurement (revision).

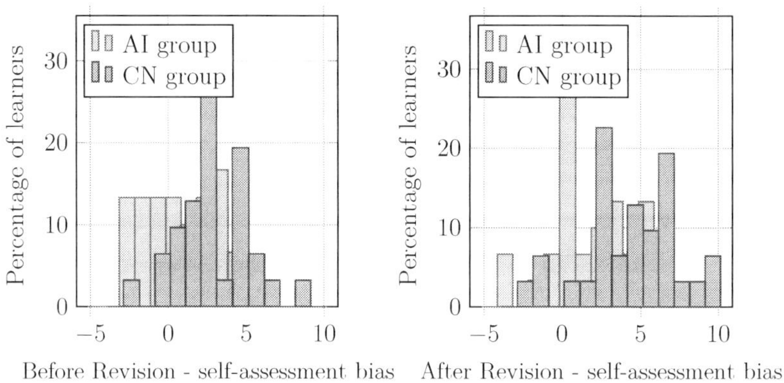

Figure 7.2 Self-assessment bias between two groups in two stages.

accuracy in comparison to the CN group. Finally, we examined the distribution of the learners' overestimation, accurate estimation, and underestimation of their writing scores. As shown in Figure 7.2, only about 10% of the learners assessed their scores accurately in stage one. In stage two, more learners from the AI group exhibited SA-Scores bias closer to zero, while the CN group saw a decrease in accuracy and an increase in underestimations. These findings demonstrated that the ChatGPT was associated with the improved accuracy of learners' self-assessment in writing.

To answer RQ2, we gathered data of learners' behavioural interactions during the experiment. This included recording keyboard and mouse events, and interactions with web controls (e.g., button clicks, hyperlink activation, text inputs). To model cognitive and meta-cognitive aspects of learners' processes, we coded learners' behaviours following an SRL measurement and analysis protocol Fan et al. (2022) to identify learners' SRL actions. After that, we obtained sequences of action labels that represent learners' meaningful SRL actions. Based on the SRL action sequences, the SRL processes from the sequence could be obtained using a trace parser Fan et al. (2022). A first-order Markov Model was used to gauge the temporal features of learners' SRL processes in which the transition probability of actions could be calculated and visualised. As shown in Figure 7.3, the nodes represent different coding labels, the line represents the transfer probability between node activities, the red line indicates that the inter-node transfer probability of the CN group is greater than that of the AI group, the green line is vice versa, and the gray line indicates that there is little difference between the two groups. It can be seen that compared with the AI group, the CN group has a higher probability of mutual transfer between MC.E (MetaCognition.Evaluation) and MC.O (MetaCognition.Orientation), that is, learners in the CN group have a deeper connection between orientation behavior and assessment behavior. However, according to the findings of RQ1, the accuracy of self-assessment in CN group did not improve, indicating that learners perform self-assessment badly without external support. In addition, we can see many red arrows pointing to the LC.FR (LowCognition.First&Re-reading), but not red arrows from this node pointing to other nodes, indicating that learners without ChatGPT support are more immersed in the reading activity and are unable to actually implement the writing task. Compared with CN group, AI group has a higher probability of shifting from MC.E to HC.EO (HighCognition.Elaboration/Organisation), indicating that ChatGPT intervention can help learners implement from meta-cognition assessment activity to actual high-cognition writing processing activity, and the self-cycle probability of HC.EO is also higher, suggesting that ChatGPT may help learners to implement writing activities, thereby reducing the degree of reduction in the accuracy of self-assessment.

7.4 IMPLICATION AND FUTURE WORK

The empirical research review conducted on the utilisation of generative AI, along with our two empirical studies, reveals the potential of generative AI in assessment. Generative AI can perform traditional assessment activities, such as grading student work and providing

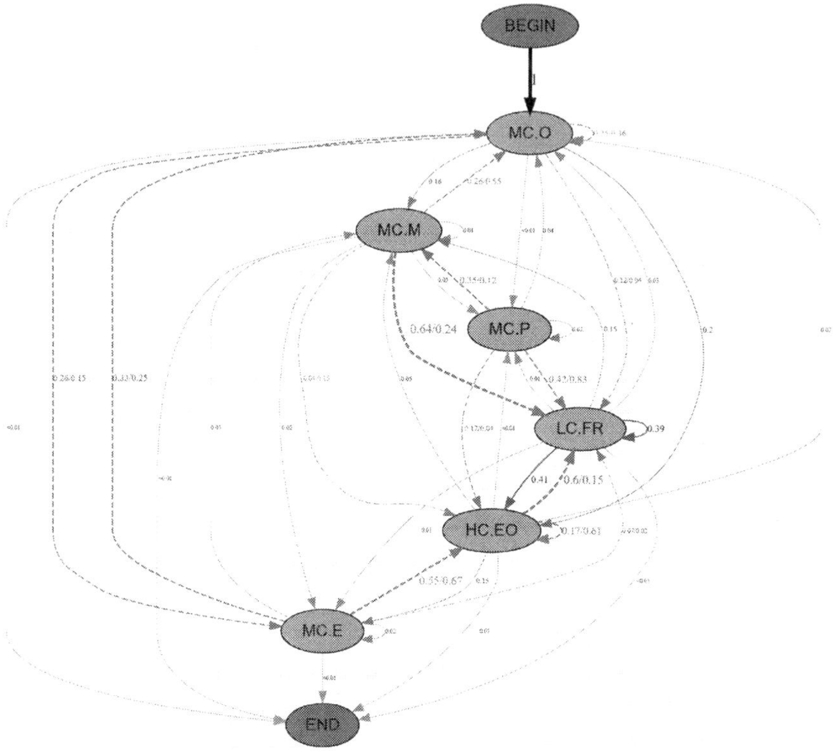

Figure 7.3 Behavioral sequences between the AI group and the CN group.

feedback, to alleviate the workload on teachers. Our research shows that ChatGPT's automatic scoring is highly consistent with human ratings in areas such as basic writing skills, academic writing skills, and essay topics. Moreover, ChatGPT can generate topics not present in reading materials and provide feedback in a concise and direct manner, indicating its potential in guiding students to improve task performance or even develop learning skills. However, ChatGPT is currently unable to reliably assess student performance in higher-order thinking skills such as creativity and critical thinking. A possible explanation is the lack of training and the absence of examples of learner essays of varying quality to accurately assess their performance. Future research should engage in prompt engineering and provide scoring samples to ensure ChatGPT's reliability in assessing student work. Furthermore, it is crucial to investigate which types of ChatGPT's feedback can effectively promote learners' study, helping ChatGPT better play the role of a teacher in guiding student learning, such as including literature with authoritative sources in feedback to strengthen students' awareness of academic ethics.

Traditional automatic assessment systems focus solely on generating the final assessment results. Generative AI (GenAI) helps us break away from this limitation. For example, GenAI can assist in generating assessment criteria before the assessment activities begin and can facilitate the conduct of self-assessment by students during the assessment activities. Our research indicates that ChatGPT's formative feedback can enhance the accuracy of learners' self-assessment. ChatGPT can explain to students why they received certain feedback, identify areas for improvement relative to the criteria, and suggest considerations for future enhancements. Additionally, the mechanism of feedback explanation makes the artificial intelligence algorithms relatively transparent, aiding in the construction of fairer assessment standards. Furthermore, our study shows that ChatGPT's formative feedback can bridge the gap between metacognitive assessment activities and the actual cognitive writing processing activities, offering support to teachers and allowing them to provide self-regulated learning to large classes in a shorter amount of time. In the future, our focus should not only be on whether GenAI can perform assessment tasks and generate results but also on how GenAI can play a significant role in facilitating the conduct of assessment activities.

Teachers and technology developers should be mindful of validation when using GenAI for assessment. While our research measured the consistency of feedback between humans and ChatGPT across different scoring dimensions we provided, it did not test their consistency in repeatedly grading the same essay. Additionally, we found possibilities for low-level errors in ChatGPT's word count in our study. Moreover, the criteria used to compare feedback from ChatGPT and humans were limited, and metrics such as sentiment and keyword usage were not specifically designed for writing feedback. There is currently a lack of comprehensive measurement standards for scoring assessments with GenAI, as well as a lack of prompts and content standards for generating feedback with GenAI. Therefore, we cannot foresee whether the content generated by GenAI may pose ethical risks beyond assessment.

Gen AI holds the promise of extending and deepening formative assessment further and also advances the implementation of stealth assessment. Stealth assessment advocates integrating assessments into students' daily lives, making them unaware of the assessment's presence (Shute, 2011). Typically based on interaction data logs in immersive games or digital learning environments, stealth assessment aims to blur the boundaries between gameplay, learning, and assessment (Shute and Ventura, 2015; Shute et al., 2022). Because the assessment is invisible and part of an engaging environment, it does not trigger test anxiety and can provide continuous feedback, adaptive support, and personalised assessment for each student (Shute et al., 2022). Many online education platforms, like Khanmigo, have begun to embed ChatGPT, offering scaffolded support to students through conversational tutoring (Kshetri, 2023). On the one hand, generative AI can provide continuous formative feedback through timely and personalised responses, facilitating the conduct of formative assessment. On the other hand, teaching platforms embedded with ChatGPT also collect students' learning behavior data and conversational logs. The rich behavioral and conversational data lay a solid foundation for analysing students' cognitive processes, aiding the conduct of stealth assessments, where the boundaries between dialogue and assessment are blurred, and the assessment is embedded in the students' conversational process. Since the assessment activities commence from the moment a student enters the learning platform embedded with generative AI and its results are continuously accumulated and updated with their actions and dialogues, the assessment is constantly generated. Based on generative AI technology, this assessment mode could perhaps be termed generative assessment.

Finally, the issue of human-computer collaboration brought about by artificial intelligence has always been a topic of discussion. Using ChatGPT for assessment may alter the traditional roles of educators, and the improvement in assessment efficiency could potentially reduce teachers' involvement in the teaching process. For example, reliance on artificial intelligence for feedback and grading might lead to a decline in teachers' critical thinking and personal interaction skills with students. Future research should explore teachers' instructional needs, guide the relationship between teachers and artificial intelligence in the educational process, and shift teachers' focus from assessment to more professional, personalised guidance and support. It should also encourage teachers to innovate assessment forms, especially those that can utilise creativity and require critical thinking, thereby better serving students' learning needs.

7.5 CHAPTER SUMMARY

In this chapter, we explore the connections between generative artificial intelligence (GenAI) and learning assessment. We begin by reviewing the classifications and practices of traditional assessments, including Diagnostic, Formative., and Summative Assessment. Additionally, we provide a concise overview of the evolution of Computer Assisted/Aided Assessment (CAA), tracing its progression from initial conventional IT-supported implementations to those enhanced by artificial intelligence and machine learning. The emergence of generative artificial intelligence as a new technology and how it could be applied to assessments warrants our consideration. Consequently, in the second part, we have collected 39 empirical studies related to GenAI and learning assessment, finding that most research focuses on formative and summative assessment. Research contents include analysing the quality of GenAI's assessments, validating the consistency of GenAI's scoring and feedback, generating innovative assessment methods and questions, leveraging existing assessment frameworks, and modifying models to enhance assessment quality. To deepen our understanding of ChatGPT's application in assessment, we present two case studies in the third part from the perspectives of learning process and product. The first study involves using ChatGPT to directly grade student essays, focusing on assess the learning product. The second study investigates ChatGPT's impact on facilitating students' self-assessment, focusing on facilitating assessment during learning process. Our findings suggest that ChatGPT can assess learning products, so it has potential as an assessment tool. Furthermore, ChatGPT also promotes self-assessment, thus enhancing the process of assessment. In summary, GenAI can be employed to conduct traditional assessment activities and has the potential to further extend and deepen learning assessment, such as embedding ChatGPT in instruction, generating real-time assessment results through the analysis of human-computer dialogues, and implementing stealth assessment and generative assessment. Moreover, educators and technology developers should also apply GenAI cautiously and focus on fostering human-computer collaboration relationships.

Bibliography

Ahmad, Z., Kaiser, W., and Rahim, S. (2023). Hallucinations in ChatGPT: An unreliable tool for learning. *Rupkatha Journal on Interdisciplinary Studies in Humanities*, *15*(4):1–18.

Akgun, S. and Greenhow, C. (2022). Artificial intelligence in education: Addressing ethical challenges in k-12 settings. *AI and Ethics*, *2*(3):431–440.

Ali, R., Tang, O. Y., Connolly, I. D., Zadnik Sullivan, P. L., Shin, J. H., Fridley, J. S., et al. (2023). Performance of ChatGPT and GPT-4 on neurosurgery written board examinations. *Neurosurgery*, *93*(6):1353–1365.

Bennett, R. E. (2011). Formative assessment: A critical review. *Assessment in Education: Principles, Policy & Practice*, *18*(1):5–25.

Bey, A., Jermann, P., and Dillenbourg, P. (2018). A comparison between two automatic assessment approaches for programming: An empirical study on moocs. *Journal of Educational Technology & Society*, *21*(2):259–272.

Bin-Nashwan, S. A., Sadallah, M., and Bouteraa, M. (2023). Use of ChatGPT in academia: Academic integrity hangs in the balance. *Technology in Society*, *75*:102370.

Black, P. and Wiliam, D. (1998). Assessment and classroom learning. *Assessment in Education: Principles, Policy & Practice*, *5*(1):7–74.

Black, P. and Wiliam, D. (2018). Classroom assessment and pedagogy. *Assessment in Education: Principles, Policy & Practice*, *25*(6):551–575.

Blayney, P. and Freeman, M. (2004). Automated formative feedback and summative assessment using individualised spreadsheet assignments. *Australasian Journal of Educational Technology*, *20*(2):209–231.

Bloom, B. S., Hastings, T., and Madaus, G. F. (1971). *Handbook on Formative and Summative Evaluation of Student Learning*. McGraw-Hill, New York.

Boud, D. (2012). Assessment and learning: contradictory or complementary? In Sambell, K., McDowell, L., and Montgomery, C., editors, *Assessment for Learning in Higher Education*, pp. 35–48. Routledge, London, UK.

Broadfoot, P. and Black, P. (2004). Redefining assessment? The first ten years of assessment in education. *Assessment in Education: Principles, Policy & Practice*, *11*(1):7–26.

Brookhart, S. M. (2011). Educational assessment knowledge and skills for teachers. *Educational Measurement: Issues and Practice*, *30*(1):3–12.

Brown, S. and Knight, P. (2012). *Assessing Learners in Higher Education*. Routledge, London, UK.

Busch, P. A. and Hausvik, G. I. (2023). Too good to be true? An empirical study of ChatGPT capabilities for academic writing and implications for academic misconduct. In *29th Americas Conference on Information Systems*, Panama City, Panama.

Cardona, M. A., Rodríguez, R. J., and Ishmael, K. (2023). Artificial intelligence and the future of teaching and learning: Insights and recommendations.

Chan, C. K. Y. and Hu, W. (2023). Students' voices on generative AI: Perceptions, benefits, and challenges in higher education. *International Journal of Educational Technology in Higher Education*, *20*(1):43.

Cheung, B. H. H., Lau, G. K. K., Wong, G. T. C., Lee, E. Y. P., Kulkarni, D., Seow, C. S., Wong, R., and Co, M. T.-H. (2023). ChatGPT versus human in generating medical graduate exam multiple choice questions: A multinational prospective study (Hong Kong Sar, Singapore, Ireland, and the United Kingdom). *PLoS One*, 18(8):e0290691.

Chufama, M. and Sithole, F. (2021). The pivotal role of diagnostic, formative and summative assessment in higher education institutions' teaching and student learning. *International Journal of Multidisciplinary Research and Publications*, *4*(5):5–15.

Cingillioglu, I. (2023). Detecting AI-generated essays: The ChatGPT challenge. *The International Journal of Information and Learning Technology*, *40*(3):259–268.

Cizek, G. J. (2010). An introduction to formative assessment: History, characteristics, and challenges. In Andrade, H. L. and Cizek, G. J., editors, *Handbook of Formative Assessment*, pp. 3–17. Routledge, London, UK.

Clark, T. M. (2023). Investigating the use of an artificial intelligence chatbot with general chemistry exam questions. *Journal of Chemical Education*, *100*(5):1905–1916.

Conijn, R., Martinez-Maldonado, R., Knight, S., Buckingham Shum, S., Van Waes, L., and Van Zaanen, M. (2022). How to provide automated feedback on the writing process? A participatory approach to design writing analytics tools. *Computer Assisted Language Learning*, *35*(8):1838–1868. http://doi.org/10.1080/09588221.2020.1839503.

Conole, G. and Warburton, B. (2005). A review of computer-assisted assessment. *ALT-J*, *13*(1):17–31.

Dai, W., Lin, J., Jin, H., Li, T., Tsai, Y.-S., Gašević, D., and Chen, G. (2023). Can large language models provide feedback to students? A case study on ChatGPT. In *2023 IEEE International Conference on Advanced Learning Technologies (ICALT)*, Orem, UT, USA, pp. 323–325.

Dixson, D. D. and Worrell, F. C. (2016). Formative and summative assessment in the classroom. *Theory into Practice*, *55*(2):153–159.

Dunder, N., Lundborg, S., Viberg, O., and Wong, J. (2023). Kattis vs. ChatGPT: Assessment and evaluation of programming tasks in the age of artificial intelligence. *arXiv preprint arXiv:2312.01109*.

Fan, Y., Lim, L., Van der Graaf, J., Kilgour, J., Raković, M., Moore, J., Molenaar, I., Bannert, M., and Gašević, D. (2022). Improving the measurement of self-regulated learning using multi-channel data. *Metacognition and Learning*, *17*(3):1025–1055.

Friederichs, H., Friederichs, W. J., and März, M. (2023). ChatGPT in medical school: How successful is AI in progress testing? *Medical Education Online*, *28*(1):2220920.

Fui-Hoon Nah, F., Zheng, R., Cai, J., Siau, K., and Chen, L. (2023). Generative AI and ChatGPT: Applications, challenges, and AI-human collaboration. *Journal of Information Technology Case and Application Research*, *25*(3):277–304.

Gardner, J., O'Leary, M., and Yuan, L. (2021). Artificial intelligence in educational assessment: 'Breakthrough? or Buncombe and Ballyhoo?'. *Journal of Computer Assisted Learning*, *37*(5):1207–1216.

Gonsalves, C. (2023). On ChatGPT: What promise remains for multiple choice assessment? *Journal of Learning Development in Higher Education*, (27). https://doi.org/10.47408/jldhe.vi27.1009.

Gross, S. and Pinkwart, N. (2015). How do learners behave in help-seeking when given a choice? In *Artificial Intelligence in Education: 17th International Conference, AIED 2015*, Madrid, Spain, June 22–26, 2015. Proceedings 17, pp. 600–603. Springer.

Hackl, V., Müller, A. E., Granitzer, M., and Sailer, M. (2023). Is GPT-4 a reliable rater? Evaluating consistency in GPT-4 text ratings. *arXiv preprint arXiv:2308.02575*.

Hahn, M. G., Navarro, S. M. B., Valentín, L. D. L. F., and Burgos, D. (2021). A systematic review of the effects of automatic scoring and automatic feedback in educational settings. *IEEE Access*, *9*:108190–108198.

Hou, W. and Ji, Z. (2023). Geneturing tests GPT models in genomics. *BioRxiv*.

Hussein, M. A., Hassan, H., and Nassef, M. (2019). Automated language essay scoring systems: A literature review. *PeerJ Computer Science*, *5*:e208.

Hutt, S., DePiro, A., Wang, J., Rhodes, S., Baker, R. S., Hieb, G., Sethuraman, S., Ocumpaugh, J., and Mills, C. (2024). Feedback on feedback: Comparing classic natural language processing and generative AI to evaluate peer feedback. In *Proceedings of the 14th Learning Analytics and Knowledge Conference*, New York, NY, USA, pp. 55–65.

Jalil, S., Rafi, S., LaToza, T. D., Moran, K., and Lam, W. (2023). ChatGPT and software testing education: Promises & perils. In *2023 IEEE International Conference on Software Testing, Verification and Validation Workshops (ICSTW)*, pp. 4130–4137. IEEE, Dublin, Ireland.

Jang, M. E. and Lukasiewicz, T. (2023). Consistency analysis of ChatGPT. *arXiv preprint arXiv:2303.06273*.

Joughin, G. (2008). Assessment, learning and judgement in higher education: A critical review. In Joughin, G., editor, *Assessment, Learning and Judgement in Higher Education*, pp. 1–15. Springer Science & Business Media, Berlin, Germany.

Jukiewicz, M. (2024). The future of grading programming assignments in education: The role of ChatGPT in automating the assessment and feedback process. *Thinking Skills and Creativity*, *52*:101522. http://doi.org/10.1016/j.tsc.2024.101522.

Keiper, M. C., Fried, G., Lupinek, J., and Nordstrom, H. (2023). Artificial intelligence in sport management education: Playing the AI game with ChatGPT. *Journal of Hospitality, Leisure, Sport & Tourism Education*, *33*:100456.

Kovanović, V., Joksimović, S., Mirriahi, N., Blaine, E., Gašević, D., Siemens, G., and Dawson, S. (2018). Understand students' self-reflections through learning analytics. In *Proceedings of the 8th International Conference on Learning Analytics and Knowledge*, pp. 389–398. ACM, Sydney, New South Wales Australia.

Kshetri, N. (2023). The economics of generative artificial intelligence in the academic industry. *Computer*, *56*(8):77–83.

Kung, T. H., Cheatham, M., Medenilla, A., Sillos, C., De Leon, L., Elepaño, C., et al. (2023). Performance of ChatGPT on USMLE: Potential for AI-assisted medical education using large language models. *PLoS Digital Health*, *2*(2):e0000198.

Kwan, C. C. L. (2023). Exploring ChatGPT-generated assessment scripts of probability and engineering statistics from Bloom's Taxonomy. In Cheung, S.K.S., Wang, F.L., Paoprasert, N., Charnsethikul,

P., Li, K.C., Phusavat, K., editors, *Technology in Education. Innovative Practices for the New Normal*, ICTE 2023. Communications in Computer and Information Science, vol 1974, pp. 275–286. Springer, Singapore. https://doi.org/10.1007/978-981-99-8255-4_24

Latif, E. and Zhai, X. 2024). Fine-tuning ChatGPT for automatic scoring. *Computers and Education: Artificial Intelligence*, *6*:100210.

Liu, Z., He, X., Liu, L., Liu, T., and Zhai, X. (2023). Context matters: A strategy to pre-train language model for science education. In Wang, N., Rebolledo-Mendez, G., Dimitrova, V., Matsuda, N., Santos, O.C., editors, *Breaking Results, Workshops and Tutorials, Industry and Innovation Tracks, Practitioners, Doctoral Consortium and Blue Sky*, AIED 2023. Communications in Computer and Information Science, vol 1831, pp. 666–674. Springer, Cham. https://doi.org/10.1007/978-3-031-36336-8_103

Lu, Q., Yao, Y., Xiao, L., Yuan, M., Wang, J., and Zhu, X. (2024). Can ChatGPT effectively complement teacher assessment of undergraduate students' academic writing? *Assessment & Evaluation in Higher Education*, *49*(5):616–633.

Luo, Z., Xie, Q., and Ananiadou, S. (2023). ChatGPT as a factual inconsistency evaluator for abstractive text summarization. *arXiv preprint arXiv:2303.15621*.

Mansour, W., Albatarni, S., Eltanbouly, S., and Elsayed, T. (2024). Can large language models automatically score proficiency of written essays? *arXiv preprint arXiv:2403.06149*.

Mao, J., Chen, B., and Liu, J. C. (2024). Generative artificial intelligence in education and its implications for assessment. *TechTrends*, *68*(1):58–66.

Mizumoto, A. and Eguchi, M. (2023). Exploring the potential of using an AI language model for automated essay scoring. *Research Methods in Applied Linguistics*, *2*(2):100050.

Moore, S., Nguyen, H. A., Chen, T., and Stamper, J. (2023). Assessing the quality of multiple-choice questions using GPT-4 and rule-based methods. In Olga Viberg, Ioana Jivet, Pedro J. Muñoz-Merino, Maria

Perifanou, Tina Papathoma, editors, *Responsive and Sustainable Educational Futures: 18th European Conference on Technology Enhanced Learning*, EC-TEL 2023, Aveiro, Portugal, September 4–8, 2023, pp. 229–245. Springer, Cham. https://doi.org/10.1007/978-3-031-42682-7_16

Nguyen, A., Ngo, H. N., Hong, Y., Dang, B., and Nguyen, B.-P. T. (2023a). Ethical principles for artificial intelligence in education. *Education and Information Technologies*, *28*(4):4221–4241.

Nguyen, H. A., Stec, H., Hou, X., Di, S., and McLaren, B. M. (2023b). Evaluating ChatGPT's decimal skills and feedback generation in a digital learning game. In Viberg, O., Jivet, I., Muñoz-Merino, P., Perifanou, M., Papathoma, T., editors, *Responsive and Sustainable Educational Futures*, EC-TEL 2023. Lecture Notes in Computer Science, vol 14200, pp. 278–293. Springer, Cham. https://doi.org/10.1007/978-3-031-42682-7_19

Nicol, D. J. and Macfarlane-Dick, D. (2006). Formative assessment and self-regulated learning: A model and seven principles of good feedback practice. *Studies in Higher Education*, *31*(2):199–218. http://doi.org/10.1080/03075070600572090.

Nikolic, S., Daniel, S., Haque, R., Belkina, M., Hassan, G. M., Grundy, S., Lyden, S., Neal, P., and Sandison, C. (2023). ChatGPT versus engineering education assessment: A multidisciplinary and multi-institutional benchmarking and analysis of this generative artificial intelligence tool to investigate assessment integrity. *European Journal of Engineering Education*, *48*(4):559–614.

Nimpattanavong, C., Taveekitworachai, P., Khan, I., Nguyen, T. V., Thawonmas, R., Choensawat, W., and Sookhanaphibarn, K. (2023). Am i fighting well? Fighting game commentary generation with ChatGPT. In *Proceedings of the 13th International Conference on Advances in Information Technology*, New York, NY, USA, pp. 1–7.

Organisciak, P., Acar, S., Dumas, D., and Berthiaume, K. (2023). Beyond semantic distance: Automated scoring of divergent thinking greatly improves with large language models. *Thinking Skills and Creativity*, *49*:101356.

Orsmond, P., Merry, S., and Callaghan, A. (2004). Implementation of a formative assessment model incorporating peer and self-assessment. *Innovations in Education and Teaching International*, *41*(3): 273–290.

Ouyang, F., Zheng, L., and Jiao, P. (2022). Artificial intelligence in online higher education: A systematic review of empirical research from 2011 to 2020. *Education and Information Technologies*, *27*(6):7893–7925.

Pantiwati, Y. and Husamah, H. (2017). Self and peer assessments in active learning model to increase metacognitive awareness and cognitive abilities. *International Journal of Instruction*, *10*(4):185–202. http://doi.org/10.12973/iji.2017.10411a.

Pearce, J. and Chiavaroli, N. (2023). Rethinking assessment in response to generative artificial intelligence. *Medical Education*, *57*(10): 889–891.

Pedró, F., Subosa, M., Rivas, A., and Valverde, P. (2019). Artificial intelligence in education: Challenges and opportunities for sustainable development. (ED-2019/WS/8):46. Accessed: 2023-12-09.

Pérez-Marín, D., Pascual-Nieto, I., and Rodríguez, P. (2009). Computer-assisted assessment of free-text answers. *The Knowledge Engineering Review*, *24*(4):353–374.

Persico, D., Passarelli, M., Manganello, F., Pozzi, F., Dagnino, F. M., Ceregini, A., and Caruso, G. (2020). Automatic feedback, self-regulated learning and social comparison: A case study. *QWERTY-Interdisciplinary Journal of Technology, Culture and Education*, *15*(2):27–44.

Pinto, G., Cardoso-Pereira, I., Monteiro, D., Lucena, D., Souza, A., and Gama, K. (2023). Large language models for education: Grading open-ended questions using ChatGPT. In *Proceedings of the XXXVII Brazilian Symposium on Software Engineering*, New York, NY, USA, pp. 293–302.

Popovici, M.-D. (2023). ChatGPT in the classroom: Exploring its potential and limitations in a functional programming course. *International Journal of Human–Computer Interaction*,*40*(22):7743–7754. https://doi.org/10.1080/10447318.2023.2269006

Rajendran, D. and Santhanam, P. (2024). Leveraging ensemble learning for stealth assessment model with game-based learning environment. *Soft Computing*, *28*:1–9.

Revell, T., Yeadon, W., Cahilly-Bretzin, G., Clarke, I., Manning, G., Jones, J., Mulley, C., Pascual, R., Bradley, N., Thomas, D., and Leneghan, F. (2023). ChatGPT versus human essayists: An exploration of the impact of artificial intelligence for authorship and academic integrity in the humanities. *Research Square*. http://doi.org/10.21203/rs.3.rs-3483059/v1.

Roy, S., Narahari, Y., and Deshmukh, O. D. (2015). A perspective on computer assisted assessment techniques for short free-text answers. In *Computer Assisted Assessment. Research into E-Assessment: 18th International Conference, CAA 2015*, Zeist, The Netherlands, June 22–23, 2015. Proceedings 18, pp. 96–109. Springer.

Salinas-Navarro, D. E., Vilalta-Perdomo, E., Michel-Villarreal, R., and Montesinos, L. (2024). Using generative artificial intelligence tools to explain and enhance experiential learning for authentic assessment. *Education Sciences*, *14*(1):83.

Scaife, J. and Wellington, J. (2010). Varying perspectives and practices in formative and diagnostic assessment: A case study. *Journal of Education for Teaching*, *36*(2):137–151.

Shepard, L. A. (2000). The role of assessment in a learning culture. *Educational Researcher*, *29*(7):4–14.

Shute, V., Lu, X., and Rahimi, S. (2022). Stealth assessment. In Spector, J. M., editor, *Stealth Assessment*, pp. 1–9. Taylor & Francis group, London, UK.

Shute, V. and Ventura, M. (2015). Stealth assessment. In Michael Spector, J., editor, *The SAGE Encyclopedia of Educational Technology*, pp. 675–676. SAGE Publications, Thousand Oaks, CA.

Shute, V. J. (2011). Stealth assessment in computer-based games to support learning. *Computer Games and Instruction*, *55*(2):503–524.

Sovrano, F., Ahley, K., and Bacchelli, A. (2023). Toward eliminating hallucinations: GPT-based explanatory AI for intelligent textbooks and documentation. In *Tokyo'23: Fifth Workshop on Intelligent Textbooks (iTextbooks) at the 24th International Conference on Artificial Intelligence in Education (AIED'2023)*, Tokyo, Japan, 3 July 2023 - 7 July 2023, pp. 54–65. CEUR-WS.

Spolsky, B., Hult, F. M., and Wiley, J. (2008). *The Handbook of Educational Linguistics*. Wiley Online Library, Hoboken, NJ.

Steiss, J., Tate, T., Graham, S., Cruz, J., Hebert, M., Wang, J., Moon, Y., Tseng, W., Warschauer, M., and Olson, C. B. (2024). Comparing the quality of human and ChatGPT feedback of students' writing. *Learning and Instruction*, *91*:101894.

Téllez, N. R., Villela, P. R., and Bautista, R. B. (2024). Evaluating ChatGPT-generated linear algebra formative assessments. *International Journal of Interactive Multimedia & Artificial Intelligence*, *8*(5):75–82.

Ullah, Z., Lajis, A., Jamjoom, M., Altalhi, A., Al-Ghamdi, A., and Saleem, F. (2018). The effect of automatic assessment on novice programming: Strengths and limitations of existing systems. *Computer Applications in Engineering Education*, *26*(6):2328–2341.

Uzun, L. (2023). ChatGPT and academic integrity concerns: Detecting artificial intelligence generated content. *Language Education and Technology*, *3*(1):45–54.

Wang, L., Chen, X., Wang, C., Xu, L., Shadiev, R., and Li, Y. (2024). ChatGPT's capabilities in providing feedback on undergraduate students' argumentation: A case study. *Thinking Skills and Creativity*, *51*:101440.

Wanner, T. and Palmer, E. (2018). Formative self-and peer assessment for improved student learning: The crucial factors of design, teacher participation and feedback. *Assessment & Evaluation in Higher Education*, *43*(7):1032–1047.

Wilby, J. (2022). Motivation, self-regulation, and writing achievement on a university foundation programme: A programme evaluation study. *Language Teaching Research*, *26*(5):1010–1033. http://doi.org/10.1177/1362168820917323.

Yancey, K. P., Laflair, G., Verardi, A., and Burstein, J. (2023). Rating short L2 essays on the CEFR scale with GPT-4. In *Proceedings of the 18th Workshop on Innovative Use of NLP for Building Educational Applications (BEA 2023)*, Toronto, Canada, pp. 576–584.

Yaneva, V., Baldwin, P., Jurich, D. P., Swygert, K., and Clauser, B. E. (2023). Examining ChatGPT performance on USMLE sample items and implications for assessment. *Academic Medicine*, *99*(2):10–1097.

Yang, A., Li, Z., and Li, J. (2024). Advancing GenAI assisted programming: A comparative study on prompt efficiency and code quality between GPT-4 and GLM-4. *arXiv preprint arXiv:2402.12782*.

Yang, A. C., Flanagan, B., and Ogata, H. (2022). Adaptive formative assessment system based on computerized adaptive testing and the learning memory cycle for personalized learning. *Computers and Education: Artificial Intelligence*, *3*:100104.

Yang, C. C. Y. and Ogata, H. (2023). Personalized learning analytics intervention approach for enhancing student learning achievement and behavioral engagement in blended learning. *Education and Information Technologies*, *28*(3):2509–2528. http://doi.org/10.1007/s10639-022-11291-2.

Yorke, M. (2003). Formative assessment in higher education: Moves towards theory and the enhancement of pedagogic practice. *Higher Education*, *45*:477–501.

Zhai, X. (2022). ChatGPT user experience: Implications for education. *Available at SSRN 4312418*.

Zhou, X., Hu, W., Lei, Z., and Liu, G.-P. (2023). Implementation and evaluation of an automatic scoring system for experimental reports based on ChatGPT. In Auer, M. E., Cukierman, U. R., Vendrell Vidal, E., Tovar Caro, E., editors, *ITowards a Hybrid, Flexible and Socially Engaged Higher Education*. ICL 2023. Lecture Notes in Networks and

Systems, vol 899. Springer, Cham. https://doi.org/10.1007/978-3-031-51979-6_45

Zhu, L., Mou, W., Yang, T., and Chen, R. (2023). ChatGPT can pass the AHA exams: Open-ended questions outperform multiple-choice format. *Resuscitation*, *188*:109783.

Zuccon, G., Koopman, B., and Shaik, R. (2023). ChatGPT hallucinates when attributing answers. In *Proceedings of the Annual International ACM SIGIR Conference on Research and Development in Information Retrieval in the Asia Pacific Region*, New York, NY, USA, pp. 46–51.

CHAPTER 8

Ethical Issues and Value Tensions in the Context of GenAI-Assisted Learning

Yuan Shen, Zhanghan Wang, and Yizhou Fan

THE RISE OF GENAI has sparked widespread discussion regarding its ethical implications, particularly in educational contexts. These ethical challenges have captured the attention of researchers, educators, and policymakers and created barriers to the deeper integration of GenAI into education systems. This chapter explores the ethical challenges associated with using GenAI in education, providing a framework for understanding how these issues intersect with human values. To gain a complete insight into ethical challenges raised by GenAI in education, we reviewed present empirical studies to overview significant ethical challenges, including privacy leakage, academic misconduct and over-reliance on GenAI. The emergence of GenAI as a new technology and how it could be applied to facilitate learning in a value-sensitive way warrants our consideration. To further investigate these issues, we present an empirical study that examines how GenAI can facilitate learning while

DOI: 10.4324/9781003632146-8

aligning with ethical values. This empirical study addresses three central questions: (1) What ethical values are prioritised by learners in online learning environments? (2) How does ChatGPT embody these values? (3) What tensions arise between ethical and pragmatic values during the learning process? Our research involved semi-structured interviews with 59 learners, revealing that learners emphasised the importance of *responsiveness*, *social comfort*, and *autonomy*. ChatGPT-4's features of being tireless, friendliness, and supporting independent decision-making embodied the value of *social comfort* and *autonomy*. However, tensions were observed between these ethical values and pragmatic considerations, underscoring the dynamic and sometimes conflicting nature of value systems in education. In summary, our analysis highlights the importance of employing GenAI in a value-sensitive manner to support ethical and effective learning. Researchers, educators, and technology developers must carefully consider how GenAI can embody critical values, ensuring its integration into educational settings aligns with human interests.

8.1 INTRODUCTION

8.1.1 Ethical Issues of Learning with GenAI

GenAI demonstrated great potential in enhancing personalised learning experiences and improving educational outcomes. However, despite promises brought by GenAI, the rise of GenAI in education also brings ethical concerns (Ferrara, 2024; Alier et al., 2024; Yan et al., 2024; Lund et al., 2023). For example, privacy leaking is a critical issue, as GenAI systems often require large datasets, including personal and sensitive information, raising the risk of unauthorised data exposure (Gupta et al., 2023; Michel-Villarreal et al., 2023). Another major concern is the propensity for GenAI to produce hallucinations, generating inaccurate or misleading information that can misguide learners (Lee et al., 2024). Furthermore, there is the danger of students developing an over-reliance on AI tools, which can undermine their critical thinking and problem-solving skills (Dasari et al., 2024; Song and Song, 2023; Liu et al., 2024). Additionally, GenAI may also facilitate academic misconduct, such as plagiarism, by making it easier for students to produce and submit AI-generated content as their own work (Yusuf et al., 2024; Narayanan, 2024).

As we continue integrating these powerful tools into educational frameworks, it becomes increasingly vital to address these ethical dilemmas head-on (Yan et al., 2024; Van Wyk, 2024). Failing to do so could lead to a future where the quality of education is weakened, and the true goals of learning, such as cultivating knowledge and creativity, may be overshadowed by convenience and expedience. Understanding, analysing, and addressing the ethical challenges that GenAI poses to education have become crucial tasks for technology developers, researchers and educators. Therefore, to develop a comprehensive understanding and analysis of the ethical issues surrounding GenAI in education, we conducted an in-depth exploration through a literature review in Section 8.2. The literature review allowed us to identify the ethical concerns commonly raised within the academic community and to establish a foundational conceptual framework.

8.1.2 Human Values Embedded in GenAI Applications

The ethical risks associated with technology in education largely stem from the intersection of technological capabilities and stakeholders' values (Friedman, 1996). Technology was conventionally perceived as neutral, merely a tool whose ethical considerations depended solely on its use and users (Miller, 2021; Greenberg, 2015). However, it has been proved that technology is far from neutral as it inherently reflects the values of its creators (Friedman and Hendry, 2019; Van Der Weij et al., 2023). The concept that values are embodied in technology has taken root in various interdisciplinary studies of technology, society, and humanity (Flanagan et al., 2008). Systems with learning capabilities such as GenAI even learn the values of users during the application process (Lund et al., 2023). Value is considered an attribute with which an individual or group consigns significance with a focus on and morality (Friedman et al., 2008, p. 70-71). Values shape human beliefs about what is morally acceptable and provide the moral compass that guides ethical behaviour and decision-making in various contexts (Mattison, 2000; Kreie and Cronan, 2000; Rezler et al., 1992).

In our view, the primary cause of ethical issues is the misalignment between values embedded in technology and prioritised by stakeholders. The value misalignment or tension occurs when multiple ethical values cannot be embodied by technology simultaneously in a specific context

(Miller et al., 2007; Muller et al., 2024; Gabriel and Ghazavi, 2023; Han et al., 2021; Yi et al., 2023). For example, a home security camera creates a tension between the value of privacy and safety. To ensure safety, it needs to record constantly, but this may compromise consumers' privacy by capturing and storing personal moments. In educational scenarios involving GenAI, value tension frequently emerges when the system's embedded values misalign with values prioritised by learners, teachers and other stakeholders, leading to ethical dilemmas. For example, the tension between *efficiency* and *autonomy* occurs when GenAI provides detailed step-by-step guidance, which can enhance learning efficiency but may undermine users' ability to independently solve problems and make decisions (Satyanarayan and Jones, 2024; Yang et al., 2024). Similarly, the tension between privacy protection and data utilisation arises when GenAI collects and analyses extensive personal data, which is essential for optimising educational strategies but raises concerns about privacy and data security among students and parents (Gupta et al., 2023). To resolve potential value tensions, it is imperative to align the value embedded in the GenAI with stakeholders' values (Friedman and Hendry, 2019; Friedman and Kahn, 2003; Bostrom and Yudkowsky, 2014; Gabriel and Ghazavi, 2023). From the perspective of human value, we carried out empirical research in Section 8.3 on the basis of the literature review. We utilised qualitative analysis of interview transcripts to comprehend learners' perceptions and attitudes toward GenAI in online learning environments. This approach enabled us to verify the characteristics and features of ethical issues in an authentic learning environment and further uncover the causes and mechanisms behind the formation of the ethical issues.

8.2 LITERATURE REVIEW

In July 2024, we conducted a literature search in the Google Scholar database using search terms including "generative artificial intelligence, GenAI, ChatGPT, ethics, ethical, values, issues, risks" to retrieve empirical research related to ethics and value topics quickly. By sorting out the retrieved studies, we found that ethical issues related to GenAI that have received more attention can be divided into three main challenges: information leaking, academic misconduct, and over-reliance

TABLE 7.5 A Summary of Research Directions on GenAI Ethical Risks

Research Direction	Studies
Information leaking	Mhlanga (2023), Wu et al. (2023), Ajlouni et al. (2023), Petrovska et al. (2024), Sebastian (2023), and Huallpa et al. (2023)
Academic misconduct	Chan and Hu (2023), Das and Madhusudan (2024), Thong et al. (2023), Fuchs and Aguilos (2023), Bergström et al. (2024), Van Wyk (2024), Pettersson et al. (2024), Isiaku et al. (2024), and Kiryakova and Angelova (2023)
Over-reliance	Mogavi et al. (2024), Das and Madhusudan (2024), Thong et al. (2023), Isiaku et al. (2024), Kiryakova and Angelova (2023), Guleria et al. (2023), and Nyaaba et al. (2024)

on GenAI. The specific research directions of these studies are shown in Table 7.5.

8.2.1 Ethical Challenge One: Privacy Leakage

What accompanies the powerful capabilities of GenAI is people's concern about information leaking. Through analysis of publications on the responsible use of AI in education, researchers have found that information leaking during the use of ChatGPT has received widespread attention (Mhlanga, 2023). Wu et al. (2023) divided the information leaking caused by ChatGPT into two types: one is due to public data exploitation, and the other is due to personal input exploitation. Essentially, large language models learn from a large amount of data to infer the content with the highest probability of occurrence, in order to make reasonable responses. This means that in order to make GenAI function effectively, it is necessary to input a large amount of high-quality data into GenAI. With the development of AI, the scenarios, scope, and quantity of personal information collection are gradually expanding, and the daily conversations, expressions, and even actions of teachers and learners may be collected by AI.

Therefore, many learners raised concerns about privacy issues when using GenAI, which hindered their use of GenAI. Previous study investigated 210 college students through a questionnaire about their views on using ChatGPT in psychological counseling programs. And 80.5% of students stated that they would not discuss their own affairs or psychological issues with ChatGPT because it may experience information leaking (Ajlouni et al., 2023). Petrovska et al. (2024) conducted a survey on learners' views on the use of GenAI in software development education. When asked about the use of GenAI in future work, almost all learners expressed concerns about potential privacy breaches in their work (Petrovska et al., 2024). In another survey, 92.5% of respondents stated that they are willing to sacrifice some features of artificial intelligence systems to enhance privacy and data protection (Sebastian, 2023). It can be seen that users have a strong demand for enhancing data protection when using GenAI.

To address privacy concerns, learners believe it is necessary to establish clear laws and regulations regarding privacy and data security (Huallpa et al., 2023; Sebastian, 2023). Information protection regulations have been established in certain regions, which impose strict requirements on collecting, processing, and storing personal data. For example, the General Data Protection Regulation (GDPR) proposed by Europe and the California Consumer Privacy Act (CCPA) (Voigt and Von dem Bussche, 2017). However, these laws and regulations are not sufficient to fully address users' concerns about information leaking of GenAI (Wu et al., 2023). Therefore, technicians also attempt to find solutions to information leaking from a technical perspective. The existing data protection technologies include data anonymisation and aggregation, differential privacy techniques, secure multi-party computation (SMPC), etc. Sebastian (2023) analysed the impact of 7 existing data protection technologies on the performance of ChatGPT. The research has found that the use of existing data protection technologies may have some negative impacts on ChatGPT's performance (Sebastian, 2023).

Sebastian (2023) mainly focused on information leaking issues related to GenAI, especially ChatGPT. Through a literature review, the study identified various privacy risks related to large language models, such as the unintended sharing of sensitive information, data leakage through model outputs, adversarial attacks, model extraction, and data poisoning. Subsequently, the researcher investigated users' attitudes towards ChatGPT privacy issues. The 75.6% of the respondents expressed concerns about privacy issues. The 78.8% of respondents stated that they were aware of the information leakage incidents caused by ChatGPT. The 94.8% of respondents stated that AI systems must comply with data protection regulations. In addition, this study evaluated existing privacy-enhancing technologies(PETs) and found that implementing PETs such as data anonymisation, differential privacy, and SMPC could help reduce privacy risks but may, to some extent, affect the performance of ChatGPT. The researcher concluded that although users had a strong demand for data protection, implementing PETs required careful balancing to avoid adverse effects on AI performance. Sebastian (2023) comprehensively analysed the information leaking problem of GenAI from three aspects, namely risks, user attitude, and solution strategies, which inspire technicians, policymakers, and researchers. The study highlights the strong demand for data protection among users and underscores the need for a careful balance when implementing specific privacy-enhancing strategies to avoid compromising GenAI performance.

8.2.2 Ethical Challenge Two: Academic Misconduct

The integration of GenAI in education, specifically tools like ChatGPT, has raised concerns about academic misconduct. In multiple surveys regarding learners' perceptions of ChatGPT usage, learners have expressed concerns about academic misconduct when using ChatGPT (Chan and Hu, 2023; Das and Madhusudan, 2024; Thong et al., 2023). Fuchs and Aguilos (2023) have conducted an in-depth analysis of learners' understanding of academic misconduct through interviews. The results showed that some learners engage in plagiarism by directly copying and pasting content generated by ChatGPT into their own articles without citation. The learners admitted that ChatGPT can quickly generate the content they want, and it was difficult not to use ChatGPT to complete learning tasks when they are lazy.

However, learners did not view all uses of ChatGPT for completing learning tasks as entirely unacceptable. For example, Bergström et al. (2024) investigated students' attitudes towards using ChatGPT in learning tasks through an academic dishonesty questionnaire. This survey aimed to understand how students perceive the use of ChatGPT in academic contexts and the extent to which they consider certain behaviours as academic misconduct. The survey was distributed online, and responses were collected from business school students in Finland. This study has found that nearly half of the respondents consider cheating acceptable in certain situations. When respondents perceive that the instructor's teaching ability is poor, they no longer firmly believe that cheating is wrong. Students generally disapproved of cheating but acknowledged that using GenAI like ChatGPT blurred the lines between acceptable and unacceptable behaviour. Using ChatGPT on mobile phones to obtain answers during exams, creating complete text from scratch using ChatGPT, and creating complete text based on other students' content using ChatGPT were considered the most incorrect behaviours (Bergström et al., 2024). Using ChatGPT to correct errors and make text smoother, using ChatGPT to generate answers to last semester's test questions, and generating personal experience notes based on student situations for project applications were considered the three least erroneous behaviours. It can be seen that learners have their own considerations regarding the acceptability of academic misconduct. Bergström et al. (2024) provided insights into the complex relationship between GenAI use and academic integrity, highlighting the need for a nuanced approach to policy development and educational strategies. The findings underscore the importance of fostering a culture of academic integrity while leveraging the potential of GenAI in education.

Faced with the widespread application of GenAI in education, educators are also very concerned about the academic misconduct caused by GenAI. In multiple surveys targeting educators, they have expressed concerns about students using GenAI to cheat and emphasised the importance of adhering to academic integrity (Van Wyk, 2024; Pettersson et al., 2024; Isiaku et al., 2024; Kiryakova and Angelova, 2023). Educators and educational researchers have proposed measures to prevent academic misconduct from multiple dimensions. In terms of institutional framework, some educators have proposed legislation to regulate and evaluate policies and guidelines related to the use of GenAI, plagiarism, academic misconduct, and ethics (Van Wyk, 2024; Pettersson et al., 2024); In terms of tools, educators have pointed out that AI detection tools can be used to detect the possibility of academic misconduct, thereby preventing students from using GenAI for plagiarism (Van Wyk, 2024); In terms of assessment strategies, educators can reduce the likelihood of students using GenAI to complete tasks by designing authentic assessment tasks (Van Wyk, 2024). For example, tasks such as case studies, problem-based projects, and writing reflections can be set up. For such tasks, it isn't easy to use GenAI to complete the writing.

8.2.3 Ethical Challenge Three: Over-Reliance on GenAI

The over-reliance on GenAI is also a concern for stakeholders. Previous studies investigating students' and teachers' views on GenAI have found their concerns about over-reliance on GenAI (Mogavi et al., 2024; Das and Madhusudan, 2024; Thong et al., 2023; Isiaku et al., 2024; Kiryakova and Angelova, 2023). If learners depend too much on GenAI, it could lead to addiction. Das and Madhusudan (2024), shallow learning habits, and hinder the development of critical thinking abilities (Mogavi et al., 2024). In addition, GenAI may exhibit model hallucinations and generate erroneous information (Ji et al., 2023). Teachers expressed concern that learners may not check the authenticity of generated content due to their complete trust in GenAI, which could have a negative impact on their acquisition of knowledge and skills (Kiryakova and Angelova, 2023). Meanwhile, over-reliance on GenAI may also lead to the spread of incorrect information. Guleria et al. (2023) tested the effectiveness of applying GenAI to academic writing and found that the content provided by ChatGPT appeared to be correct, but the references cited were not correct and might have been created by ChatGPT.

Thong's study in 2023 explored students' attitudes, perceptions, and ethical concerns regarding the use of GenAI tools like ChatGPT in educational settings (Thong et al., 2023). The research highlighted potential risks, including shallow learning, addiction, and the erosion of critical thinking skills due to over-reliance on GenAI. Employing a quantitative research design and a cross-sectional survey methodology, the study involved 60 students from diverse geographical regions and educational backgrounds (Thong et al., 2023). The findings revealed significant dependence on GenAI for completing learning tasks, particularly among urban students, and while students recognised ChatGPT's usefulness, they expressed concerns about its accuracy and ethical implications (Thong et al., 2023). Thong suggested the need for clear ethical guidelines and improvements in GenAI accuracy, advocating for a balanced approach that avoids over-reliance and ensures the retention of critical thinking and verification skills (Thong et al., 2023). The study also calls for systematic solutions, such as regulations and human supervision, to maintain academic integrity and enhance educational outcomes (Thong et al., 2023).

Currently, few studies have proposed systematic solutions to the problem of over-reliance. Researchers have pointed out the need to establish regulations for the use of ChatGPT in academia and research, to some extent regulating learners' use of GenAI (Guleria et al., 2023). In addition, several learners have emphasised the necessity of integrating GenAI tools with human supervision to address concerns regarding data validity and ensure a balance between the two (Nyaaba et al., 2024).

From the existing ethical research on the application of GenAI in education, we can identify that privacy leakage, academic misconduct, and over-reliance are the primary concerns raised by both teachers and students. Current studies mainly focus on highlighting potential ethical risks, with conclusions often drawn from interviews with learners and teachers. In most cases, researchers directly ask them whether they have any concerns, and based on their responses, potential solutions are proposed. However, there is still a lack of comprehensive and deeper analysis regarding the fundamental causes and underlying mechanisms of these ethical issues, as well as the potential connections and complexities among them. Given the abstract and subjective nature of ethical concerns, directly questioning teachers and learners about these issues may not accurately pinpoint the root causes, which could, in turn, affect the development of effective solutions. Therefore, we conducted an empirical analysis to explore these ethical issues through the lens of value-sensitive design (VSD).

8.3 EMPIRICAL STUDY: VALUE ANALYSIS IN THE ONLINE LEARNING ENVIRONMENT

The theory of VSD advocates for creating technology that thoughtfully considers social, cultural, and institutional contexts to enhance human flourishing and societal benefits. By aligning values, developers ensure that AI systems act in accordance with human values and ethical principles (Friedman and Kahn, 2003; Friedman et al., 2017; Friedman and Hendry, 2019; Friedman et al., 2008). VSD was conceived by its founders, Batya Friedman and others in the field of information and communication technologies (Friedman, 1996). VSD advocates embedding stakeholders' ethical values such as freedom, autonomy, equality, and justice, which manifest intrinsic correctness into the design at the early stages of technology development, addressing value tensions as they arise (Miller et al., 2007; Umbrello, 2020; Friedman et al., 2017). VSD has been conducted in learning contexts in the past 10 years, and values of accountability, transparency, trust, autonomy, privacy, self-image, social well-being, and freedom from bias were identified in previous research (Chen and Zhu, 2019; Ahn et al., 2021; Buckingham Shum et al., 2019; Hakami and Hernández Leo, 2020).

Methodologically, VSD offers a three-part framework in which conceptual, empirical, and technical investigations are applied iteratively and integratively, with new investigations building on results from earlier studies (Miller et al., 2007; Friedman and Hendry, 2019). Conceptual and empirical investigation provides a solid foundation for improving technology design. Friedman and Hendry (2019) proposed a framework of 13 values with ethical importance implicated in system design. This framework includes *human welfare, ownership and property, privacy, freedom from bias, universal usability, trust, autonomy, informed consent, accountability, courtesy, identity, calmness,* and *environmental sustainability.* This authoritative framework provided a robust basis for identifying value tensions encountered by stakeholders in the educational settings with GenAI, which is an inherently value-laden tool. However, current ethical discussions on the application of GenAI in education are primarily conceptual analyses based on general ethical principles (Yang et al., 2021; Dwivedi et al., 2023; Cotton et al., 2024; Sharples, 2023; Viberg et al., 2023). The empirical evidence is currently under-explored. Also, few practical strategies exist to address tensions among a diverse group of values as they unfold during the design and deployment process (Miller et al., 2007).

In the literature review, we found that privacy leaking, academic misconduct, and over-reliance are the risks most frequently highlighted in current empirical research. However, there is still a lack of sufficient practical evidence regarding the underlying mechanisms behind these ethical issues and their potential solutions. Limited empirical evidence has been discovered to show whether stakeholders prioritise values identified in the conceptual investigation, whether new values have emerged, or whether existing values have gained new meanings during online learning. Therefore, we conducted an empirical investigation of VSD to delve deeper into these challenges. In this experiment, we investigated what values learners prioritise during online learning and how they perceive ChatGPT's performance in embodying values. This empirical investigation allowed us to further uncover the causes and mechanisms behind the development of ethical issues.

In post-task stage, a total of 59 participants accepted to participate in semi-structured interviews after completing the two-stage task (i.e., 33 participants in the AI Group and 26 participants in the HE Group). Interviews were conducted as one-on-one audio conferencing interviews with an average duration of 35 minutes. The interviews consisted of three main parts, including background and overall feedback, writing experience, and revision experience (For example, How was your experience while revising your essay under the guidance of an AI/human facilitator? What characteristics do you think a good facilitator should have? Which facilitator do you prefer, ChatGPT or a human expert? Do you worry about any risks associated with using ChatGPT during online learning?). By inviting learners to respond to these questions, we focused on three key research questions:

1. What values do learners consider critically important during online learning?
2. How do ChatGPT and human experts differ in embodying these values?
3. What kinds of value tensions arise when GenAI assists online learning?

The transcribed interview data were analysed using a thematic analysis assisted by NVivo 12. We coded all 59 participants with Group+Number (AI01-AI33, HE01-HE26). Two researchers participated in the coding process and followed the systematic process suggested by Richards and Hemphill (2018). A total of 356 open codes were generated, out of which 261 open codes pertained to ethical values and

95 addressed practical values. After filtering, merging, and refining all codes identified, a thematic structure was further established, including eight value themes: *responsiveness, social comfort, autonomy, freedom from bias, privacy, efficiency, accuracy and development.*

8.3.1 Learners' Prioritisation of Responsiveness, Social Comfort and Autonomy

Through thematic analysis, we found that learners' expectations of facilitators in the ethical dimension mainly concentrated on three key values: *responsiveness*, *social comfort*, and the ability to support learners' *autonomy*.

Responsiveness commonly refers to the specific ability of a system to complete assigned tasks within a given time (Ali and Ali, 1988).In our analysis, we defined *responsiveness* as the facilitator's capability to promptly and appropriately interpret and react to learners' needs, intentions, and emotions (Chen et al., 2021; Reis and Gable, 2015). A total of 26 participants conveyed the expectation that the facilitator would be able to grasp their intentions during online learning in 95 excerpts. Participants expressed willingness to seek help from facilitators who perceived their state of mind. Participant AI23 noted that a good facilitator should intuitively comprehend what they are trying to convey and what they want to ask, even in cases of poor expression. Participant AI32 recounted how the human expert offered active encouragement throughout the revision session, employing positive phrases like *I know what you want to say* and *Your structure is clearer* in the feedback. These findings highlight the significance of *responsiveness* as a crucial value in online learning, emphasising learners' demands for being comprehended by facilitators.

Social comfort was identified as another essential value, which was mentioned as a local concept by the 20 participants when they described the human-AI interaction. The value of *social comfort* underlined the facilitator's capability to alleviate the interpersonal stress of learners and to provide them with a sense of ease and reassurance. Participants highlighted the social pressure linked to facilitation and explained that interacting with the human expert made them more mindful of their phrasing and attitude. For instance, participant HE22 stated, *If my English were poor or I didn't follow their [the human expert's] advice,*

I would worry that not doing well might cause their dissatisfaction. Participants also expressed concern that the questions they asked were *too simple* (AI20), fearing that this might create a negative impression on the human expert. Participants noted that the facilitator they sought help from should possess ample patience. According to participant HE03, *I hope the facilitator will never get tired and judgemental during long question and answer sessions.* These findings highlight learners' concerns about the social interaction process and the desire for friendly and patient facilitation, which is vital for creating a supportive online learning environment.

Autonomy was typically defined as the ability of individuals to decide, plan, and act in ways they believe will help them achieve their goals (Friedman and Hendry, 2019). In this study, we defined *autonomy* in the GenAI-assisted online learning environment as respecting learners' freedom to make their own choices and enabling them to monitor their own learning process. Participants expressed the desire to decide how to make revisions on their own. 18 participants expressed their demand for the freedom to make choices and monitor themselves. For example, a participant expressed that facilitators should respect their opinions without attempting to change them or suggesting that their perspective is incorrect (HE04). Participant HE22 expressed concern that online facilitation might lead to a reduction in *self-monitoring efficiency*. Learners might unconsciously lower their own standards on writing, which differs from the impact of having a teacher provide direct instruction in person. These findings indicate the need for a balanced approach in online learning facilitation that encourages self-regulated learning and respects learners' freedom to choose, decide and monitor themselves.

8.3.2 Complementary Relationship between Human and AI in Embodying Values

We also identified a complementary relationship between ChatGPT and human experts in embodying certain values. ChatGPT faced challenges in accurately assessing learners' conditions and carried risks of information leakage, demonstrating a weaker capacity for responsiveness and privacy protection compared to human experts. On the other hand, ChatGPT's relentless availability, neutrality, and encouragement of independent choices effectively reflected the values of social comfort and autonomy.

Notably, ChatGPT was favoured for reducing the social pressure often associated with face-to-face communication. Participants reported that interacting with ChatGPT felt more *comfortable and relaxing* (AI12) compared to conversing with a human expert. By incorporating ChatGPT, some of the social pressure was alleviated, providing learners with an environment where they could engage without fear of social judgement. ChatGPT facilitated smooth communication, even in cases of grammatical or vocabulary challenges. Additionally, ChatGPT did not display emotions such as frustration, nor did it become fatigued, impatient, or irritated. Participant AI15 emphasised a major benefit of utilising ChatGPT for feedback, pointing out the ease of requesting assistance without being concerned about emotions and judgement, which reduced the psychological burden when seeking corrections or improvements.

Participants praised ChatGPT for giving them the autonomy to decide independently whether to revise their work. One participant shared their revision experience with ChatGPT, highlighting the freedom it provided:

(ChatGPT) gave me the answer directly. Then, I chose whether to accept it. I have a greater power of selectivity and decision-making [with ChatGPT]. Even though it [ChatGPT] may have some differences in logic or description thinking compared to the human expert, I could still convey what I wanted to express. The most important thing for me was having the autonomy to decide whether to revise my work independently.(AI13)

In contrast, the human expert was seen as having more control over learners' actions, which tended to make them more passive during the revision process. Our observations showed that the human expert often instructed learners to follow specific steps or recommended particular changes. For example, in the conversation log of HE09, the human expert explicitly advised revising the first paragraph to "include a detailed description of the future classroom." Since no explanation was provided for this suggestion, the learner felt "obligated to make these changes," as HE09 mentioned during the interview.

We also found that the human expert displayed responsiveness more effectively than ChatGPT. In our experiment, both ChatGPT and the human expert were provided with the same contextual information,

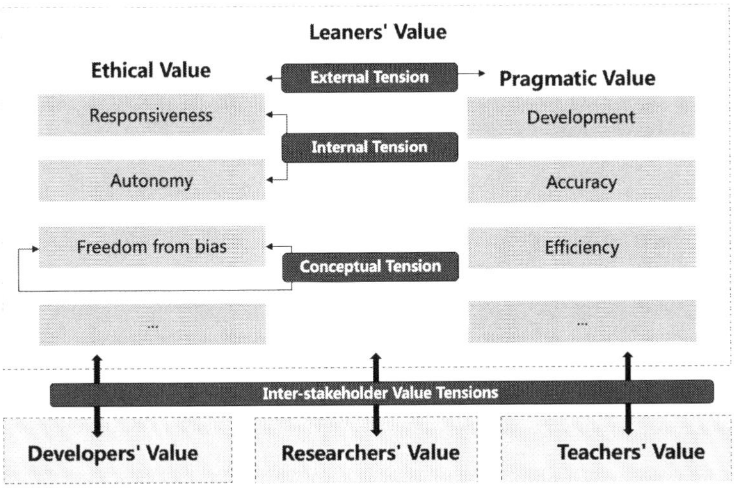

Figure 8.1 Human value framework in the context of GenAI in education.

including learners' essays, instructional materials, and writing rubric questions. However, participants felt that the human expert had a better grasp of their intentions. Participant HE09 shared: *With just a brief explanation, the expert understood what I meant and guided me appropriately.* On the other hand, participants often found it challenging to get the desired responses from ChatGPT due to its reliance on well-crafted prompts. The way students phrased their questions and the context they provided significantly influenced the quality and relevance of the feedback ChatGPT could offer. ChatGPT was able to deliver better responses when the questions were more structured and clear. Participant AI10 remarked: *ChatGPT struggled to interpret questions correctly if they're not phrased precisely, often leading to confusion or a complete lack of understanding.*

8.3.3 Value Tensions between Ethical Values and Pragmatic Values

Addressing value tensions is crucial for fostering ethical and effective GenAI integration into society. Petersen (2021) differentiated between three kinds of possible value tensions: (1) **conceptual tensions arise within one single value and involve different interpretations of the single value.** For example, different interpretations of "transparency" may lead to confusion in estimating whether an algorithm is transparent or not (Petersen, 2021); (2) **internal tensions arise between different ethical values.** For example, sharing more information in a social networking system supports the value of identity but reduces the value of privacy, which users may be concerned with (Friedman and Hendry, 2019); (3) **external tensions arise between ethical values and pragmatic values.** For example, an isolated local area network without wireless connectivity and disconnected from the Internet may provide both privacy and security, but hinder the pragmatic value of access (Friedman and Hendry, 2019). Based on the classification of value tensions proposed by Petersen (2021), we identified value tensions between ethical values versus other pragmatic values such as accuracy and development (see Figure 8.1).

We found tensions between the value of social comfort and accuracy. When ChatGPT demonstrated friendliness, intimacy, and patience, it also created the misconception that the feedback was high quality. Participant AI01 noted that *It [ChatGPT] was very patient in revising academic expressions, and the answers it gave seemed correct. But I found that ChatGPT secretly changed the meaning I wanted to express.* Interestingly, we found that a number of the participants were willing to compromise the reliability and standardisation of the facilitator's feedback in exchange for a greater sense of social comfort. Participant AI12 described their trade-off process, saying, *Even if the answer given by ChatGPT is not very accurate and I may need to make more modifications based on its answer, I will still be more inclined to use it. For me, it is easier to express my ideas to ChatGPT than to reveal my shortcomings to a real teacher.* This sentiment was echoed by participant AI08, who stated, *If I know that my writing isn't very good, or my English level is relatively low, or the problem seems quite basic to be asked, I would be more willing to ask ChatGPT about it and let it help me with the initial revisions. Because the teacher may think that my English is poor, but ChatGPT will not [judge].*

We also observed value tension between ethical values and the pragmatic value of development. Development, as a pragmatic value, involves a facilitator's role in enhancing learners' performance. ChatGPT, while offering friendly and polite feedback, often delivered comments that were decontextualised and emphasised social comfort over development. For instance, ChatGPT provided feedback like *Your paper is well-structured overall, but it might benefit from a clearer introduction* and *Keep refining your arguments and supporting them with evidence.* Although these comments were encouraging, they lacked specificity and did not offer detailed guidance on how to improve the introduction or strengthen the arguments.

In contrast, the human expert provided feedback that was more contextualised, targeted, and at times, assertive. The expert suggested to participant HE24 that the focus of the manuscript *should be on education and how AI can help education from the beginning of the first paragraph.* and *use more conjunctions to make the article more logical.* We further found that the participants were inclined to prioritise development over *social comfort* when they had clear learning objectives. For example, one participant noted, *In tasks that are crucial to my personal development, such as revising documents for studying abroad, I refuse to let my social anxiety hinder my progress* (HE07).

Additionally, we identified value tension at the individual level between *accuracy* and *responsiveness*. This was exemplified by Participant AI33 during the interview, where they expressed a weighing of these values. The participant noted, *I rely on ChatGPT because I trust its accuracy. However, I believe that communicating in a more human-like manner is more important. A native speaker might make some grammatical errors, but they can convey things in a more authentic way. I prefer this kind of interaction.* This reflects the complex psychological dynamics that individual users experience when utilising GAI tools in online learning.

For more details and findings about this study, see the paper led by Yuan Shen and Yizhou Fan "Aligning and Comparing Values of ChatGPT and Human as Learning Facilitators: a Value-Sensitive Design Approach" Shen et al. (2025).

8.4 IMPLICATION AND FUTURE WORK

Since the purpose of developing GenAI in education is to serve learners' needs, satisfy learner desires and maximise the realisation of learners' values (Gabriel, 2020; Yudkowsky, 2011; Han et al., 2021), the value sensitivity of designing and implementing GenAI is critical for ethical usage. Ethical dilemmas occur when GenAI tools are not appropriately designed or used, especially when multiple ethical principles cannot be simultaneously upheld within a specific context. To effectively integrate ethical principles and human values into technology design and application, developers, researchers, and educators must deeply understand the ethical risks that arise in the use of generative AI in education (Liberman and Chaiken, 1991)

Our findings highlight that the ethical issues are highly context-specific. From the literature review and the empirical study, we found that the values learners prioritised and the hypothesised risks are different. Rather than the issues of privacy and academic misconduct often mentioned in many conceptual studies, we found that participants in our research demanded for facilitators with social comfort and responsiveness. Also, the values identified in this study go beyond the critical competencies of a "good facilitator" proposed by previous research (e.g., promoting interaction, conducting needs assessments, developing a systems perspective of thinking) (Dabbagh and Kitsantas, 2004). Our findings strongly suggest that value prioritisation is highly dependent on the context, so more empirical research is required. Moreover, the ethical landscape of GenAI in education is not static. The emergence of new values, shifts in value meanings, and the trade-offs learners are willing to make illustrate the complexity and fluidity of ethical issues in GenAI-assisted learning. Previous studies have shown that factors such as gender, learning environment, personal characteristics, prior experiences, preconceived notions about AI, self-efficacy, and learning objectives play a crucial role in how learners navigate value trade-offs (Strzelecki and ElArabawy, 2024; Cercone, 2008; Hodges, 2008; Trigwell et al., 2013). Our findings support this, as participants prioritised self-development over social comfort when focused on improving writing skills, demonstrating how learning objectives can influence value hierarchies. Additionally, our experiment revealed tensions between the values of learners, researchers, and developers. While ethical concerns such as academic misconduct or the malicious use of GenAI tools are typically anticipated by researchers (Weidinger et al., 2021; Yi et al., 2023; Farhi et al., 2023; Imran and Almusharraf, 2023), these issues did not emerge as primary concerns among learners in an online learning context. As stakeholders engage more deeply with GenAI and gain experience, these value tensions may shift or diminish over time since human values evolve alongside human cognition (Wang et al., 2021; Chong et al., 2022; Friedman and Hendry, 2019). This dynamic nature of value prioritisation calls for GAI developers, researchers, and other practitioners to remain adaptable and sensitive to emerging conflicts or shifts in value meanings.

The findings of our study underline the need to reconsider the underlying limitations of current GenAI designs and improve them in a value-sensitive way. While LLMs excel in generating coherent and readable text, they often fall short of fully capturing the nuances of user interactions and embodying values like responsiveness and accuracy. This is because LLMs rely on statistical patterns of word association rather than genuine comprehension of content (OpenAI, 2022; Liu et al., 2023). The discrepancy between the values prioritised by learners and those assumed by technology companies and developers highlights the need for a more tailored approach to GenAI tool development by closely aligning the design and functionality of GenAI tools with the specific needs, preferences, and ethical concerns of the end-users, emphasising the importance of moving beyond mere functionality and readability. Future research and development should focus on creating GenAI tools that not only respond effectively but also align more closely with human values. This could involve enhancing prompt engineering, developing AI models with emotional intelligence, and tailoring AI responses to individual learning needs. Additionally, embedding strategies that support collaborative learning and conducting longitudinal impact studies on GenAI-facilitated education can further refine the alignment between GenAI tools and learner needs. By prioritising these areas, we can make GenAI a more effective and ethically grounded tool in education. Moreover, expanding the VSD methodology to encompass the entire technology life cycle, rather than restricting it to the design phase, would offer a more holistic approach to ethical AI development (de Reuver et al., 2020; Van Der Weij et al., 2023; Vernim et al., 2022). This ongoing commitment to ethical consideration throughout the development, deployment, and usage phases can significantly enhance the alignment between AI tools and the diverse needs of their users, ultimately fostering a more responsible and human-centric evolution of technology.

The empirical study revealed that human experts and ChatGPT may complement each other in embodying learners' values. This discovery prompts a reconsideration of the relationship between GenAI and humans. Previous research on teacher-AI collaboration suggests that achieving intended learning outcomes is most effective when AI and human facilitators work together, rather than relying on one or the other alone (Holstein et al., 2020; Bower, 2019; Jeon and Lee, 2023; Holstein et al., 2019a). For educators, this highlights the importance of leveraging the strengths of GenAI tools in specific areas. For example, ChatGPT is well-suited to serve as a patient assistant, helping learners practice their spoken language or debate skills. These tasks often intimidate learners, as they may feel embarrassed practising with human experts. These applications create a supportive learning environment where students feel comfortable asking questions, reducing the pressure and embarrassment often associated with seeking help (Karabenick and Dembo, 2011; Holstein et al., 2019b). However, to maximise the potential of AI in education, educators must also address socio-technical challenges such as unequal access to technology, resistance to new teaching methods, and gaps in digital literacy. Ensuring that all students benefit equally from advanced AI tools requires attention to these issues (Ng et al., 2021; Tammets et al., 2013). Moreover, educators should recognise their irreplaceable role in accurately assessing students' needs and providing personalised support. They should integrate AI in ways that complement and enhance their professional expertise rather than replace it. In the future, human-machine collaboration is likely to become mainstream in the education domain, which raises questions. For example, is the current effort to humanise machines truly necessary? Where should the boundaries between humans and machines be drawn? How can we optimise the efficiency and effectiveness of human-machine collaboration? Moreover, what implications might this new working model have for intellectual property? These questions require a broader, more comprehensive perspective, and further empirical research is essential to address them adequately.

8.5 CHAPTER SUMMARY

In this chapter, we explored the ethical challenges in a GenAI-assisted learning environment. We began by introducing the ethical risks commonly discussed by researchers and the public. Then we introduced the perspective of human value analysis to decode ethical risks. To gain a full insight into ethical challenges raised by GenAI in education, we reviewed present empirical studies to overview significant ethical challenges, including privacy leakage, academic misconduct and over-reliance on

GenAI. The emergence of GenAI as a new technology and how it could be applied to facilitate learning in a value-sensitive way warrants our consideration. To deepen our understanding of the ethical issues of GenAI's application in facilitating learning, we presented one empirical study from the perspective of value analysis. We answered three questions, including what ethical values were prioritised by learners, how ChatGPT embodied these values and what value tensions occur during online learning. We conducted semi-structured interviews with 59 learners. Our findings suggested that learners prioritised responsiveness, social comfort and autonomy during online learning. ChatGPT-4's features of being tireless, friendliness, and supporting independent decision-making embodied the value of social comfort and autonomy. Furthermore, value tensions occurred between ethical values and pragmatic values, which alerts us to pay attention to dynamic value systems. In summary, GenAI should be employed to facilitate learning in a value-sensitive way. Researchers, educators, and technology developers should also apply GenAI cautiously and take great advantage of GenAI features to embody values of social comfort and autonomy.

Bibliography

Ahn, J., Campos, F., Nguyen, H., Hays, M., and Morrison, J. (2021). Co-designing for privacy, transparency, and trust in k-12 learning analytics. In *LAK21: 11th International Learning Analytics and Knowledge Conference*, Irvine, CA, USA, pp. 55–65.

Ajlouni, A., Almahaireh, A., and Whaba, F. (2023). Students' perception of using ChatGPT in counseling and mental health education: The benefits and challenges. *International Journal of Emerging Technologies in Learning (iJET)*, *18*(20):199–218.

Ali, M. and Ali, M. (1988). *Industrial and Engineering Applications of Artificial Intelligence and Expert Systems*, volume 1. CRC Press, Boca Raton, FL.

Alier, M., García-Peñalvo, F., and Camba, J. D. (2024). Generative artificial intelligence in education: From deceptive to disruptive. *International Journal of Interactive Multimedia and Artificial Intelligence*, *8*(5):5.

Bergström, J., Repo, V., and Tuunainen, V. (2024). Challenges to academic integrity from new tools: A survey of students' perceptions and behaviors of employing ChatGPT. *Proceedings of the 57th Hawaii International Conference on System Sciences*, Honolulu, USA.

Bostrom, N. and Yudkowsky, E. (2014). *The Ethics of Artificial Intelligence*, pp. 316–334. Cambridge University Press, Cambridge.

Bower, M. (2019). Technology-mediated learning theory. *British Journal of Educational Technology, 50*(3):1035–1048.

Buckingham Shum, S., Ferguson, R., and Martinez-Maldonado, R. (2019). Human-centred learning analytics. *Journal of Learning Analytics, 6*(2):1–9.

Cercone, K. (2008). Characteristics of adult learners with implications for online learning design. *AACE Review (Formerly AACE Journal), 16*(2):137–159.

Chan, C. K. Y. and Hu, W. (2023). Students' voices on generative AI: Perceptions, benefits, and challenges in higher education. *International Journal of Educational Technology in Higher Education, 20*(1):43.

Chen, B. and Zhu, H. (2019). Towards value-sensitive learning analytics design. In *Proceedings of the 9th International Conference on Learning Analytics & Knowledge*, Tempe, AZ, USA, pp. 343–352.

Chen, J.-S., Le, T.-T.-Y., and Florence, D. (2021). Usability and responsiveness of artificial intelligence chatbot on online customer experience in e-retailing. *International Journal of Retail & Distribution Management, 49*(11):1512–1531.

Chong, L., Zhang, G., Goucher-Lambert, K., Kotovsky, K., and Cagan, J. (2022). Human confidence in artificial intelligence and in themselves: The evolution and impact of confidence on adoption of AI advice. *Computers in Human Behavior, 127*:107018.

Cotton, D. R. E., Cotton, P. A., and Shipway, J. R. (2024). Chatting and cheating: Ensuring academic integrity in the era of ChatGPT. *Innovations in Education and Teaching International, 61*(2):228–239. http://doi.org/10.1080/14703297.2023.2190148.

Dabbagh, N. and Kitsantas, A. (2004). Supporting self-regulation in student-centered web-based learning environments. *International Journal on E-learning*, *3*:40–47. Association for the Advancement of Computing in Education (AACE).

Das, S. R. and Madhusudan, J. (2024). Perceptions of higher education students towards ChatGPT usage. *International Journal of Technology in Education*, *7*(1):86–106.

Dasari, D., Hendriyanto, A., Sahara, S., Suryadi, D., Muhaimin, L. H., Chao, T., and Fitriana, L. (2024). ChatGPT in didactical tetrahedron, does it make an exception? A case study in mathematics teaching and learning. *Frontiers in Education*, *8*:1295413.

de Reuver, M., van Wynsberghe, A., Janssen, M., and van de Poel, I. (2020). Digital platforms and responsible innovation: Expanding value sensitive design to overcome ontological uncertainty. *Ethics and Information Technology*, *22*:257–267.

Dwivedi, Y. K., Kshetri, N., Hughes, L., Slade, E. L., Jeyaraj, A., Kar, A. K., et al. (2023). "So what if ChatGPT wrote it?" Multidisciplinary perspectives on opportunities, challenges and implications of generative conversational AI for research, practice and policy. *International Journal of Information Management*, *71*:102642.

Farhi, F., Jeljeli, R., Aburezeq, I., Dweikat, F. F., Al-shami, S. A., and Slamene, R. (2023). Analyzing the students' views, concerns, and perceived ethics about Chat GPT usage. *Computers and Education: Artificial Intelligence*, *5*(4):100180.

Ferrara, E. (2024). GenAI against humanity: Nefarious applications of generative artificial intelligence and large language models. *Journal of Computational Social Science*, *7*(1):1–21.

Flanagan, M., Howe, D. C., and Nissenbaum, H. (2008). *Embodying Values in Technology: Theory and Practice*, pp. 322–353. Cambridge Studies in Philosophy and Public Policy. Cambridge University Press, Cambridge.

Friedman, B. (1996). Value-sensitive design. *Interactions*, *3*(6):16–23.

Friedman, B. and Hendry, D. G. (2019). *Value Sensitive Design: Shaping Technology with Moral Imagination.* MIT Press, Cambridge, MA.

Friedman, B., Hendry, D. G., and Borning, A. (2017). A survey of value sensitive design methods. *Foundations and Trends in Human-Computer Interaction, 11*(2). http://doi.org/10.1561/1100000015.

Friedman, B., Kahn, P. H., and Borning, A. (2008). Value sensitive design and information systems. In Zhang, P. and Galletta, D. F., editors, *Human-Computer Interaction in Management Information Systems: Foundations*, pp. 348–372. M. E. Sharpe, New York.

Friedman, B. and Kahn Jr, P. H. (2003). Human values, ethics, and design. In Andrew Sears, Julie A. Jacko, Julie A. Jacko, editors, *The Human-Computer Interaction Handbook*, pp. 1177–1201. CRC Press, Boca Raton, FL.

Fuchs, K. and Aguilos, V. (2023). Integrating artificial intelligence in higher education: Empirical insights from students about using ChatGPT. *International Journal of Information and Education Technology, 13*(9):1365–1371.

Gabriel, I. (2020). Artificial intelligence, values, and alignment. *Minds and Machines, 30*(3):411–437.

Gabriel, I. and Ghazavi, V. (2023). The challenge of value alignment: From fairer algorithms to AI safety. In Véliz, C., editor, *Oxford Handbook of Digital Ethics*, pp. 336–355. Oxford University Press, Oxford.

Greenberg, B. A. (2015). Rethinking technology neutrality. *Minnesota Law Review, 100*:1495.

Guleria, A., Krishan, K., Sharma, V., and Kanchan, T. (2023). ChatGPT: Ethical concerns and challenges in academics and research. *The Journal of Infection in Developing Countries, 17*(09):1292–1299.

Gupta, M., Akiri, C., Aryal, K., Parker, E., and Praharaj, L. (2023). From ChatGPT to threatgpt: Impact of generative AI in cybersecurity and privacy. *IEEE Access, 11*:80218–80245. http://doi.org/10.1109/ACCESS.2023.3300381.

Hakami, E. and Hernández Leo, D. (2020). How are learning analytics considering the societal values of fairness, accountability, transparency and human well-being? A literature review. In Martínez-Monés, A., Álvarez, A., Caeiro-Rodríguez, M., and Dimitriadis, Y., editors. *LASI-SPAIN 2020: Learning Analytics Summer Institute Spain 2020: Learning Analytics. Time for Adoption?*, pp. 121–141, Valladolid, Spain. CEUR, Aachen.

Han, S., Kelly, E., Nikou, S., and Svee, E.-O. (2021). Aligning artificial intelligence with human values: Reflections from a phenomenological perspective. *AI & SOCIETY*, *37*(1):1–13.

Hodges, C. B. (2008). Self-efficacy in the context of online learning environments: A review of the literature and directions for research. *Performance Improvement Quarterly*, *20*(3-4):7–25.

Holstein, K., Aleven, V., and Rummel, N. (2020). A conceptual framework for human-AI hybrid adaptivity in education. In *Artificial Intelligence in Education: 21st International Conference, AIED 2020*, Ifrane, Morocco, July 6–10, 2020, Proceedings, Part I 21, pp. 240–254. Springer.

Holstein, K., McLaren, B. M., and Aleven, V. (2019a). Co-designing a real-time classroom orchestration tool to support teacher-AI complementarity. *Grantee Submission*, *6*(2):27–52.

Holstein, K., McLaren, B. M., and Aleven, V. (2019b). Designing for complementarity: Teacher and student needs for orchestration support in AI-enhanced classrooms. In *Artificial Intelligence in Education: 20th International Conference, AIED 2019*, Chicago, IL June 25-29, 2019, Proceedings, Part I 20, pp. 157–171. Springer.

Huallpa, J., Flores Arocutipa, J., Diaz Panduro, W., Chauca Huete, L., Flores Limo, F., Espinoza Herrera, E., et al. (2023). Exploring the ethical considerations of using Chat GPT in university education. *Periodicals of Engineering and Natural Sciences*, *11*(4), 105–115.

Imran, M. and Almusharraf, N. (2023). Analyzing the role of ChatGPT as a writing assistant at higher education level: A systematic review of the literature. *Contemporary Educational Technology*, *15*(4):ep464.

Isiaku, L., Kwala, A. F., Sambo, K. U., and Isiaku, H. H. (2024). Academic evolution in the age of ChatGPT: An in-depth qualitative exploration of its influence on research, learning, and ethics in higher education. *Journal of University Teaching and Learning Practice*, *21*(06):67–91.

Jeon, J. and Lee, S. (2023). Large language models in education: A focus on the complementary relationship between human teachers and ChatGPT. *Education and Information Technologies*, *28*: 15873–15892.

Ji, Z., Lee, N., Frieske, R., Yu, T., Su, D., Xu, Y., Ishii, E., Bang, Y. J., Madotto, A., and Fung, P. (2023). Survey of hallucination in natural language generation. *ACM Computing Surveys*, *55*(12):1–38.

Karabenick, S. A. and Dembo, M. H. (2011). Understanding and facilitating self-regulated help seeking. *New Directions for Teaching and Learning*, *2011*(126):33–43.

Kiryakova, G. and Angelova, N. (2023). ChatGPT—a challenging tool for the university professors in their teaching practice. *Education Sciences*, *13*(10):1056.

Kreie, J. and Cronan, T. P. (2000). Making ethical decisions. *Communications of the ACM*, *43*(12):66–71. http://doi.org/10.1145/355112.355126.

Lee, D., Arnold, M., Srivastava, A., Plastow, K., Strelan, P., Ploeckl, F., Lekkas, D., and Palmer, E. (2024). The impact of generative AI on higher education learning and teaching: A study of educators' perspectives. *Computers and Education: Artificial Intelligence*, *6*: 100221.

Liberman, A. and Chaiken, S. (1991). Value conflict and thought-induced attitude change. *Journal of Experimental Social Psychology*, *27*(3):203–216.

Liu, M., Zhang, L. J., and Biebricher, C. (2024). Investigating students' cognitive processes in generative ai-assisted digital multimodal composing and traditional writing. *Computers & Education*, *211*: 104977.

Liu, Y., Han, T., Ma, S., Zhang, J., Yang, Y., Tian, J., He, H., Li, A., He, M., Liu, Z., Wu, Z., Zhao, L., Zhu, D., Li, X., Qiang, N., Shen, D., Liu, T., and Ge, B. (2023). Summary of ChatGPT-related research and perspective towards the future of large language models. *Meta-Radiology, 1*(2):100017. http://doi.org/10.1016/j.metrad.2023.100017.

Lund, B. D., Wang, T., Mannuru, N. R., Nie, B., Shimray, S., and Wang, Z. (2023). ChatGPT and a new academic reality: Artificial intelligence-written research papers and the ethics of the large language models in scholarly publishing. *Journal of the Association for Information Science and Technology, 74*(5):570–581.

Mattison, M. (2000). Ethical decision making: The person in the process. *Social Work, 45*(3):201–212.

Mhlanga, D. (2023). Open AI in education, the responsible and ethical use of ChatGPT towards lifelong learning. *Education, the Responsible and Ethical Use of ChatGPT Towards Lifelong Learning (February 11, 2023).*

Michel-Villarreal, R., Vilalta-Perdomo, E., Salinas-Navarro, D. E., Thierry-Aguilera, R., and Gerardou, F. S. (2023). Challenges and opportunities of generative AI for higher education as explained by ChatGPT. *Education Sciences, 13*(9):856.

Miller, B. (2021). Is technology value-neutral? *Science, Technology, & Human Values, 46*(1):53–80.

Miller, J. K., Friedman, B., Jancke, G., and Gill, B. (2007). Value tensions in design: The value sensitive design, development, and appropriation of a corporation's groupware system. In *Proceedings of the 2007 ACM International Conference on Supporting Group Work*, Sanibel Island, FL, USA, pp. 281–290.

Mogavi, R. H., Deng, C., Kim, J. J., Zhou, P., Kwon, Y. D., Metwally, A. H. S., et al. (2024). ChatGPT in education: A blessing or a curse? a qualitative study exploring early adopters' utilization and perceptions. *Computers in Human Behavior: Artificial Humans, 2*(1):100027.

Muller, M., Weisz, J. D., Houde, S., and Ross, S. I. (2024). Drinking chai with your (AI) programming partner: Value tensions in the tokenization of future human-AI collaborative work. In *Proceedings of the 3rd Annual Meeting of the Symposium on Human-Computer Interaction for Work,, CHIWORK'24*, New York, NY. Association for Computing Machinery.

Narayanan, N. (2024). *The Era of Generative AI: Transforming Academic Libraries, Education, and Research*. St. Agnes College, Mangaluru, Karnataka.

Ng, D. T. K., Leung, J. K. L., Chu, S. K. W., and Qiao, M. S. (2021). Conceptualizing AI literacy: An exploratory review. *Computers and Education: Artificial Intelligence*, *2*:100041.

Nyaaba, M., Kyeremeh, P., Majialuwe, E. K., Owusu-Fordjour, C., Asebiga, E., Barnabas, A., et al. (2024). Generative AI in academic research: A descriptive study on awareness, gender usage, and views among pre-service teachers. *Journal of AI*, *8*(1):45–60.

OpenAI (2022). How ChatGPT and our language models are developed. OpenAI Help Center.

Petersen, T. S. (2021). Ethical guidelines for the use of artificial intelligence and the challenges from value conflicts. *Etikk i praksis-Nordic Journal of Applied Ethics*, *1*(1):25–40.

Petrovska, O., Clift, L., Moller, F., and Pearsall, R. (2024). Incorporating generative AI into software development education. In *Proceedings of the 8th Conference on Computing Education Practice*, Durham, United Kingdom, pp. 37–40.

Pettersson, J., Hult, E., Eriksson, T., and Adewumi, T. (2024). Generative AI and teachers–for us or against us? A case study. *arXiv preprint arXiv:2404.03486*.

Reis, H. T. and Gable, S. L. (2015). Responsiveness. *Current Opinion in Psychology*, *1*:67–71.

Rezler, A. G., Schwartz, R., Obenshain, S., Lambert, P., McLGibson, J., and Bennahum, D. (1992). Assessment of ethical decisions and values. *Medical Education*, *26*(1):7–16.

Richards, K. A. R. and Hemphill, M. A. (2018). A practical guide to collaborative qualitative data analysis. *Journal of Teaching in Physical Education, 37*(2):225–231.

Satyanarayan, A. and Jones, G. M. (2024). Intelligence as agency: Evaluating the capacity of generative AI to empower or constrain human action. *An MIT Exploration of Generative AI*. https://mit-genai.pubpub.org/pub/94y6e0f8.

Sebastian, G. (2023). Privacy and data protection in ChatGPT and other AI chatbots: strategies for securing user information. *International Journal of Security and Privacy in Pervasive Computing (IJSPPC), 15*(1):1–14.

Sharples, M. (2023). Towards social generative AI for education: Theory, practices and ethics. *Learning: Research and Practice, 9*(2): 159–167.

Shen, Y., Tang, L., Le, H., Tan, S., Zhao, Y., Shen, K., Li, X., Juelich, T., Wang, Q., Gasevic, D., and Fan, Y. (2025). Aligning and comparing values of ChatGPT and human as learning facilitators: A value-sensitive design approach. *British Journal of Educational Technology*, 1–24. https://doi.org/10.1111/bjet.13562

Song, C. and Song, Y. (2023). Enhancing academic writing skills and motivation: Assessing the efficacy of ChatGPT in ai-assisted language learning for efl students. *Frontiers in Psychology, 14*:1260843.

Strzelecki, A. and ElArabawy, S. (2024). Investigation of the moderation effect of gender and study level on the acceptance and use of generative AI by higher education students: Comparative evidence from Poland and Egypt. *British Journal of Educational Technology, 55*(3):1209–1230. http://doi.org/10.1111/bjet.13425.

Tammets, K., Pata, K., and Laanpere, M. (2013). Promoting teachers' learning and knowledge building in a socio-technical system. *International Review of Research in Open and Distributed Learning, 14*(3):251–272.

Thong, C. L., Butson, R., and Lim, W. (2023). Understanding the impact of ChatGPT in education: Exploratory study on students' attitudes, perception and ethics. ASCILITE Publications, pp. 234–243.

Trigwell, K., Ashwin, P., and Millan, E. S. (2013). Evoked prior learning experience and approach to learning as predictors of academic achievement. *British Journal of Educational Psychology, 83*(3):363–378.

Umbrello, S. (2020). Imaginative value sensitive design: Using moral imagination theory to inform responsible technology design. *Science and Engineering Ethics, 26*(2):575–595.

Van Der Weij, F., Steinert, S., Van De Poel, I., Allcblas, J., Melnyk, A., and De Wildt, T. (2023). Value change and technological design. *IEEE Technology and Society Magazine, 42*(3):25–32.

Van Wyk, M. M. (2024). Is ChatGPT an opportunity or a threat? Preventive strategies employed by academics related to a GenAI-based LLM at a faculty of education. *Journal of Applied Learning and Teaching, 7*(1):35–45.

Vernim, S., Bauer, H., Rauch, E., Ziegler, M. T., and Umbrello, S. (2022). A value sensitive design approach for designing AI-based worker assistance systems in manufacturing. *Procedia Computer Science, 200*:505–516.

Viberg, O., Jivet, I., and Scheffel, M. (2023). Designing culturally aware learning analytics: A value sensitive perspective. In Viberg, O. and Grönlund, Å., editors, *Practicable Learning Analytics*, pp. 177–192. Springer, Berlin, Germany.

Voigt, P. and Von dem Bussche, A. (2017). The EU general data protection regulation (GDPR): A Practical Guide. *A Practical Guide*. Springer, Heidelberg, Germany.

Wang, Q., Saha, K., Gregori, E., Joyner, D., and Goel, A. (2021). Towards mutual theory of mind in human-AI interaction: How language reflects what students perceive about a virtual teaching assistant. In *Proceedings of the 2021 CHI Conference on Human Factors in Computing Systems*, Yokohama, Japan, pp. 1–14.

Weidinger, L., Mellor, J., Rauh, M., Griffin, C., Uesato, J., Huang, P.-S., et al. (2021). Ethical and social risks of harm from language models. *arXiv preprint arXiv:2112.04359.*

Wu, X., Duan, R., and Ni, J. (2023). Unveiling security, privacy, and ethical concerns of ChatGPT. arxiv. *URL: https://arxiv. org/abs/ 2308.10092.*

Yan, L., Sha, L., Zhao, L., Li, Y., Martinez-Maldonado, R., Chen, G., Li, X., Jin, Y., and Gašević, D. (2024). Practical and ethical challenges of large language models in education: A systematic scoping review. *British Journal of Educational Technology*, *55*(1):90–112.

Yang, S. J., Ogata, H., Matsui, T., and Chen, N.-S. (2021). Human-centered artificial intelligence in education: Seeing the invisible through the visible. *Computers and Education: Artificial Intelligence*, *2*:100008.

Yang, Y., Luo, J., Yang, M., Yang, R., and Chen, J. (2024). From surface to deep learning approaches with generative AI in higher education: An analytical framework of student agency. *Studies in Higher Education*, *49*(5):817–830. http://doi.org/10.1080/03075079.2024.2327003.

Yi, X., Yao, J., Wang, X., and Xie, X. (2023). Unpacking the ethical value alignment in big models. *arXiv preprint arXiv:2310.17551.*

Yudkowsky, E. (2011). Complex value systems in friendly AI. In *Artificial General Intelligence: 4th International Conference, AGI 2011*, Mountain View, CA, August 3–6, 2011. Proceedings 4, pp. 388–393. Springer.

Yusuf, A., Pervin, N., and Román-González, M. (2024). Generative AI and the future of higher education: A threat to academic integrity or reformation? Evidence from multicultural perspectives. *International Journal of Educational Technology in Higher Education*, *21*(1):21.

CHAPTER 9

Future Vision and Key Topics of Learning with GenAI: Conceptual Constructions Rooted in Empirical Studies

Yizhou Fan

In this final chapter, I discuss the insights gathered from diverse empirical studies in the fields of educational technology and learning analytics, highlighting the complex and multifaceted interactions facilitated by Generative Artificial Intelligence (GenAI) in learning settings. I briefly introduce and discuss emerging key concepts anticipated to be crucial in shaping future learning environments, such as human-AI co-evolution, synergy regulation, generative assessment, metacognitive laziness, and value tension. Each concept reflects unique opportunities and challenges presented by the integration of AI in education. This chapter also projects potential research directions, focusing on the development of conversation-based pedagogical agents, new assessment frameworks aligned with GenAI's affordances, and the design of regulation scaffoldings that support strategic learning with AI. By providing both a visionary outlook and theoretical foundation for the integration

 DOI: 10.4324/9781003632146-9

of GenAI in education, this chapter aims to pave the way for innovative practices and robust theoretical advancements.

9.1 WHAT DO MULTI-DIMENSIONAL EMPIRICAL STUDIES TELL US?

The empirical studies in the previous chapters provide a comprehensive analysis of how generative AI, particularly ChatGPT, shapes learning experiences across multiple dimensions. They reveal that GenAI tools can enhance specific learning outcomes, such as writing performance, self-assessment accuracy, and task engagement. AI-driven feedback, characterised by immediacy and precision, supports iterative improvement but may lead to over-reliance, reducing learners' self-regulation and metacognitive skills. Emotional dynamics, such as boredom and focus recovery, further highlight the nuanced interactions between learners and AI tools. Crucially, comparisons with human instructors reveal that while AI excels in structured and task-specific support, it struggles with fostering deeper cognitive engagement, critical thinking, and creativity. Ethical considerations also emerge, with learners valuing responsiveness, autonomy, and freedom from bias. The studies underscore the importance of balancing AI integration with human facilitation to mitigate risks like over-reliance and cognitive offloading, ensuring that AI tools complement human instructors in fostering holistic, critical, and ethical learning environments. These insights advocate for thoughtful, value-sensitive design in AI-augmented education, promoting both efficiency and equity.

9.2 EMERGING KEY CONCEPTS IN FUTURE LEARNING WITH GENAI

Based on the previous chapters' empirical studies and discussions, here I list five concepts that are emerging as pivotal topics in future learning with GenAI.

9.2.1 Human-AI Co-Evolution

The concept of human-AI co-evolution revolves around the idea that learners and AI agents grow together in a mutually beneficial manner (Järvelä et al., 2023). Unlike traditional educational technologies, GenAI has the capacity to learn from its interactions, which allows it to adapt its responses over time. This evolving dynamic requires rethinking the nature of teacher-learner relationships, shifting towards a more collaborative model where AI acts as a partner in the learning journey. In this context, learners are encouraged to engage deeply with the content while leveraging AI to extend their problem-solving capabilities. Empirical studies have shown that students interacting with AI-driven tutors can achieve significant improvements in areas like critical thinking and problem-solving, largely because of the adaptive support that evolves based on the learner's progress.

9.2.2 Synergy Regulation

Synergy regulation refers to a collaborative and dynamic process in which human-led and AI-supported learning and regulation activities are mutually reinforcing. Unlike traditional models of regulation, synergy regulation emphasises co-evolution, where both human and AI agents adapt, learn, and improve in response to each other. This approach enables a continuous feedback loop where human insight and AI-driven precision generate a superior level of learning and regulation that neither could achieve independently. This concept is relevant but different from hybrid human-AI regulation and human-AI shared regulation (Molenaar, 2022), with the emphasis on creating a combined effect that exceeds the sum of their individual contributions (one plus one bigger than two effects) (Nguyen, 2025).

The challenge lies in harmonising these roles to create an effective educational experience. GenAI provides opportunities for learners to receive instant feedback, but it lacks the nuanced understanding of context that human educators possess. The concept of synergy regulation involves creating an equilibrium where the strengths of AI—such as scalability and personalisation—are effectively complemented by the empathetic and contextual insights of humans. Recent studies demonstrate the importance of designing systems that help learners regulate their interactions with AI, ensuring they engage meaningfully without over-relying on automation. This concept of regulation aims to foster productive collaboration where both human and AI inputs are optimised.

9.2.3 Generative Assessment

Generative assessment represents a shift from traditional summative and formative assessments towards a more dynamic, real-time evaluative process. By leveraging GenAI's ability to provide instant, context-specific feedback, assessments can be integrated into the learning process itself, enabling continuous adaptation and learning enhancement and ultimately achieving stealth assessment in the learning process (Fan et al., 2024). Generative assessment is especially promising in environments where individualised learning paths are crucial. It facilitates personalised feedback loops that adapt to a learner's progress, providing tailored challenges and guidance. Empirical studies indicate that such assessments can significantly enhance learning outcomes by focusing on the process rather than merely the final product, promoting a deeper understanding and retention of knowledge.

9.2.4 Metacognitive Laziness

The concept of metacognitive laziness refers to the risk of learners becoming overly reliant on AI-generated answers, thereby neglecting the cognitive and metacognitive processes necessary for critical thinking and self-regulation (Fan et al., 2024). While GenAI can serve as a powerful tool for scaffolding learning, its accessibility, and ease of use may encourage superficial engagement rather than deep cognitive processing. Empirical evidence suggests that students who frequently use GenAI without adequate guidance may develop a habit of bypassing essential reflective and evaluation practices (Chen et al., 2025), thereby limiting their metacognitive growth. This phenomenon necessitates the design of educational interventions that encourage students to actively reflect on AI-provided information and integrate it meaningfully into their learning processes.

9.2.5 Value Tension

Value tension refers to the ethical and moral dilemmas that arise from using GenAI in educational contexts (Shen et al., 2025). These tensions often stem from conflicting values such as efficiency versus fairness or personalisation versus privacy. For instance, while AI can provide highly individualised learning experiences, it may also inadvertently reinforce biases present in its training data. Empirical studies have highlighted concerns regarding privacy, bias, and academic integrity. Addressing these value tensions requires a collaborative effort among educators, developers, and policymakers to create AI systems that align with educational values while mitigating ethical risks.

9.3 POTENTIAL FUTURE RESEARCH DIRECTIONS

9.3.1 Conversation-Based and Role-Play Pedagogical Agents

One promising direction for future research is the development of conversation-based and role-play pedagogical agents. These AI-driven systems simulate real-life scenarios, allowing learners to engage in immersive and experiential learning. Role-play agents can provide learners with opportunities to practice problem-solving in a low-stakes environment, thus enhancing both their cognitive and social skills. Empirical studies support the potential of such pedagogical agents to improve learner engagement and retention by making learning more interactive. Future research could focus on optimising these agents for diverse educational contexts, ensuring that they are culturally responsive and capable of addressing individual learner needs.

9.3.2 New Generation of Assessment in the Age of GenAI

The traditional models of assessment are insufficient to capture the dynamic and evolving learning processes facilitated by GenAI. There is a need for a new generation of assessments that can evaluate not only the final output but also the learner's engagement, creativity, and the quality of interactions with AI. Future research should aim to develop assessment frameworks that integrate real-time data from AI interactions to provide holistic evaluations of student learning. Such frameworks could leverage machine learning algorithms to track learner progress continuously, providing educators with actionable insights to support personalised learning.

9.3.3 Regulation Scaffoldings on Strategic Learning with GenAI

The integration of GenAI in education necessitates new forms of regulation scaffoldings that help learners manage their interactions with

AI effectively. These scaffoldings could include tools and prompts that encourage learners to think critically about the information provided by AI, ensuring that they engage in meaningful cognitive processing rather than passive consumption. Future research could explore the design and implementation of such scaffoldings, focusing on enhancing learners' self-regulation skills. By supporting strategic learning, these scaffoldings can help mitigate the risks of metacognitive laziness and foster deeper engagement with learning materials.

9.4 CONCLUSION

The concluding chapter of this book offers a forward-looking perspective on the integration of GenAI in educational environments, emphasising the need for theoretical constructs that are firmly grounded in empirical evidence. By addressing key concepts such as human-AI co-evolution, synergy regulation, generative assessment, metacognitive laziness, and value tension, the book establishes a comprehensive framework for understanding the opportunities and challenges posed by GenAI in education.

Looking ahead, the future of learning with GenAI holds immense potential for reimagining education as a collaborative and dynamic process between humans and AI. Personalised, responsive, and co-regulated learning environments will emerge, enabling learners to engage in meaningful interactions with AI-driven agents. The development of intelligent conversational agents, role-play simulations, and adaptive regulatory scaffolds will support strategic, reflective, and ethical learning behaviours. Central to this vision is the call for rigorous empirical research, which serves as the cornerstone for understanding and shaping human-AI relationships. Such research is essential for uncovering how human cognition and AI responses co-evolve, ensuring that AI-driven education remains ethical, effective, and human-centred. By refining theoretical models and expanding empirical inquiry, the vision for GenAI-driven learning is one of synergy, adaptability, and human flourishing, with AI serving as an enabler of critical thinking, creativity, and lifelong learning.

As we envision the future for our next generation, we extend our heartfelt wishes for a future where they thrive in a world where AI and human ingenuity converge to unlock their true potential. May they be bold in their exploration, wise in their use of technology, and compassionate in their pursuit of knowledge. In this ever-evolving landscape of human-AI collaboration, we hope they grow as critical thinkers, creative innovators, and ethical leaders, ready to shape a more just, inclusive world filled with boundless possibilities.

Bibliography

Chen, A., Xiang, M., Zhou, J., Jia, J., Shang, J., Li, X., Gašević, D., and Fan, Y. (2025). Unpacking help-seeking process through multimodal learning analytics: A comparative study of ChatGPT vs human expert. *Computers & Education, 226*:105198. https://doi.org/10.1016/j.compedu.2024.105198.

Fan, Y., Tang, L., Le, H., Shen, K., Tan, S., Zhao, Y., Shen, Y., Li, X., and Gašević, D. (2024). Beware of metacognitive laziness: Effects of generative artificial intelligence on learning motivation, processes, and performance. *British Journal of Educational Technology*, 1–42. http://doi.org/10.1111/bjet.13544.

Järvelä, S., Zhao, G., Heikkilä, J., Järvenoja, H., Mikkonen, K., and Kaleva, S. (2023). Hybrid intelligence–human-AI co-evolution and learning in multirealities (HI). In Lukowicz, P., Mayer, S., Koch, J., Shawe-Taylor, J., Tiddi, I., editors, *HHAI 2023: Augmenting Human Intellect*, pp. 392–394. IOS Press, Amsterdam, Netherlands.

Molenaar, I. (2022). The concept of hybrid human-AI regulation: Exemplifying how to support young learners' self-regulated learning. *Computers and Education: Artificial Intelligence, 3*:100070.

Nguyen, A. (2025). Human-AI shared regulation for hybrid intelligence in learning and teaching: Conceptual domain, ontological foundations, propositions, and implications for research. *Proceedings of the 58th Hawaii International Conference on System Sciences (HICSS-58)*, 7–10 January 2025, Waikōloa Village, HI.

Shen, Y., Tang, L., Le, H., Tan, S., Zhao, Y., Shen, K., Li, X., Juelich, T., Wang, Q., Gasevic, D., and Fan, Y. (2025). Aligning and comparing values of ChatGPT and human as learning facilitators: A value-sensitive design approach. *British Journal of Educational Technology*, 1–24. https://doi.org/10.1111/bjet.13562

Index

Made in the USA
Las Vegas, NV
19 September 2026

15f822c1-c296-446a-90bc-c890c04b9046R02